The Amateur

THE STORY OF
THE AMATEUR GOLF CHAMPIONSHIP
1885-1995

The Amateur

THE STORY OF
THE AMATEUR GOLF CHAMPIONSHIP
1885-1995

by

John Behrend

with statistics
by
John Littlewood

GRANT BOOKS, WORCESTERSHIRE 1995

ISBN 0 907186 60 2

also by John Behrend
John Ball of Hoylake
Golf at Hoylake (with John Graham)
St. Andrews Night and Other Golfing Stories

Typeset and printed by Severnside Printers Limited
Upton-upon-Severn, Worcestershire, England

Published in a limited edition of 975 copies
by
Grant Books
The Coach House, Cutnall Green,
Droitwich, Worcestershire WR9 0PQ

The Amateur

THE STORY OF
THE AMATEUR GOLF CHAMPIONSHIP
1885 - 1995
is
published in a limited edition of 975 copies
of which the first 75 copies are the Author's Edition

Copy No: **908**

GRANT BOOKS, WORCESTERSHIRE 1995

Contents

Acknowledgements   *i*

Foreword – by Michael Bonallack   *iii*

Introduction   *vi*

One – The Gutty Years   *1*

Two – Hoylake Heroes   *35*

Three – Between The Wars   *70*

Four – American Domination   *121*

Five – The Bonallack Era   *152*

Six – Double Champions   *178*

Seven – The Transient Years   *198*

Eight – Ninety Nine Not Out   *231*

An Appreciation of Bobby Jones – by Charles R. Yates   *237*

Results and Statistics – by John Littlewood   *239*

Index   *250*

Acknowledgements

Research is one of the most enjoyable parts of producing a book like this. Many interesting hours have been spent in the University Library at St. Andrews, in the British Golf Museum and in the library at Royal Liverpool and my thanks go to those establishments.

I have had help from a large number of individuals and, in naming some of them, I recognise that others, not named, have assisted me and I hope that they will not be offended by their omission. I am grateful to Margaret Tait, Mrs. Wethered, Mrs. Tweddell, Tony Duncan and John Blackwell, all of whom allowed me access to family scrapbooks. Jean Ward Thomas sent me copies of Pat's "Country Life" articles on the Amateur. The following took the trouble to contact me with recollections or enclose press cuttings or photocopies – Ken Gordon, Peter Ryde, Tom Harvey, Bill Campbell, Reid Jack, John Beharrell, Michael Lunt, Trevor Homer, Peter McEvoy and Louis de Banzie, archivist for the Glasgow Golf Club. To them I must add the name of Leslie Edwards. I am amazed and gratified at his recall.

I have renewed acquaintances with countless golf books and club histories and I acknowledge particularly the writings of Horace Hutchinson, Harold Hilton, Robert Harris, Francis Ouimet, Peter Lawless and Guy Farrar. Short extracts have been quoted from their books, also from "Green Memories" by Bernard Darwin, which have been reproduced with the permission of A. P. Watt on behalf of Ursula Mommens, Doctor Paul Ashton and Lady Darwin. I have also used some passages from early editions of "The Field", "The Scotsman" and "The St. Andrews Citizen".

Turning to the illustrations, I am indebted to Gordon Munro of Golf World for access to their picture library and for all his help. I acknowledge with thanks. permission to reproduce photographs from Popperfoto (H. W. Neale Collection), The University Library of St. Andrews (Cowie Collection), and Mark Newcombe. I would also like to thank Brian Bowness, John Graham, Tony Hawkins, Philip Truett, Royal and Ancient Golf Club, Royal Liverpool Golf Club and Royal St. George's Golf Club for providing additional photographs.

Michael Bonallack, Charlie Yates and John Littlewood have also made immensely important contributions to the book and I am deeply indebted to them. Lastly my thanks go to Audrey Ellison who has spent many hours at her word processor on my behalf.

Foreword

In the contemporary world of golf the amateur game is understandably, but regretably, overshadowed by the professional game and the ever increasing levels of prize money won by the leading players. It is therefore of great pleasure to all those still interested in amateur golf to know that John Behrend has, as a labour of love, produced a history of the Amateur Championship from its birth to the present day, covering a period of one hundred and ten years and marking the hundredth Championship which will take place at Royal Liverpool in 1995. This is most appropriate because it was at Hoylake that the first Championship was played and it will be the seventeenth held there, putting it ahead of any other venue.

In the early days the great amateurs, John Ball, Harold Hilton, both from Royal Liverpool, together with Freddie Tait, Royal & Ancient, and John Laidlay, the Honourable Company, were all capable of taking on and beating the leading professionals, with John Ball winning the Open Championship in 1890 and Harold Hilton following him in 1892 and 1897. However it was twenty-nine years before another amateur was to win. That was the great Bobby Jones who repeated his success in 1927 prior to completing the Grand Slam in 1930. It is inconceivable that an amateur could ever again win an Open.

As a youngster of eleven, just starting to play golf, my two heroes were Bobby Jones and Henry Cotton. It is hardly surprising as they were the two golfers everyone knew. However, because Bobby Jones was an amateur who had beaten the professionals in both Open Championships, my ambitions soon focused on his achievements and like countless other young golfers I dreamt of winning the Amateur Championship. Nowadays, children of that age probably have the same fantasies about the Open, but at that time we spent most of our time playing match play, for which I got a liking and we were not so concerned with the, as yet untelevised, seventy-two hole stroke play events.

Having progressed through club and county junior golf I found myself playing in the 1951 Boys Championship at Prestwick, the scene of so many Amateurs and Opens. Sadly my stay was short as I lost in the first round.

ix

Next year at Formby I holed one or two putts and eventually won the Championship at the thirty-seventh hole beating Alec Shepperson in the final. This gave me the taste for championship golf. It was not until 1956 that I played in my first Amateur, held at Troon. This time I managed to win my first round match against an Australian but lost two and one to an American, Joe B. Golden, in the second. Nevertheless, I stayed on to watch some of the players whose names were now becoming familiar to me, Reid Jack, Phillip Scrutton, Gerald Micklem and the American Joe Conrad. Unfortunately Joe Carr, who I particularly wanted to see, had like myself lost in the second round.

So for a few years I served my apprenticeship. In 1957 I reached the fourth round and in the following year, on the Old Course at St. Andrews, I lost to the player who epitomised all that was best in amateur golf, Joe Carr. That was in the semi-final, which was played over 36 holes then. My first Amateur win came in 1961 at Turnberry and I can still remember the final hole of the match, the thirty-second, as if it was yesterday. The rain was pouring down and I was oblivious to it. The other Championships were all satisfying and memorable, but there is nothing to compare with winning for the first time.

John Behrend's history of the Amateur has reminded me of some of the happiest days of my life. Competing in match play against friends on the finest championship courses in the world is an experience that is probably now only available to those playing in the Amateur. I believe he has captured the essence of the game of golf which is the same today as it was in 1885.

I am sure this book will give enormous pleasure to the thousands of golfers who have played in the Amateur or who have been there as spectators and I would like to think that there are eleven year olds who might read the book and, as I did, dream that one day they too might hold the magnificent silver cup engraved with the names of golfers and courses which together form the history of the Amateur Championship.

Michael Bonallack
Royal and Ancient Golf Club
of St. Andrews

Michael Bonallack – five times Champion. Now R & A Secretary

Introduction

This book celebrates a landmark – the hundredth Amateur Championship. It is the story of a "grand tournament" that grew into a great championship, but which, in public perception, no longer captures the imagination or the headlines.

Through twelve decades "The Amateur" has progressed in many ways. The standard of golf is now higher than ever. Through the attention to detail and administrative skill of the Royal and Ancient, there are few better organised events. The field has world wide representation, from Europe, from across the Atlantic and from the southern hemisphere. On the other hand the average age of the competitors is not much more than twenty and for many of them it is one of the stepping stones to a professional career. This is not surprising, as media coverage is now directed largely towards the professional game. Whereas around the turn of the century and even between the wars, the Amateur generated more column inches in the press than the Open, now the miserly editors allocate only a few hundred words to it. The names of the top amateurs were then as well known and as well respected as their professional counterparts, but now even the avid supporters of amateur golf may be hard pressed to name the last five winners of the championship.

Television has brought great rewards to top sportsmen, not least in golf, and ambitious young players naturally look towards the fame and riches available on the professional tour. Each year the cream from the amateur game, together with some of the skimmed milk, cross the divide. This is no criticism. The questions they need to ask – are they good enough to have a chance of success and what are the alternatives to a career as a professional golfer? For most of them the decision "to give it a try" is right, though some of them will regret their decision, particularly when they realise what they have left behind, the enjoyment and companionship of the amateur game. This defection from the amateur ranks has not been to the benefit of the championship, as it has meant that there are no longer the recurring names that give continuity.

Clubs and balls, clothing, the length and condition of the courses have all changed, but the challenge of matchplay golf has not. One shot, good or bad, a giant putt holed or a drive out of bounds can swing the initiative. A long lead disappearing sees one player's confidence and serenity give way to uncertainty and despair, whilst the hope and determination of his opponent grows. All golfers who have competed in a close match, whether it be a championship or a club captain's prize know that feeling of tension as they prepare to drive from the final tee ..... think rhythm, or at the moment of truth, when they face a yard putt to win, and they battle to prevent the hands tightening on the grip of the putter, in the slender hope of producing a smooth slow stroke. Sometimes they do and there is the joy of winning against the odds and sometimes it is the pain of defeat, when victory had seemed assured.

This book is a collection of stories about individuals who have experienced all these emotions. It has no heroes and no villains, just winners and losers. Maybe there is one inanimate hero, the great Championship Cup purchased in 1886 from the contributions of twenty four clubs. The donor clubs were:

Alnmouth	Royal Aberdeen
Bruntsfield	Royal Albert (Montrose)
Dalhousie	Royal and Ancient
Formby	Royal Blackheath
Gullane	Royal Burgess
Honourable Company	Royal Liverpool
Innerleven	Royal North Devon
Kilspindie	Royal St.George's
King James VI	Royal Wimbledon
New North Berwick	Tantallon
Panmure	Troon
Prestwick	West Lancashire

The cup is the symbol of the fierce yet fair and friendly competition of match play golf, the spirit of the game,

CHAPTER ONE

The Gutty Years

Sitting at the head of the table in a private room at the Windsor Hotel, Edinburgh, on August 9th 1886 was a tall, powerfully built man with a booming confident voice. He was B. Hall Blyth, a prominent Edinburgh man, a civil engineer and a keen if somewhat erratic golfer, whose vigorous swing caused more discomfort to the gutty ball than it did to the opposition. Around him were delegates from a number of the leading golf clubs – the Royal and Ancient, the New Club at North Berwick, Dalhousie Club of Carnoustie and Luffness. Hall Blyth was representing the Honourable Company and the Royal Liverpool, of which club he was the immediate past captain. They were meeting to finalise arrangements for a competition, the winner of which would be the Champion Amateur Golfer for the year.

Decisions were taken, doubtless in accordance with the chairman's wishes, as he was a man who normally got his own way. St. Andrews would be the venue for the championship in some six weeks time. Earlier plans that North Berwick should host the event had been changed as the dates proposed were not convenient to them. In the two following years the championship would be held at Hoylake and Prestwick. A trophy was to be purchased by subscription from the leading clubs at a cost not exceeding £100, and the entry money of one guinea would go to the host club, who would provide the medals and other prizes and would make all the arrangements. The meeting agreed also on the definition of an amateur golfer:

"An amateur golfer shall be a golfer who has never made for sale golf clubs, balls or any other article connected with the game; has never carried clubs for hire, or received any consideration for playing in a match, or giving lessons in the game; and who for a period of five years prior to the 1st September 1886 has never received a money prize in any open competition."

The way was now clear for the first championship, or was it the first?

The Edinburgh meeting would not have taken place but for the initiative of the Royal Liverpool Golf Club. Fifteen months earlier at the time of their Spring Meeting they had held a Grand Tournament, with the hope that it would lead to

1

the establishing of an Amateur Championship. It had still required a letter from them to the Royal and Ancient in January, suggesting that they should take the lead in promoting it. Wheels turned slowly. Although the R & A Green Committee favoured the idea it was decided that it should be put to a General Meeting of the Club, to be held in May. It was as a result of this meeting that the representatives of the leading clubs had gathered in Edinburgh.

The concept of a tournament to establish a champion golfer is a natural one. Prestwick had inaugurated the Championship for the famous belt in 1860, but this was largely for professional golfers, who at the time were mostly the caddies, the club makers and the keepers of the green, very much the artisans of the game. Before that, the Royal and Ancient had held their Grand National Tournament of 1858 which, "by a series of single matches to be decided by holes not by strokes," would determine who was champion. This was to be open to members of any golf club and gave rise to the first amateur status decision. Ronald Ross, a respectable young man from the Bruntsfield Allied Club of Edinburgh, had his entry money refunded before teeing off on the first morning of the tournament on the grounds that, as a venetian blind maker, he was an artisan and not therefore qualified. Despite protests that others in the field were in no higher position in society, the tournament went ahead without him and was ultimately won by Robert Chambers, who "had twice drawn a bye, beaten one man a weak player at the outset by 4 and after that had three halved matches in succession, and then won the deciding heat by a single hole." Although the format was not deemed to be totally satisfactory, a similar tournament was held the following year with scratch and handicap classes but the venture was then discontinued. In the years that followed there was much talk and press speculation about a national golf trophy for amateurs, but twenty-five years elapsed before positive action was taken.

Towards the end of 1884, so the Royal Liverpool minute book reveals, Thomas Owen Potter, the Secretary, brought up the subject of a tournament to be played during the Royal Liverpool Spring Meeting the following year, open to all amateur golfers. No decision was taken then, but soon plans had been prepared which were put to a general meeting of the club held in Liverpool on the 28th January 1885 under the chairmanship of the club captain James Cullen. The minutes read:

"Captain Cullen stated that their indefatigable Secretary Mr. T. O. Potter, who he was sorry to say was absent that day through ill health, had made a very valuable suggestion which he was sure all lovers of the noble game of golf would appreciate, which was that a golfing tournament be held at Hoylake during the Spring Meeting with a view to establish an Amateur Golf Championship, something similar to that which existed amongst professionals, in the belief that if the idea was started and carried out at Hoylake, it would be taken up by other clubs, and would result in making the game more popular and lead to better play. Mr. Potter's idea was a tournament open to all amateur golfers to be played by holes, one round of the links to constitute a match, all ties to be played off the same day as far as possible, and that the club grant the sum of £50 out of it's funds in furtherance of the scheme."

There was lengthy discussion on two issues – the amount of the grant and who should be entitled to play. Captain Cullen pressed that the tournament should be restricted to members of invited clubs. After all, he argued, it was not in the best interest of the game for a fisherman or a weaver from Scotland to win such a valuable prize. In the end the issues were resolved. It would be open to members of "recognised" golf clubs and the home club would put up twenty-five guineas towards the event. When one considered the annual subscription of a member was then one pound and ten shillings, that represents a significant amount.

A further problem arose once the tournament had been advertised and entries were filed. One was received from Douglas Rolland, who had finished equal second in the previous year's Open Championship and had received a money prize. Some felt that he was not truly an amateur, but it was then pointed out that Hoylake's Johnny Ball, as a teenager, had won one pound for finishing fifth in the 1878 Open Championship. The rule that was drafted enabled the committee to "exclude any player who has accepted a money prize in a competition open to allcomers; at the same time if it is many years since the player has done that, there seems no reason why he should not by lapse of time be held to have regained his status as an amateur". So it was that Ball was eligible and Rolland was not, a fact that caused Horace Hutchinson, a prominent and respected member of the tournament committee, to resign.

1885

Forty four entries were received with twelve clubs represented. A dozen of the players were locals but others came from London, Edinburgh, Glasgow and one from Dublin. From the twenty two first round matches due to be played on the Monday morning, four players moved in to the second round with walk- overs and another four as a result of a rule that both players in a tied match proceed to the next round. This meant twelve matches in the second round, and it was not therefore surprising that by Tuesday evening, the end of the second day, three competitors remained, which is not a good number to contest the semi-finals or final. They were Johnny Ball and Horace Hutchinson who were to play off for the privilege of a final against Allan Macfie. He was one of those to have reached the second round by halving his first game and had won by a single hole in his fourth round against W.de Zoete doing the Rushes (fourteenth hole) in one, "a very lucky coincidence in such an evenly contested game." The third day of the meeting was given over to the club's Spring Medal. Most of the championship competitors played, and Johnny Ball completed his round in a magnificent 77, the lowest medal score yet recorded at Hoylake, to win the Club Gold Medal. The locals therefore expected him to beat Hutchinson when the championship was resumed next morning.

It was a splendid golfing day with a fresh wind from the south west. The early holes were exchanged and after eight the match was all square. Ball's long game was magnificent and so too was Hutchinson's recovery work, as evidenced by the description of play at the Dowie (then the eighth hole). "Mr. Ball in driving off from the tee at the Dowie hole played a beautiful cleek shot laying himself on the green within three yards of the hole. Mr. Hutchinson was badly rushed, but with true pluck layed himself dead in two, the hole being halved." Hutchinson found trouble at the next two holes, which left Ball two up with eight to play and his supporters confident that their man would win. Four holes later their hopes had evaporated. Hutchinson with 4, 3, 4, 3 had won them all. The next two were halved with Hutchinson holing from twelve yards to match Ball's 4 at the Lake (sixteenth). Ball won the Dun (seventeenth) in 3, but Hutchinson at the final hole in front of the Royal Hotel put his second shot inches from the pin and Ball conceded the hole and match. All who had watched were agreed that it was

Hoylake, 1885, Royal Green

one of the finest matches ever played at Hoylake. Both were round in 80, excellent golf over the rough terrain with seven or eight clubs and a gutty ball, which even the top players could not propel much beyond 200 yards.

The afternoon was an anti-climax, as reaction set in for Hutchinson. Allan Macfie played steadily, completing the first nine holes in 41 to turn five up, and the match ended on the twelfth green.

One story from the final was of a spectator who came up beside Macfie and congratulated him on a splendid shot. This was ignored and so the spectator repeated his congratulatory observations, but again without response, so he walked away muttering, "What a surly brute". Unknown to the spectator, Macfie was stone deaf – literally stone deaf as a result of a fall from a horse on to a heap of stones in his childhood in Australia. He could lip read effectively face to face but could never identify the remarks of someone at his side. As to his golf he was not a long hitter, but his preciseness and attention to detail ensured accuracy on short shots and particularly on the green, where apparently "he could putt with anything from a fire shovel to a Philp". Although he never achieved similar success in the championships, he won scratch medals both north and south of the border and proved himself worthy of pride of place on the championship trophy, though it was many years before that honour was bestowed upon him.

1886

The championship had been fixed for the week prior to the R & A Autumn Meeting. Coincidentally forty four players had again entered. Two of those were disqualified prior to teeing off on the grounds that they did not conform with the rules on amateurism. One was J. Kirk of the St. Andrews Thistle Club, who earlier that month had collected £10 of plate as winner of a tournament for amateurs at Troon, but he had apparently "carried clubs for hire".

Allan Macfie, Horace Hutchinson, Leslie Balfour and Mure Fergusson were all St.Andrew's specialists and expected to do well, as were Johnny Laidlay, who had recently become a member of the R & A, and Johnny Ball from

A. F. Macfie (From a water colour drawing by the late T. Hodge)

Hoylake, even though he had as yet failed to find the key to the mysteries of the Old Course. These were the names that were to dominate the early years of the championship.

Ball the youngest at 24, Laidlay 26, and Hutchinson 27 had all made their mark as teenagers. Of the three, Ball without doubt had the most elegant swing and the greatest natural talent. At Hoylake he was unstoppable and had won many of the scratch medals there since joining the club in 1881. Although he had finished fifth in an Open Championship at the age of 16, there were questions about his temperament for the big occasion and his ability to succeed away from Hoylake.

Laidlay, whilst still at school at Loretto, had done nine holes at Musselburgh in 36, an outstanding score when compared with those compiled in the Open Championships there during the '80s. At 18 he had won the Medal at Luffness as a new member and he repeated the feat on joining the Honourable Company in 1883 and the Royal and Ancient in 1885. He was not however noted for his style. It is said that a student of the game, going to North Berwick to watch him play, returned with the comment that he had every known fault that one was taught to avoid. That was certainly not true of his grip, as he was the first to use what later became known as the Vardon grip. He did however play all the shots from drive to putt off his left foot, and was not as graceful at golf as at cricket, another game at which he excelled.

Hutchinson had at the age of 16 committed the "blazing indiscretion" of winning the Captain's Medal at Westward Ho!, which carried with it the captaincy for the year. Thus young Horace took the chair at club meetings, which caused some consternation. He had started golf at the age of 13. In his own words, "I had the luck to be constantly ill when I was a boy, so that I could only occasionally be at school. I spent a good deal of the time, when I was enjoying ill health, at golf." He learnt the game, as did most young boys at the time, by watching his peers at Westward Ho!, though Johnny Allen the eldest of the three golfing professional brothers gave him friendly guidance. Bernard Darwin described his swing as "rather loose and flamboyant", and this applied to his wristy putting action as well. He was not endowed with a totally placid temperament but his success came more from his determination and ability to play the critical shots well. Bunkers held no fear for him and his recovery shots undermined many of his opponents, but it was his holing out that destroyed them.

Leslie Balfour (Balfour Melville as he became known) and Mure Fergusson were in their early 30s and whilst they were not perhaps as consistently successful as the other three, they were men to be avoided in the draw. The former was a great games player, who not only represented Scotland at cricket and rugby, but won the Scottish Lawn Tennis Championship. Cricket and his profession as an Edinburgh lawyer meant that he had only limited time for competitive golf. As one would expect from an all round athlete with a fine physique, he had a sound style and hit a long ball. If there was any fault it was his putting, which lacked the confidence of the rest of his game. Mure Fergusson was large, red faced and formidable. His presence alone was sufficient to unnerve timid opponents and some terse comment often added to their discomfort. One opponent who is said to have called him by his christian name was put firmly in his place. "Mr.Fergusson to you from ten to four and after that I don't know you." His driving was somewhat erratic as a result of a long and free swing. It was his putting that earned him much of his success. "He was a magnificent putter, standing straight up, noticeably far from the ball, and hitting it straight in. It really looked as if the ball knew better than to disobey him."

So much for the likely candidates for the title of Champion Amateur Golfer, but Horace Hutchinson's caddie had different ideas. "There's a man Fogie from Earlsferry, he's going to win the championship. He's a terrible fine player," the caddie had told his master who had noted that, if he won his first match, he would play Foggo in the next round. It was with some relief that he heard next morning that the potential champion had lost his first match to a Dr. McCraig, against whom Hutchinson that afternoon was to find himself seven up after seven holes.

Next day it was Laidlay that took the crowds for his match with Macfie. An interesting account of the game appeared in "The Field":

"Both men are fine exponents of the game and were looked upon as very equally matched, and this was the case all through, first one and then another having the lead, but never more than two holes separating them, and the match was at the close only decided by a putt. Both led off with fine tee shots and both crossed the Burn in 2, Mr. Macfie however being short. The latter with his third shot carried upon the Road, and Mr. Laidlay who lay well on the green with the like holed out in 4 and won the first honour...."

This description of the play at the first hole is clear evidence that the left hand course was being played. A combination of this and the blustery conditions may account for the fact that the scores in this and other games were somewhat higher than might have been expected.

Having beaten Macfie, Laidlay played Ball in the afternoon, the first of many contests they were to have in championships over the years. There was disappointment for the Scottish crowd both in the result, Ball winning by three and two, and in the play, as "the scoring was rather high, but it must be remembered that scores are secondary in a hole match".

Hutchinson versus Chambers and Lamb versus Ball were the semi-final games to be played next morning. Hutchinson won with some ease and as

H. G. Hutchinson

the news of the other semi-final came through, there was once again cause for relief. The final he had anticipated against Johnny Ball would not be taking place. Despite improved conditions described as "very auspicous", Ball had taken 54 strokes to reach the turn and lost by seven and six. "His troubles seemed to be as many as Job's. He was entirely off both driving and putting and it seemed as if he had retired from the business." Lamb was not much better in the final, scoring 51 for the first nine holes and Hutchinson, playing them steadily in 45, took control and won the match and championship at the twelfth hole.

It was a disappointing day's golf for the spectators. There was however one exciting match, as there was a play off for third place between Ball and Chambers. "The encounter was exceedingly close, the former only leading by one, and winning at the last hole by a putt."

1887

The 1887 Championship was fixed for early August at Hoylake. The date was clearly not a popular one, as the entry was only thirty-three, and many of the leading Scottish players – Laidlay, Balfour, Mure Fergusson and others were not present. As one would expect there was a strong representation from the home club and this included an 18 year old named Harold Hilton, playing in the event for the first time. He won his first match before succumbing to the senior John Ball, Johnny's father and the proprietor of the Royal Hotel, who won again in the next round for a place in the semi-final. He was to play Horace Hutchinson, the holder, whilst his son was matched against John Tait from Edinburgh.

At the halfway stage both games were going against expectation, with father two up against Hutchinson and son three down to Tait. Johnny, playing ahead, pulled round his match with a succession of well played holes and won it at the Dun hole (seventeenth). This news came back just as father, still one up, had played his second shot to that hole. Tempting fate, he turned to Hutchinson and said, "It would be a funny thing if father and son had to play it off together." Hutchinson was quick to respond "Wait a bit, Mr. Ball, you haven't done with me yet." Whether this exchange was the cause of it or not, old man Ball missed his third shot, dropping it into the cross-bunker short of the green, lost the hole, and the eighteenth, where Hutchinson holed his putt for a 3 and the match. So father was to have the more accustomed role of spectator, watching his son play the final amidst a large partisan crowd. It was hot work, as "all day the scorching rays of the sun beat down on the parched turf." Two years earlier the two of them had battled to the last hole and this was another close and tense affair.

Both were out in 42 and the match was still square as they went to the short fourteenth. The report from "The Field" describes those last five holes:

"At the Rushes Mr. Ball played a magnificent stroke. His opponent missing the putt left a dead stymie, and the Hoylake player after calculating the circumstance of the situation resolved to make for the hole. By sheer skill he twisted his ball round that of his opponent, and in it dropped to the hole. The crowd cheered the feat vociferously. Ball accordingly obtained for the first time in the match a lead. After the next hole had been divided he heeled away; it sped into the enclosed field, which, according to the rules of the green, is regarded as an unplayable spot. Taking another ball and counting a stroke, he made a second bid for the hole. This time the shaft of his brassie gave way..... These two mishaps proved too much for Mr. Ball and the game stood all even, and two holes to play. Here was a pretty fight for the championship. These two holes were to decide on whose shoulders the honour would fall of being the best amateur golfer of the year. As might be expected in such exciting circumstances, the play was not too good. The question at issue became more one of nerve than pure golf. Both men drove from the tee, but Ball topped his cleek approach, and on the green there was very lose play. Putts of a very ordinary character were missed on either side, and the hole was divided. Driving for the last hole Mr. Ball had the evil fortune to send his ball into the artificial bunker which faces the teeing ground. Before he got to the green he had played 4. The mishap lost him the hole and with it the Championship."

So Hutchinson had won the championship again, although a round of 84 in favourable conditions was not exceptional golf. This was a great disappointment to Ball's many local supporters. They were beginning to wonder if he did have the courage and character to win the championship.

In the minute book of the Royal Liverpool Golf Club the results of all the matches are recorded in elegant handwriting. Below them are the accounts for the championship. Entrance fees of £34.13.0 had been collected, of which four guineas were refunded to the four semi- finalists. The four medals had cost £6.9.6. and the other expenses – postage, printing and advertising £5.12.9. This left a balance of £18.6.9 which was divided amongst the medalists – goods to the value of £9 to the winner (£1 more than the Open Champion received), £4.10.0 to the runner-up, £3 for third place and £1.16.9 for the fourth. No play off took place for third and fourth place as Mr. Ball senior preferred to concede that honour to John Tait, to enable him to watch his son in the final.

1888

The championship was held at Prestwick during the second week in May, once the Spring Meetings at the premier clubs had been contested. Prestwick was a popular and challenging venue. Disaster lurked everywhere, with the Railway, the Cardinal's Nob, the Pow Burn, the Himalayas, the Dyke and the Alps all generating fear, and calling for long hitting and high flighted shots. A strong field had assembled with all but Mure Fergusson of the best Scottish players in attendance, so a worthy champion would emerge. Four first round matches were played and in the first of these James Kirk of Glasgow unexpectedly beat Allan Macfie. The latter had been ahead most of the way and was two up with three to play. "Whether or not confidence begat carelessness, he lost all three holes, the last one by missing a very easy putt," was the unsympathetic report in "The Field". Those that are all square playing the final hole, having lost the previous two, know that no putt on the home green is an easy one. Another of the first round matches was not so close. "Mr. Andy Stuart's treatment of his virtual namesake was cavalier. He won the first ten holes right off the reel, surely a severe dressing to one bold enough to venture into the champion arena." John Stewart of Prestwick was the victim.

Johnny Laidlay recovered from three down with seven to play against David Bone of Glasgow in his second round match and then proceeded smoothly through the top half of the draw. Johnny Ball and Horace Hutchinson looked to be probable semi-final opponents in the lower half, and the former must have been grateful to Stuart for deposing the champion. Stuart and Hutchinson had been paired together a week earlier in the R & A Spring Meeting and had tied with Laidlay for the scratch medal. The three of them went out again later that day for the play off, and Hutchinson won the medal. This time Stuart got his revenge. The match will however be remembered for an extraordinary incident. At the seventh hole Hutchinson sliced his second and was left with a blind shot over a high dune to the right of the green. The player described what happened next:

"I went over the ridge, with my caddie, to play the ball, and pitched it over, with a loft, to the place where I thought the green to be. Then I ran up to the top of the ridge, and looked, but could see no ball. I asked then, as I came down over the ridge, where the ball was. There was a small concourse of perhaps a score of spectators. "Oh," they said, "the ball has not come over." "Not come over!" I repeated, filled with astonishment. "Why, I know it has!" As a matter of fact it had been lofted high into the air and both I and the caddie had seen it with the most perfect distinctness. Still, it appeared that it was not there; it almost seemed as if the ordinary operations of nature's laws had been suspended and the solid gutty had been dissolved into thin air in mid flight. Then, as we all were looking about, in much surprise, a man spoke up. He was a Mr. Kirk, a townsman of St. Andrews and a fine golfer. He took part in the first amateur championship when it was played at St. Andrews, but he had come to this one as a spectator only. He said, "Well – I think I felt a tug at my pocket." And at that he looked into the outside breast pocket of his coat; and there the ball lay, on his handkerchief, like an egg in a nest."

After some discussion the ball was dropped where the spectator had been standing at the time and from there Hutchinson played the ball, but Stuart who had been on the green in two shots won the hole. Indeed he led all the way, though Horace did not surrender without a fight, as, three down with four to play, he won the fifteenth and sixteenth holes. He could not however match Stuart at the Alps, and lost by two and one.

For quality of play, the match of the championship was that between Johnny Ball and James Mansfield from the Honourable Company. Mansfield took an early lead, but Ball, out in 36, was two up at the turn. He lost them both, but came again to win at the seventeenth. Next morning he beat Stuart by four and three, whilst Laidlay was winning comfortably against Balfour.

The best of England versus the best of Scotland promised well for the final, but "it not infrequently happens that when Greek joins Greek, the tug of war is not characterised by any remarkable deeds of derring do." So it was. Ball drove onto the railway at the first hole and lost it, but thereafter it was Laidlay who made the mistakes and Ball reaching the turn in 43, playing no better than was necessary, won by five and four. Thus Johnny Ball had allayed the doubts of his supporters, and the Prince of Hoylake had been crowned.

In addition to winning the gold medal, he was allowed to purchase an item to the value of £8, the winner's share of the balance of the entrance money after the expenses of the championship had been paid. His choice was a double–barrelled shot gun, doubtless for use in keeping down the rabbits on the links at Hoylake.

1889

Ball, Hutchinson, Laidlay, and Balfour were all competing at St. Andrews in 1889 and, whilst the winner was expected to come from that quartet, there were some others who caught the eye. Allan Macfie and H. S. C. Everard had won the scratch prizes at the R & A Spring meeting the previous week and Harold Hilton, in practice, had completed a round in 84 shots on this his first visit to St. Andrews. In the event Everard and Hilton did not make much progress, with Everard losing in the first round to A. M. Ross, despite a four hole lead after seven holes, and Hilton losing to Laidlay in a close contest in the third round. They were all square with two to play, but Hilton was on the road at the seventeenth, losing the hole to a 6 and he could only halve the eighteenth. Whilst he was satisfied at taking such a fine player so far, he had lost his way in the middle of the round, confessing afterwards that, "at one period I had a lead of one, and the prospect of winning so frightened me that I went to pieces for the next three holes."

The draw brought Ball and Hutchinson, the two previous champions, together in the second round and they took most of the spectators with them. The match was not of the highest quality. Both were in the burn at the first and Hutchinson followed that with three putts. The game swung in favour of Ball round the loop. He was three up after halving the eleventh and "after this Mr. Hutchinson began to foozle, was repeatedly bunkered, and Mr. Ball won the next two holes." He finished the match at the fifteenth. Ball then moved on to meet Laidlay in the first semi-final whilst Balfour played W. S. Wilson of Prestwick in the other. This went according to expectation with Balfour winning comfortably.

Laidlay versus Ball, a repeat of the previous year's final, turned out to be the match of the championship, "indeed no grander match than this has yet marked the annals of the championship." Laidlay who had started with a 3 was two up at the turn and still two up with five to play. Ball holed a good putt at the fourteenth and with Laidlay bunkered at the sixteenth, they were level again. Both were on in 3 at the seventeenth and "were two club lengths from the hole and it fell to Mr. Laidlay to give the odds. His line was not deadly enough to get him home, and Mr. Ball had this for the hole. A trifle weak and the opportunity slipped from his hands, and the fight was transferred to the Home hole." Ball had the better of it there but just failed to obtain his 4 and a fine approach enabled Laidlay to get the half.

At the first extra hole Laidlay was across the burn in 2, but with three putts he failed to capitalize on the advantage. At the twentieth Ball played his second shot first and it disappeared over the brow at the front of the green going straight for the flag. Whilst Laidlay was preparing to play his shot there were signals from the green that his opponent's ball had run on into the pot bunker at the back of the green. Whether this relieved the pressure on Laidlay, one will never know, but he played another outstanding shot and won the hole with a 4.

In the final Laidlay reached the turn in 41 and was four up after ten holes but Balfour fought gallantly. Three down with four to play, he won both the fifteenth and sixteenth and at the Burn hole, as the seventeenth was then known, he overhit his fourth shot "upon the footpath, and though he cleverly regained the green, Mr. Laidlay with a fine shot won the hole".

1890

This was Johnny Ball's year. The championship was back at Hoylake, already recognised by all golfers for the quality of its putting greens. The post and rails of the old racecourse were disappearing, "the golfers wrath and niblick and the people's need of firewood having almost made an end of them." The rabbit burrows were not however disappearing, despite the Ball family and their guns, and it was suggested that "no wild driver should come to Hoylake without a ferret trained to draw gutta-percha." That apart, the hazards were much as they are today, the low turf walls or cops denoting the out of bounds and the benty sandhills. Much of the trouble was on the left and it was said at the time that players "are better on the heel than on the pull."

The championship followed the Spring meeting and many of the competitors had played in that. Laidlay and Hutchinson respectively had won the Club Gold Medal and the Kennard Medal, whilst "Mr. Ball was off his game." The following day Ball and Charles Hutchings played Laidlay and Hutchinson in a foursome but lost easily.

Things were different when the championship started and Johnny cruised through to the final winning his four matches by six and four, eight and seven, three and two, and six and four. Only Hilton in the quarter-final put up any resistance. The previous day, he had demolished his opponent by nine and seven and carried on to complete the round in 80. This time it was Ball who was round in 80, although the younger player held the master to the turn. Having lost the tenth and eleventh he won the Rushes with a 3 and was still only one down with four to play. "After which the fickle fortune forsook him and the luck went dead against him, as he was badly bunkered twice or thrice, and though he fought with undiminished nerve, Mr. Ball scored the fifteenth and sixteenth and so won a most interesting struggle."

Leslie Balfour (driving) against Alexander Sinclair – 2nd round, clubroom of Royal Hotel in the background

Meanwhile Johnny Laidlay was working his way through the bottom half of the draw, but not with such consummate ease. He was one down with two to play against Horace Hutchinson in the quarter-final but a 5 at the seventeenth and 4 at the eighteenth where Hutchinson missed a short putt were enough to clinch the match. Again in the semi-final Laidlay found himself one down and two to play against D.Leitch and this time produced a 5 and a 3, all that was required.

So to the final. The start was delayed by a thunderstorm, but when they set off they were "accompanied by a larger crowd than ever, and though the rain came down again in occasional torrents, it could not damp the ardour of the spectators, who tramped every inch of the round with undiminished interest to the exciting end". Ball drew first blood. He took the opening hole with a 4 and the second, where Laidlay drove into "forbidden ground." By the turn, which he reached in 37, the lead had been extended to six up. Brilliantly though Laidlay played from there, with 4, 4, 4, 4, 2, 5, he could win only two of the holes and Ball had won by four and three. "As for the crowd, the pent up enthusiasm of the natives at once found full vent, and amidst round upon round of hearty cheering, the winner was hoisted onto willing shoulders, which bore him in gratified triumph from the links to the clubroom." For the record Ball required two 4s and a 5 for a 76, and Laidlay was also heading for a round of less than 80.

That was only the start of a memorable year, for in September at Prestwick he became the first amateur and the first Englishman to win the Open Championship. Johnny however remained unaffected by it all, with the same quiet modesty pervading his words and actions. A few weeks after his victory at Prestwick a visitor arrived at Hoylake as Ball was teeing off. "Can you tell me, is the Open Champion playing here today?" the visitor inquired. "Yes, I believe he is," Johnny replied and the visitor went happily on his way across the links to find the champion. On another occasion a journalist came to interview him. "Tell the Editor that I can't think of anything that the readers would find of interest," was all that Johnny would say.

John Ball recovering from the Cop bunker

1891

In early May the competitors gathered again at St. Andrews. That it was there, and not at Prestwick, was the cause of adverse comment in the press. St. Andrews, Hoylake and Prestwick had been chosen as the first three venues, and it had been assumed that this rota would be maintained. There was, however, a counter move to have the championship alternately in England and Scotland, and the proposal of the representatives from the Royal and Ancient and Royal

Liverpool was that St. Andrews and Hoylake should take the championship in turn. Clear resentment by the west of Scotland contingent at this made it appropriate for the question of venues to be re-opened during the meeting of the dozen or so delegates from the leading clubs held during the championship. The England/Scotland rotation was confirmed, but Sandwich would be introduced to the rota for 1892 and Prestwick retained for 1893 before the championship returned to Hoylake in 1894 and St. Andrews in 1895. Some rules matters were also discussed amongst the delegates and it was reported that a proposal to alter the rule regarding the stymie was rejected.

Leslie Balfour and Horace Hutchinson were missing from the draw, but the first day was not without incident and surprise. Ball, the double champion, struggled in the first round to beat J. Kirk of Glasgow by a single hole and then against R. B. Sharp of Dundee, who was playing in the championship for the first time, he found himself three down with five to play. He won them back and came to the eighteenth all square, but there he hooked his second. His pitch through the Valley of Sin was well enough played but it lost pace and only just reached the top from where he took three putts, leaving Sharp a putt for his 5 and the match, which, "though he was labouring under some nervousness," he holed. "Mr. Ball's defeat it should be pointed out was not due to any falling off on his part." Sharp, having started 6, 6 to lose the first two holes, was one under 4's for the next ten.

With Ball eliminated it was left to Harold Hilton to carry the English flag. With a bye and a walk-over he found himself in the last sixteen without playing a shot. This can be a disadvantage and in his first match against A. Morrison of Troon he came to the sixteenth tee two down. From here he saved himself with a 4, 5, 5 finish, winning all three holes. Two further victories against lesser players put him into the final against Laidlay.

The 22 year old Hilton had been marked as a potential champion at St.Andrews two years earlier when he had lost that close match with Laidlay. He was to impress the locals again on this occasion, not least for his fighting spirit, though Hilton himself was not so impressed with the spectators, who demonstrated their patriotism by applauding a missed putt early in the round. Laidlay had the better of the first nine holes and was three ahead. The next four holes changed hands, two to each of them, and so Laidlay was left at three up with five to play. Hilton with a 5 and a 4 at the fourteenth and fifteenth brought himself back into the game. Two halves followed,

Johnny Laidlay

15

and at the eighteenth a fine approach to three feet gave Hilton the chance to square the match. In his own words, "he scrambled it in." Let the report from "The Scotsman" tell the story of the extra holes:

"For the first time the final of the championship resulted in a tie, the rule being that the players must go out again until one or other wins a hole. The crowd in the excitement of the unusual, not to say unexpected occurrence, allowed the excitement to get so much the better of them that it was with difficulty that the course could be cleared. When a way was at length made and when both players had got across the Burn in 2, it was found that Hilton had much the advantage of the position and with a not very unusual putt might have holed in 3. Mr. Laidlay's ball did not get on to the green and there was a rising ground between him and the hole. By a very pretty approach he was well up and down in 4, his opponent over-running the hole in 3 also getting down in 4. But the struggle was nearing conclusion. Both played their second shot for safety out of the line of intervening bunkers and the conflict was transferred to the short game. It was evident that Hilton had not got his nerves under perfect control. He failed to be up in a putt of about two yards, and he thus gave his opponent a chance of being down in the like. Laidlay was equal to the occasion......"

Thus Laidlay had won a second championship like Hutchinson and Ball.

1892

The decision to include Sandwich on the rota was unpopular with the Scots. Even so half of the competitors came from north of the border. A dozen or so members of the home club had been encouraged to play to ensure that no criticism could be laid at the club for a less than satisfactory entry. All of them had however been eliminated by the end of the third round.

First time visitors to Sandwich, many of whom had competed in the St.Georges' Grand Challenge Cup earlier in the week, found the course a severe challenge of about 6000 yards with blind drives over dunes and sandy wasteland. "Sahara", "Maiden" and "Hades" all set their problems as did the ditch at the fourteenth, then known as "Swilken" – now as "Suez". Of the greens it was said, "Rain would undoubtedly have made the ball travel more truly on the putting greens, which were tricky and the non-holing of short putts was far from being a rarity." The fairways were however good.

"Where ten years ago were wide wastes of sand, now stretch broad sweeps of smooth turf, though always undulating as though the swell of the neighbouring sea had been seized upon and solidified for ever. To carry the simile further in places we have great Atlantic waves suddenly arrested when at their height, for rising above the rest are mounds of fifty feet in height from a summit of which the greater part of the links can be seen as a panorama."

The draw looked well balanced. Laidlay, Hilton and Fairlie, who had won the Grand Challenge Cup with a record 79, were in the second round, all at the top.

Hutchinson, Balfour and Ball were in the lower half, though during the course of the first morning it appeared that the last named would play no further part in the championship. He was four down to some excellent golf by Andy Stuart, who had reached the turn in 39. Stuart topped from the eleventh tee and this was just the encouragement that Ball needed. He won three holes in a row, squared the match at the sixteenth and won it at the last where Stuart overran the hole and missed the return putt.

Johnny Ball continued his progress with three more of the closest matches, playing in turn Mure Fergusson, Horace Hutchinson and Leslie Balfour. He won the first of them on the seventeenth when Mure Fergusson, one down at the time, had some putting difficulties, "the effort being certainly not helped by the click of a photographic apparatus, which articles were numerous on the ground and were a source of terror to the more nervous players," not that Mure Fergusson fitted the image of a nervous player. Against Hutchinson, and Balfour in the semi-final, Ball saw a lead of four holes evaporate, but each time he won with a good putt at the eighteenth.

Meanwhile Harold Hilton was having less difficulty, avoiding the big guns, until he met Johnny Laidlay in the semi-final. Playing his best golf, he reached the turn in 36, as he had done the previous morning, and was four up. He finished on the fourteenth and was full of optimism about his match against the other Johnny in the final. The optimism turned out to be unfounded, as recounted by Hilton himself in "My Golfing Reminiscences":

"It was not a great game as regards play but there was never much in it and at the twelfth hole we stood all square. Then came one of those little turns of fortune which tend to decide a match. At the thirteenth hole he ran down quite a longish putt for a 4 and at the same time for the hole. To the fourteenth I had the best of the wooden club play my second being quite close to the bunker guarding the green whilst his was some way short, and as the approach was downwind and the green keen I held a distinct advantage. His approach was not a good one; it was far too merry and looked like finishing in the rushes beyond the green, but it struck the guiding post on the far edge of the green and bounced back. My third finished some 7 or 8 yards past the pin. His run up he played beautifully and nearly holed it, the ball finishing about a foot past the hole. Now my approach putt had to be played on a slippery green with a ball just beyond the hole. The rules of golf decree that if your opponent's ball is in the way and the distance between the balls is more than six inches, you have to play your ball as it lies. This fact crossed my mind and I played this approach very gingerly, with the result that I was five feet short and then missed the subsequent putt."

So Ball led by two holes and he held on to win at the seventeenth thus taking the championship for the third time, leaving Hilton as runner up for the second year in succession.

This was not the end of Ball and Hilton's golfing achievements that year, for at Muirfield in the Open Championship the two amateurs finished first and second, the order reversed, Hilton winning by three shots from Ball who was tied with Hugh Kirkcaldy and Sandy Herd.

1893

The Open and Amateur Champions were heavily engaged on the first day at Prestwick. Ball, with his first title five years earlier followed by the Open Championship victory in 1890, had the happiest of memories of the links. He was drawn against the best of the locals, W. S. Wilson, a semi-finalist in 1889, and, from four up with five to play, he lost three holes in a row and struggled home with a less than convincing performance. Hilton was drawn against F. G. Tait, who had played without success in the championship at Sandwich. He was building a reputation for himself at St. Andrews both as a tenacious competitor and a powerful hitter. A drive of 340 yards at St. Andrews in January had received much publicity. He was not however expected to be a match for the Open Champion, and after six holes he was three down. Unaccountably Hilton did not win another hole. His putting normally so secure failed him and he lost six of the next seven and the match by three and two, a reverse that was to have deep consequences.

If Hilton's putting had let him down, it was nothing to the problems that Ball had on the second day in his match against Mure Fergusson. Two down after eight holes, he looked like winning the next:

"Mr. Ball was lying well on the edge of the green in 3, while his opponent having been trapped in a new bunker from the tee and thereby penalised, lay badly in long grass in the like. Mr. Ball lay dead in the next while Mr. Fergusson played away to the left but made up for the mistake by getting in a fine long putt. Mr. Ball then made one of those unaccountable mistakes which lost him the match. He was lying dead for a half, but missed the putt and lost the hole. At the tenth hole the balls lay for a half on the green, and the Hoylake champion, by a repetition of his last blunder, again threw away the hole."

He missed one more of about three feet to surrender the match at the sixteenth.

Only one Englishman survived to the quarter-final and that was another Hoylake player, Charles Dick. He lost narrowly to Mure Fergusson and the semi-finals were contested by four Scots. Tait was drawn against Laidlay and Mure Fergusson against Peter Anderson, a 21 year old student at St. Andrews University with no previous championship form, who had worked his way quietly through an easier section of the draw. Laidlay versus Tait was as close as had been expected. All square with six to play the remaining holes were done in 25 strokes by each player with both the seventeenth and eighteenth halved in four, but at the nineteenth Tait overran the hole with his putt. Left with a four footer to keep the game going, "he took great care and although he putted straight for the hole a tuft of grass threw the ball off line, completely spoiling his effort". In the other match Mure Fergusson, who had played fine golf to this point, was suffering from an attack of gout, which severely handicapped him and opened the way for Anderson to win by two holes.

Surely Laidlay would have no problem in winning his third title. So it seemed as he won the first two holes against some nervous play by his opponent, doubtless overawed by the huge crowd. "Indeed the crowd was so great in the afternoon as to be almost beyond control and it required most strenuous efforts on the part of Charlie Hunter and old Tom Morris to secure an open course for the finalists." At the third hole, with Anderson struggling again, Laidlay topped his second into the Cardinal bunker in front of him. He lost a hole he should have won and never quite recovered his composure. Meanwhile Anderson was settling into some steady play with splendid putting. Even so Laidlay was two up with five to play, but Anderson stole the fifteenth with a long putt and halved the sixteenth despite a topped drive. At the Alps hole Anderson played safe whilst Laidlay went for the green, which in the morning he had reached with a fine second shot. This time he was short, in the sleepered bunker, and took two to recover. The tortoise had caught the hare. "The excitement among the great gallery of onlookers was now at fever pitch and the expostulations of old Tom Morris and Mr.Hart were as futile as the efforts of the constables who were on the ground." At the final hole it was Anderson who was left with a putt of four feet for the championship and he made no mistake.

For the first time the Amateur had produced an unexpected winner. Anderson's golf on this third and final day was certainly not exceptional. Two rounds of 87 were good enough to win his matches, scores that were several shots more than those returned by Laidlay, Tait and Mure Fergusson in the early part of the championship. His golfing ability was however confirmed a week later when, playing in the St. Andrews Medal, a competition open to members of all the St. Andrews clubs, he holed the Old Course in 80 shots, a new record in stroke play. He played again next year in an unsuccessful attempt to defend his title, whereafter there is no record of competitive appearances. He became a clergyman, and for health reasons emigrated to Australia, joining his brother Mark, who coincidentally won the unofficial Australian Amateur Championship of 1893.

1894

The committee at Hoylake was concerned about the condition of the course prior to the 1894 championship held at the end of April. The previous year's drought had ravaged some of the normally smooth putting surfaces and temporary greens had been brought into play during the winter. The decision as to which holes should be played was left to the last moment and in the end there was just one change, a new short sixteenth hole between the Lake and Dun holes, to replace the eleventh.

The first day saw one outstanding match between Horace Hutchinson, the newly installed captain of the club, and Freddie Tait. It was a tense match of the highest quality, with both round in 80. Hutchinson described the nineteenth hole in his review of the championship and his feelings will be familiar to many golfers who have faced a similar experience.

"The golf had been good, with Mr. Tait's approaching and holing out being quite remarkable. The nineteenth hole looked like being somewhat in favour of Mr. Hutchinson after the second stroke, but he ran for the hole in three and over-ran; then with slight nervous irritation, as no-one knows better than the writer, at Mr. Tait's repetition of his approaching and holing out practice, missed the putt back for the four, and so lost the match – very simple in the telling, very painful in the fact."

Horace Hutchinson watches Freddie Tait putt, Alps green – 2nd round

Next day Tait was again involved in a match that attracted a large crowd, his quarter-final against Harold Hilton. The former, as he had done all week, lost the first two holes, but by the time they had reached the fifteenth they were back to all square. Here Hilton topped his second into a rabbit scrape. Under the rules at that time, "subject to the loss of a stroke, the player may take it out, change the ball if he pleases, and drop it behind the hazard." This cost him the hole and, with the remaining holes halved, the match.

Meanwhile Johnny Ball had reached the semi-final without going beyond the fourteenth hole in any of his earlier matches. Once again he faced Laidlay who was not at his best and Ball won that by five and three and waited for the anticipated clash in the final with Freddie Tait. It was not to be, as Mure Fergusson was too steady for him, and so Ball was to play the man who had beaten him in the previous year's championship.

As had happened in 1890 the start was delayed by heavy rain but this did not deter the vast crowd, bigger than those seen in Scotland and estimated at about 4000. The finalists were continually required "to drive down a living lane of humanity," and this had a greater effect on Mure Fergusson than Johnny, who took the first four holes, but they began to slip away and when this happens tension creeps into the game. With just two holes left to play he had lost his lead and thoughts of the previous year's defeat may have been on his mind. The Scottish supporters were in full cry, "Johnny Ball's beaten – he's funking." This however was the moment for one of his great strokes. The second shot at the Dun hole at that time had to be played with the Field intruding on the right, and, if the green was to be reached, over a fearsome cross-bunker. Mure Fergusson had played short, but Johnny, taking courage into his hands, went for the green with his favourite brassie. The ball soared over the Field, carried the cross-bunker and ran to within ten yards of the pin. This was the shot that won him his fourth Amateur.

Mure Fergusson was clearly upset both by the crowd control and by some press comment relating to his play in the final, and he made his feelings known through a letter to the editor of Golf:

Sir,

I amused myself yesterday by reading extracts from different papers on the final heat for the Amateur Championship, and among other accounts I read that of Mr. Horace Hutchinson in your paper. I am surprised he should take so much pains to point out that he thought the play, especially on my part, so inferior. But I doubt, even if Mr. Horace Hutchinson had played instead of me, whether he would have been able to pull out his true form. He seems to ignore the fact of our having to drive off the tee down a lane of people, having a feeling all the time that one would probably injure someone, which is not calculated to make one drive well and thus affects the whole part of the game. The approach shots also were very difficult to play, caused by the difficulty in determining the distance, owing to the deep crowds standing at the back of the hole.

I fancy I am not singular in my view that as a rule a match of this sort is not calculated to produce low scoring... As Mr. Horace Hutchinson has played so often in these sort of contests, I think he should extend a little more charity to those not so successful as himself trying to win first honours. Apologising for the length of this letter I am,

Sir, etc.

S. Mure Fergusson.

As a further postscript to the championship, it can be recorded that Freddie Tait stayed on one further day to play "the final that might have been." They played two rounds, producing some fine golf with Ball round in 78 in the morning, winning by three, and by one hole in the afternoon with a 77. It says as much for the champion's stamina and resilience as for Tait's enthusiasm.

1895

St. Andrews again proved a popular venue and, with a record sixty-eight entries, a fourth day was required for the championship. The locals were there in force with nineteen R & A members and ten from other St. Andrews clubs. Of these, six reached the quarter-finals with Andy Stuart, a member of the Honourable Company, and a solitary Englishman, Johnny Ball making up the numbers.

The earlier rounds had been played without surprise results, but one noteworthy third round match between William Turpie from Edinburgh and W. E. Fairlie of Prestwick was all square after eighteen holes, and they required another seven holes to decide the tie, which included Turpie, the eventual winner, negotiating a stymie at the twenty-first hole to keep the game alive. Reaction set in when he resumed later that afternoon in the fourth round against Stuart, who had received a walk over in the morning, and he lost by seven and five.

Next day Leslie Balfour Melville fought his way to the final at the expense of two young locals, Willie Greig and Laurie Auchterlonie. Balfour Melville put Greig under severe pressure with an outward half of 38 for a lead of four holes, but the latter clawed his way back into the match and was just one down with one hole left. Greig looked certain to lose but his opponent, with two putts from four yards for the match, left the first two feet short and missed the next. One can imagine Balfour Melville's feelings when he saw his second shot at the nineteenth disappear into the Swilcan. Surely the match had been thrown away;

4.5 on the Stimpmeter. Leslie Balfour Melville putts against Laurie Auchterlonie in the semi-final

but Greig followed him in, dropped out and took three more shots, one too many. Against Auchterlonie in the afternoon Balfour Melville once again established a lead at the turn. This time he was out in 41 and three up. Again the holes dribbled away and if Auchterlonie had holed from eighteen inches on the sixteenth he would have taken the lead. As it was he did take the lead at the next, where it was Balfour Melville's turn to miss from close range. However a brilliant second at the eighteenth secured a 3 and levelled the match. This time at the nineteenth he carried the burn with his second and Auchterlonie did not.

Meanwhile the other semi-final was the match the locals wanted to see. The champion, Ball, against Scotland's hero, Tait, who had been crushing all his opponents by substantial margins. They were in for a disappointment. Tait missed his putts on each of the first two greens and lost the third hole as well. He never regained the honour and Ball playing steadily rather than brilliantly won by five and three.

The final commenced at 11 a.m. next day with a large gallery, which, with heavy betting on the outcome and the natural partisanship, became a little unruly and the club Captain had to administer a strong rebuke at their applause when Ball missed a short putt. Balfour Melville had however suffered similarly when playing young Greig the previous day. Ball missed once again from close range at the twelfth to go one down and then at the thirteenth he bunkered his tee shot. In playing his mashie recovery the ball rebounded into the club and "Mr. Ball gave up the hole." Still two down with four to play, he won the fifteenth but bunkering his drive lost the next. A 5 and a 4 at the last two holes were however good enough to tie the game and yet again Balfour Melville found himself playing the nineteenth:

"Neither of the players were foolish enough to try to carry the burn in 2 and the Reverend R. A. Hull, referee, was called upon to decide which player should be the first to negotiate the hazard. Agreeable to his decision Mr. Balfour Melville gave the odds. He pitched over well, but Mr. Ball with the like, took the ground, foozled the stroke and was in the burn."

So for the third time the Swilcan came to the aid of Balfour Melville and he gained the Gold Medal to add to his championship collection of one silver and three bronze medals.

For Ball, round in 90 and a disastrous shot played at a critical moment, it must surely have been one of his greatest disappointments. Why had he chosen his pitching club in preference to the mashie which he normally used for such shots? As for the crowd behaviour, there were no complaints from Johnny and apologies in "The Scotsman". The behaviour "was very far indeed from being directed against him personally. I'm afraid the truth may be that we Scots are an excitable lot. Personally I blame the porridge and oatcakes, not the whisky."

1896

A decision had been taken at the previous year's delegates' meeting that, with the increased entry causing the championship to run into a fourth day, the final would be played over 36 holes. Another more contentious and significant matter, due to be raised at the meeting of delegates in Sandwich, was the possible formation of a Golf Union, which would take over from the Royal and Ancient their role relating to the rules. This had the support of a number of clubs south of the border, including the Royal Liverpool who had authorised their delegate James Cullen to vote in favour. In the end Hall Blyth, who had introduced the motion, sought leave to withdraw it as clearly there was no consensus.

It would not have been difficult to pick Freddie Tait as the likely winner, not just because he had won the St. George's Grand Challenge Cup, the stroke-play prelude to the championship, but he had shown a liking for the course with some previous successes including ninth place in the 1894 Open. However when the draw was made, his task did not look easy. It was, to say the least, unbalanced with "the most noted players together in a heap near the head of the list." Tait, Ball, Laidlay, Hutchinson and Mure Fergusson who were to meet in the first round, and Leslie Balfour Melville, the holder, were all in the top half, with only Hilton of the elite in the lower half.

Tait after an easy first round match played successively Hutchings, Laidlay, Ball and then Hutchinson in the semi-final. He kept his own golfing diary recording the scores in every match he played, whether a competition or friendly round, noting against them some brief comments. His account of this championship was as follows:

"First round. C. G. Broadwood played a good game out in 35 – 4, 5, 4 first three holes in. My opponent was evidently off his game. Very heavy rain during the last part of the round."
"Second round. C. Hutchings – CH went rather off his game against the wind. A beastly day v. wet and windy. Won four."
"Third round. J. E. Laidlay – the wind increased to a gale with very cold rain. Golf v. difficult to play. A very good match up to the tenth hole. JEL not driving very well."
"Fourth round. J. Ball – FGT played a very strong game and rather demoralised the ex champion. Out in 36 in 5, 4, 5, 6, 5. Putting very well. Won the match by five up and four to play. John Ball very steady. Fairly strong wind."

He was now to face Horace Hutchinson in the semi-final. This was the stage at which he had lost in each of the three preceding years, and he must have been fearful of a similar result when he started badly and was two down at the turn. His diary continued, "But after that I played a good game, especially after a row with HGH at the twelfth hole about my caddie. Holed a fine putt to win the match at the sixteenth hole. HGH putted v. well." It is interesting that reference to the row with the caddie was excluded in Low's biography of Tait, which otherwise records verbatim the diary reports of all the matches. The account in "The Scotsman" on the play at the first three holes home may give some background to the altercation.

"Approaching the tenth green, which is a nasty pitch, Mr. Hutchinson duffed his shot and was badly bunkered. In his effort to recover he failed, was caught in another trap, and Mr. Tait had the hole in hand. Now only one down Mr. Tait put himself on equal terms with his opponent. At the next hole both were on the green in two, and Mr. Hutchinson was strong in his long putt. Mr. Tait played the like safe for holing, and Mr. Hutchinson failed with his chance from eight feet. Two good drives brought the Scotsman, who was now playing a splendid game, to the twelfth green. The Westward Ho! player had rather a nasty stand from which to play his second. He failed to get a hold of it and was wide with his next......"

So Hutchinson had lost his lead and, maybe with it, his normal equanimity. He lost the thirteenth as well and as the diary recounted, Tait closed him out by three and two.

Hilton, as expected, reached the final, but not without a difficult third round game against Harry Colt of Rye in the very worst of the weather. At the bottom of the draw he was out late, "and at about 12 o'clock there was an ominous appearance in the sky. That something was coming was very evident, as the sky was black as ink. ... Without a moment's notice the wind swept down the course carrying everything before it. ..." The luncheon marquee was flattened and the press tent was only saved by "the united efforts of its occupants." Hilton and Colt, the former one up at the time, had driven from the tenth tee as the storm intensified. They sheltered for twenty minutes before resuming.

"When the unwelcome visitation had passed over, we proceeded to find the balls; his was easily found, but mine was not so easy to discover. Eventually we found it tucked up hard against the face of the pot bunker lying to the left of the big bunker which has to be crossed with the second shot. It must have been over 300 yards from the tee and yet that ball could not have carried over 100 yards. The force of the wind in that storm must have been extraordinary. I never got out of that bunker; my hands were so cold I could not hold my club. The play for the remainder of the round approached the farcial. We were both so cold that we could hardly hit the ball at all."

Hilton found himself two down with five to play but some how scrambled home at the twentieth. In the semi-final he beat his young Hoylake friend Jack Graham, playing in the championship for the first time.

As for the final, Tait's diary sums it up as follows: "Played a particularly strong game 36 + 41 = 77. With the exception of a few short putts the score could not have been improved upon. FGT six up at the end of first round. Hilton played a v. plucky uphill game. 83 first round. Second round FGT v. steady except first hole. 39 out. Hilton again very plucky and holed some good putts." Despite the pluck Hilton could take him no further than the eleventh green and he too agreed that Tait "was in most merciless mood, and I never had a chance. Not that I way playing even indifferent golf, far from it, but the truth was simply that I was outplayed in every department of the game." Tait's score for his first round, 76 according to the press reports, would have been a course record in stroke-play. He was indeed a worthy winner.

The end of the morning round. Tait studies his putt

1897

Muirfield, the home of the Honourable Company, became a new venue for the championship in 1897. There had been some criticism of the recently opened links at the time of the Open Championship in 1892, but not now, as it was in fine condition and there had been major changes, with the course lengthened by 500 yards to nearly 6000. At the meeting of delegates held prior to the championship to discuss the further rotation, a proposal to add Westward Ho! to the list, as a third English venue, was rejected. Hoylake would stage the championship again next year followed by Prestwick in 1899, Sandwich 1900, St. Andrews 1901, and Hoylake once more in 1902 before it came back to Muirfield.

By the end of the first day both Ball and Laidlay had been eliminated. Robert Maxwell accounted for the former. He was a young man of 20, playing in his first championship, having joined the Tantallon Club a few months earlier, so that he could enter. In North Berwick he was known to be a fine player and when he took an early lead of two holes against the great man, local spectators were nodding knowingly. Ball recovered and led by a hole playing the eighteenth, but young Maxwell holed there and Ball missed. The first four extra holes were halved in 3, 5, 4 and 4 before Maxwell holed from seven feet at the twenty third for the match.

Tait and Hilton were defeated on the second day. Tait, never in the lead, lost a fine match to Greig by a single hole. He was round in 83 to Greig's 82, and Robert Maxwell further enhanced his stature by beating Hilton who had temporarily lost his form. Once again there was a solitary Englishman in the quarter-final with seven hungry Scots.

The Englishman was Edmund Spencer from Hoylake, aged 21, who was developing into a good player. He had beaten John Ball in practice and was expected to win against John Low a young member of the Royal and Ancient in the quarter-final. His game was however sabotaged by a private dinner party that evening. "When I say that we were played home to our hotel (John Ball, Jack Graham, Harold Janion and one or two others) by the celebrated golfer Freddie Tait of the Black Watch, and up the stairs at the New Inn Gullane with FGT blowing lustily on his pipes, it seems obvious that my chances were not improved!" Low won by three and two.

In the top half of the draw the 19 year old James Robb from St. Andrews earned his place in the final by beating Low, who was three down with four to play. By means of a pitch and run dead, a putt from the edge of the green and a stymie, he squared the game. When Robb missed from two and a half feet at the nineteenth and hooked his tee shot near the wall at the twentieth it looked as though his chances had gone, but he luckily halved that hole and despite another hook from the tee at the twenty-first won the match there.

Meanwhile Jack Allan, a young medical student from Edinburgh who played at Braid Hills and was competing in his first championship, was working his way through to the final with narrow victories against Auchterlonie and Balfour Melville in the quarter-final and semi-final. There were a number of unusual features about his play. His style had "a good deal of individuality ... standing almost upright he has a long easy slow, and what at first glance might appear, a loose swing." He was also criticised for his pitching and half shots on the grounds that "he has not mastered the wrist stroke." All were agreed however that he was a splendid putter. "Another of Dr. Allan's peculiarities was the eschewing of anything approaching a nail in his golfing shoes and like our statesman golfer he preferred to play bareheaded. On each of the four days over which play extended he travelled from Edinburgh to Drem by rail and bicycled the four miles to Muirfield. His caddie was the smallest of small boys, picked up on the Gullane road, so that of caddie's counsel he had none. Calm and imperturbable, he fought his own fight; of all there, he seemingly the least concerned."

27

A leader in "The Scotsman" commented on the success of the younger element ...

"It may be premature to suggest that because all recognised masters of the game have fallen by the way, and two young and comparatively unknown players have been left to fight out the final match, the days of the select ring have passed away. But in truth everything now points to the likelihood of the trophy passing each year into different hands. For one man that played ten years ago, ten play today and every year the entry for the championship grows larger and the chances of any individual immeasurably smaller. ... The game is for those who have youth and strength and are as yet innocent of nerves."

It was indeed premature to write off the "recognised masters" as the next few years were to demonstrate and as to the contestants being "innocent of nerves", there was no evidence from the early play in the final that this was so. Robb made an inauspicious start with 6s at the second, third and fourth holes, losing all three. With Allan one up at the halfway stage, Robb again started badly after lunch, losing three of the first five holes. He was back to two down playing the eleventh but here his chances of recovery disappeared due to an unfortunate incident. Allan hooked his second shot towards the wall. The ball could not be found. The search continued for some time, until eventually it was identified in the pocket of Robb's caddie. Presumably it had rebounded some considerable way from the wall, and the caddie had been seen picking up a ball, but as to whether he had done it wilfully or through some misconception one will never know. Robb himself had nothing to do with the incident but lost the hole. From three down with seven to play he was unable to make further progress and lost the match by four and two.

Whether Allan's rich potential would ever have been fulfilled is a question that tragically was left unanswered. He qualified as a doctor that summer but early next year he contracted a serious chest infection and died.

Jack Allan

1898

There was considerable optimism at Royal Liverpool that, as on the last two occasions the championship had been held there (1890 and 1894), they would again cheer a home bred winner. Fifteen out of the seventy-eight entries were from the home club, including Harold Hilton, who had won the previous year's Open Championship over the Hoylake links. He had maintained this form at the start of the new season with medal wins at Westward Ho!, Lytham St. Annes and Hoylake. John Ball was, as always, a force to be reckoned with, though an injury to a muscle in his left arm, which he had sustained some weeks earlier, was still giving him trouble and there were doubts as to whether he would play. Graham, Dick, Spencer and Hutchings were also expected to do well. Those who had watched the preliminary play might have placed a pound or two on Freddie Tait, for in practice he was round in 74 in a four ball match, partnered by Jack Graham against Ball and Hilton. With Graham contributing usefully the other pair never won a hole. On the day before the championship started a match was played between Tantallon and Royal Liverpool. Tait, playing top for the Scottish club, met Ball and took five holes from him over the two rounds.

The draw for the championship meant that a clash between Hilton and Tait was a probability in the fourth round. Hilton won his first three matches with ease, whilst Tait scraped through at the nineteenth hole against Hutchings in the third round. All Liverpool seemed to be there to see "the match of the week". At the second hole Hilton with a possible putt for a win, missed it and the one back to lose the hole. He topped his tee shot at the next, missed a short putt at the Cop hole, and the match became a procession and the anticlimax of the week. A dispirited Hilton and disappointed hordes were walking back to the clubhouse from the thirteenth green.

The home chances were however still alive as Graham and Ball won their fourth round matches for places in the quarter-final, but next morning Ball fell to Robb who was round in 78. Meanwhile, Tait, who was staying at the Graham family home close to the links, was having a somwhat nervy encounter with his host, which Graham should have won, but for missing two of the shortest putts. The second of these, to take the match to extra holes, was described by Hilton who was watching as "about the shortest I have ever seen missed in a championship." So after all the high hopes four Scotsmen all from St. Andrews were left to contest the semi-finals. Tait versus Low and Robb versus Mure Fergusson. The second match went to Mure Fergusson. He came from behind against Robb who was unable to repeat his fine form of the morning.

The previous year Low had lost at the twenty-first in the semi-final. This time he was to go one hole further but with the same result. The match, though not of the highest standard, was full of drama. Low played the steadier golf, whilst Tait alternated erratic strokes with remarkable recoveries. At the sixteenth, having driven into the ditch guarding the out of bounds, he could only move the second a short distance forward. From there he played a stroke of 200 yards or more to the green – reminiscent of the one that Ball had played in his final against Mure Fergusson four years earlier. Tait got his half there and the match was still level after eighteen holes and then, as Hilton describes:

"The fun still continued in the play off. The first hole was halved, but the end seemed certain to come at the twentieth hole, as Freddie half topped his approach, and ran past the hole into the grip beyond. His third was again an indifferent one leaving him some seven or eight yards away. In the meanwhile John Low placed his third dead, and this putt of seven or eight yards had to be sunk or all was over. Down it went, but I cannot help thinking that that putt was a lucky one, as he hardly took the trouble to look at it, a most unusual thing for him; he simply walked up and hit. Another nasty obstacle overcome. There were more however in the offing, as he pulled his next tee shot to square leg, and out of bounds it went, so that he had to drop another and lose one. John Low was eventually on the green in 3, and everything depended upon Freddie's fourth, a full wooden club shot; it was well played, but always seemed to be working away to the right of the hole. When it pitched, however, it got a most extraordinary kick towards the pin, and finally finished up but a few yards away, and down he ran his putt once again. The finish came at the next hole, where John Low failed in his putting and his enemy did not."

The final was not such a memorable match. Tait was too strong for Mure Fergusson. There was however one notable moment, when the latter with a wayward drive at the third hole onto the fourteenth green, dropped clear into a dreadful lie. Freddie instantly stepped forward and gave the ball a decent lie. The crowd yelled "Bravo Tait," and his friends muttered, "That's Tait all over." For the record Tait was round in 80 in the morning, out in 39 for the second round and won by seven and five. He further endeared himself to the locals at the prize giving. Acknowledging receipt of the Cup and Gold Medal, he said, "Thank you for the way in which you have received my fluky win. I ought to have been beaten twice yesterday, but I got off. I played better today but I really don't deserve the championship." The report continued – "The crowds called for Mr. Tait to come out onto the balcony with his bagpipes, but Mr. Tait remained in the seclusion of the club lounge."

There are other stories of him and his bagpipes, that he played them marching down Market Street the night before the final and that he played them standing on the dining room table in the Graham household. Whether they are true or not, they fit the popular image of Freddie Tait.

1899

At Prestwick the championship entry exceeded 100 for the first time which meant a very full opening day's play. The draw brought Balfour Melville and Robb, and Laidlay and Graham together in the second round. Robb was not in form against Belfour Melville and lost by four and three. That was not true of Graham who reached the turn in 37 but Laidlay was better still and, 35 out, was two up at the turn and went on to win at the sixteenth, although the newspaper report, after giving details of the scores for nine holes, simply added, "Play was not concluded until 7 o'clock." This may have been one of the reasons for the

Tantallon representative at the delegates meeting making the proposal that, "a day's play at scoring be held on the first day of the Amateur meeting, the best scores afterwards to engage in matchplay." The report of the meeting concluded brusquely – "the motion not being seconded, fell to the ground."

Play on the second day proceeded largely according to form and resulted in two more clashes of the giants in the quarter finals on the third morning. Ball was to play Maxwell in a repeat of their outstanding match at Muirfield two years earlier and yet again Hilton was to face Tait. They had played on the day prior to the championship, when a return match between Tantallon and Hoylake took place, Tait beating Hilton by two holes. Hilton had been somewhat lucky to beat John Gairdner from Richmond at the twentieth hole in the fourth round, having halved the preceding hole despite an excursion onto the railway line. Against Tait the luck ran the other way. Tait's hooks at the fifteenth and sixteenth deserved punishment but found lies from which he was able to reach the green and retain his one hole lead. At the eighteenth Tait, for variety, sliced wildly towards the fourteenth green. The shot looked scarcely possible, but from there he played a miraculous pitch and run, up and over a bank, onto the green. Even then Hilton was well inside him with hopes of levelling the game, but Tait's putt left him with a dead stymie and robbed him of any chance. So for Hilton the Tait bogey had still not been laid.

Ball against Maxwell had been just as exciting with Ball establishing an early lead, four up after six holes. From the seventh, Maxwell held the honour for the rest of the match and the holes slipped away from Ball, until, missing a four foot putt at the eighteenth for the match, they were back to all square. Maxwell hit the longer tee shot at the nineteenth, but Ball played his second with a brassie to within twenty yards of the pin. Maxwell failed to match this with his cleek and this time Ball's short putt for a four and the match found the hole.

The two winners of those morning clashes had less trouble that afternoon. Ball was out in 35 against Whigham, a young member of the home club, and won at the twelfth, whilst Tait came through at the seventeenth against Williamson from Musselburgh. So the final that everyone had been waiting for had at last materialised. Scotland was to play England, the champion against the five times winner, Freddie Tait versus Johnny Ball, the two most popular and respected figures in amateur golf.

Bernard Darwin, who had been beaten in the fourth round, stayed on to watch the final and subsequently wrote, "The more matches I watch, the more I think that this was the greatest, the most prostratingly exciting of them all." Play had been even for the first few holes until Freddie drew ahead, in part through his own good play and in part through Johnny's old fallibility with the short putts. He missed three of them in quick succession, and after fourteen holes had plunged to five down. By the end of the round he had recovered two of them and so, with more positive thoughts, he spent most of the interval on the eighteenth green, with Harold Hilton in attendance to advise him, trying a number of different weapons. Tait meanwhile was resting on a sofa in the clubhouse, pondering no doubt on the loss of those two holes.

When a big lead begins to disappear, it breeds that feeling of insecurity and this will have been heightened when he pushed his tee shot on to the railway at the first hole in the afternoon and another one was gone. By the sixth the match was all square and the initiative firmly with Ball. So it remained until he missed another short putt at the eleventh. This surely was a critical moment and the opportunity for Tait to draw ahead again but, with the honour, he hooked far and wide, over the Burn and out of bounds, and his lead had gone again. Ball won the sixteenth to become one up. The seventeenth at Prestwick, the Alps hole, measured 370 yards and the second shot, if the green was to be reached, had to carry a high range of sandhills and a large bunker guarding the green, a bunker which at the time was more than half filled with water. This hole in the 1899 Amateur Championship final has been immortalised by the writing of Bernard Darwin and is as much part of golf history as is the final hole at Turnberry in the 1977 Open Championship. Tait played his second shot first and, failing to carry the bunker, was in the water. Ball followed with a fine shot, but signals from the hill indicated that it had just failed to make the carry and lay on wet sand close to the sleepered face of the bunker. Tait waded in, the water being a foot or so deep, and the ball bobbled with his ripples. He waited a moment for it to settle and then splashed out:

"It was a grand shot, no doubt of that, and as the hero waded out again he was helped up the bank by willing hands, like another Horatius emerging from the Tiber. Long before the cheering had ceased Mr. Ball had played an almost equally great shot from horrid, hard, wet sand with the boarded face close to him. He has always however had a genius all his own for making the ball get up almost vertically if he wants to, and out it came apparently with the utmost ease."

The hole was halved, but Tait with three perfect shots at the eighteenth squared the match.

Huge crowds followed them to the first hole. Amongst them was Harold Hilton who had found a place on the hill to the left of the green to watch the second shots. On this occasion Johnny had the longer drive and Tait's shot to the green ...

"... was not at all well treated, as it seemed to get a shooting fall, the ground just short of the hole being very hummocky. In any case, whether it was owing to the way in which the stroke was played or to the unfortunate fall, the fact remains that it left the striker a putt of some seven to ten yards. Johnny Ball's approach was also ruled on the pin. What would it do? Skid over the green like the other, or pull up? We were not long in doubt, as from the very first bounce it was evident that it was not going to travel far and it gently trickled on until it passed the hole by about seven feet. Freddie Tait had a most difficult putt. He made a good bid, but it never looked like going in and everything depended upon Johnny's seven footer. A man standing beside me remarked, 'These are just the ones he misses.' I thought to myself, 'No these are just the ones he holes.' Had it been three or four feet I should have been more anxious. From where we stood we could not see the outline of the hole, and it was impossible to tell whether the ball was going in or not, but I liked the look of the striker as the ball was travelling. I knew his attitudes well, and was not at all surprised when the ball disappeared."

Tait's disappointment at letting slip a match in which he led by five holes, and at his failure, during the earlier part of the second round, to play up to his own high standard was quickly forgotten and typically at the presentation he spoke warmly of Johnny Ball – if he was to lose, there was no other man by whom he would rather be beaten.

When Johnny returned to Hoylake next day there were crowds five deep on the platform of Hoylake station to greet him and whisk him away to the clubhouse for further celebration. Over the next few months dinners were held and presentations made. The members subscribed £300 and this went towards a portrait for the club, to be painted by the Liverpool artist R. E. Morrison, a new clubhouse clock and a gold hunter pocket watch for Johnny himself, not that he was looking for any such approbation.

Little did the golfing public realise that they would never again be following the golfing exploits of Freddie Tait and for a couple of years Johnny Ball would be missing from the championship scene. Tait was a soldier and when the Boers declared war in October he was full of enthusiasm at the prospect of sailing to South Africa with the Black Watch to fight them. For Johnny, although there was a strong element of patriotism in him, the decision to enlist was more surprising. He had previously participated as a territorial in the Wirral troop of the Earl of Chester's Yeomanry and attended camp with them. They had been disbanded a few years earlier and some of his friends had transferred to the Denbighshire Yeomanry. They encouraged him to volunteer, even though it was doubtful whether, because of his age, he would be accepted for active service. In the end he was accepted, completed his training at Aldershot and sailed from London in early February.

A few days later the tragic news broke that Freddie had been killed leading a counter attack against the Boers at Koedoesberg. It was received with stunned disbelief not just by the golfing world. Tait was a household name and he was everybody's hero. His infectious humour, his high spirits and his friendly disposition were combined with generosity and modesty, all of which endeared him to fellow soldiers and fellow golfers alike.

1899 had been a year of great golfing achievement for him. In addition to the Prestwick silver medal he had won the St. George's Grand Challenge Cup, the three major medals at the Royal and Ancient and the Calcutta Cup. His final match, before sailing, was another challenge against Johnny Ball played in early October, thirty-six holes at Lytham, and there he avenged his Prestwick defeat, winning on the last green.

His record in Amateur Championships was outstanding. He played on eight occasions winning thirty of his thirty-six matches with two gold, one silver and three bronze medals to show for it. Almost more remarkable was the fact that in the last four Open Championships he finished third twice, fifth and seventh. Only Harry Vardon achieved a lower aggregate score over those sixteen rounds. Tait was however no part-time golfer. His golfing dairies reveal how much he played. He recorded each game on one line – seventeen lines to the page – and in 1898 there were fifteen pages, and another thirteen pages from January to October 1899. That represents an average of five rounds each week.

He was just 30 years old. One can only conjecture what records might have fallen to him had he been spared that Boer's bullet.

Freddie Tait

John Ball

CHAPTER TWO

Hoylake Heroes

1900

It was no surprise that the first fifteen years of the championship had seen the entry increase from forty to more than a hundred. The growth in popularity of the game was such that the number of clubs had increased more than eightfold since 1885 from just over 160 to 1350. South of the border golf had become socially acceptable, the railway system had made courses more accessible and the mass production of clubs and balls had reduced the cost of the game. All this meant more competition and an improvement in standards. More players were capable of reaching the closing stages or springing a surprise by beating one of the established "cracks". A few interested spectators had watched in 1885 at Hoylake and the following year at St. Andrews, but through the later part of the 90s several thousand followed the main matches, creating crowd control problems which had yet to be solved. With this wider public interest newspaper coverage had also increased dramatically. At Prestwick in 1893 the local postmaster and one clerk had handled the telegrams but, six years later, eleven extra hands had been called in from Glasgow. Whilst overall control remained with the delegates from the leading clubs, who met each year during the championship to discuss future venues and possible changes in format, the detailed organisation was in the hands of the host club, who took the entry money, paid the ground expenses, advertising and cost of medals, leaving the balance to be distributed in kind to the medallists. Johnny Ball had purchased two bicycles with his 1899 prize voucher of £30, a figure that equated the Open Championship winner's prize of the previous year.

"A championship without Mr. Ball and Mr. Tait would not appear like a championship," one of the golfing scribes had written in an early preview for 1900. In the event it was quantity not quality that caused concern at Sandwich. The entry was only sixty-eight with just seventeen travelling from north of the border, although none of the potential winners were missing. Laidlay, Balfour Melville, Mure Fergusson and Maxwell made the journey, as did Robb, Whigham

35

and Williamson, all recent medallists. It was just as well that there was a strong entry from Oxford and Cambridge, which included John Bramston, a 19 year old Oxonian, who had excelled in a match at Westward Ho! a few weeks earlier by beating Horace Hutchinson and Harold Hilton on the same day. There had been rumours too that an American team would be coming to play some matches and then in the championship. As it turned out, only one, A. G. Hamilton from Baltusrol, entered and he lost by eight and seven to Charles Hutchings on the first day in the vilest weather, a strong north-easterly wind and driving rain. He must have wondered whether his journey was worthwhile. Laidlay and Hutchinson, two of the three past champions playing, also met on the first day, and their golf matched the weather conditions. It was just as well there were not many spectators to watch it, as Hutchinson was off his long game and Laidlay was making errors on the green. The former's problems were the more serious and Laidlay won by four and three.

The two favourites for the title, Hilton and Maxwell, met on the second morning. On the day prior to the championship Maxwell had won the Grand Challenge Cup, with scores of 77 and 78, and his long game was said to be magnificent. Hilton had reached the final on his two previous visits to Sandwich and had been playing well in club events. He was strongly tipped to win "with the spell of the personality that so often barred his way removed." (Tait had beaten him five times in the previous seven years.) In this match of giants, Maxwell started strongly and took an early lead, but Hilton won the fourth and fifth. The sixth was crucial and he describes it:

"I had the best of the tee shot, and had nearly holed in 2. Maxwell had a comparatively easy putt for a half but he missed it. Still he did the next best thing to holing it, as he laid me a dead stymie, his ball being only an inch or so from the hole. Now, the green at the Maiden hole at Sandwich is almost an ideal one on which to attempt to loft stymies, as it has plenty of grass on it, and it is consequently very easy to get under the ball; under ordinary conditions, I should have had no hesitation in going for the stroke, but this was a championship, and had I knocked it in, as I certainly would have done had I hit his ball, I should have lost a hole which I had every right to win. In addition to the actual loss of the hole there was also the moral effect to take into account, as although the match was still in its comparative infancy, it was certainly at a critical stage. I eventually went for the shot, and luckily brought it off making me two up."

Hilton won the next as well, holing from seven feet whilst Maxwell, who had reached the green with two fine shots, took three more. That turned out to be the key to victory.

Hilton went on to reach the final, easily beating his fellow club member Jack Graham in the semi-final. It had begun badly for Graham, as whilst the two of them were searching over the back of the green for Hilton's ball, a spectator shouted over, "It's in the hole." Hilton had holed his second shot with a brassie. The other semi-final was a closer affair. Young Robb from St. Andrews, having reached this stage for the third time, was matched against Bramston. The latter had the stronger long game, but Robb, by means of excellent holing out, stayed with him and the match was all square after fourteen holes. At the fifteenth Bramston topped his mashie second shot into a bunker and after several abortive hacks conceded the hole. He topped again at the sixteenth, into a water hazard. Having picked out, he played disinterestedly towards the pin, losing that hole as well. A fluffed approach at the next brought the match to a speedy conclusion. Afterwards he was asked about his collapse and he answered, "It was not a matter of nerves, I was in a state of absolute paralysis."

The final was as one-sided as the Tait versus Hilton game had been four years earlier, but this time Hilton was in control against his Scottish opponent. He was never behind, and drawing ahead during the second part of the morning round he lunched three up. Loss of rhythm affected Robb's driving in the afternoon and Hilton, reaching the turn in 36 shots, became nine up. The game ended two holes later. So Hilton in his fourth appearance in the final had won and achieved "his fondest ambition." No champion had previously won with such apparent ease. Only Maxwell had taken him beyond the fourteenth green and in the seven rounds he had only to play ninety-four holes.

1901

The attraction of St. Andrews resulted in a record entry of 116 competitors of whom more than two-thirds came from north of the border, although sadly one of the favourites for the title, Robert Maxwell, who had shown fine form in the annual match between Tantallon and Royal Liverpool prior to the championship, was forced to withdraw due to a family bereavement. Of the previous year's medallists, Bramston was also absent. In his case parental pressure had resulted in him giving priority to his new city job.

Capain W. H. Burn, the recently retired secretary to the delegates' committee, had the longest first day, which ended in honourable disappointment. Having disposed of a fellow Scot on the twentieth green in the morning, he reached the same point in the afternoon against F. McKenzie from the St. Andrews Thistle Club. With both players on in two, all the day's good work was undone when he accidentally moved the ball with his putter. He called the penalty on himself and duly lost the match. By contrast, on the second day, Hilton, having disposed of Laidlay in the morning at the sixteenth, was matched against W. Herbert Fowler of the R & A in the afternoon. Fowler was as surprised to find himself in the last sixteen as were his fellow members. The report of the match read: "Mr. Hilton and Mr. Fowler claimed the attention of the crowd, although the result was considered a foregone conclusion. Mr. Fowler lost hole after hole, and wisely retired at the High hole, where Mr. Hilton was leading by seven." Herbert Fowler became better known for his golf course architecture than for his competitive successes. Walton Heath, the Berkshire and Saunton were three of his finest layouts.

For all the Scottish entry, only two from clubs from north of the border reached the quarter-final, although two of the others, both from Royal Liverpool, Graham and Dick, could claim Scottish ancestry. With Hilton and Hutchings also there that made it four from Hoylake. The latter lost by a hole to Horace Hutchinson with three putts on the eighteenth after a fine second shot to the green, whilst Dick's undoing was a putting lapse on the sixteenth, which allowed Low to take the lead and win at the Home hole. Both the semi-finals were close. Hilton playing first was one down to Hutchinson after twelve holes, but wrested the initiative and won on the seventeenth. He was soon up on the balcony of the clubhouse to see the end of Low's match against Graham as it came to the eighteenth, and...

"In the room behind me there was a table, around which were grouped four men deep in the intricacies of bridge, one of whom I noticed had apparently something to do with the management of the meeting, at least he sported the badge of a club official. I was casually asked

Tom Morris watches Harold Hilton drive against John Low

38

how the games were going. I replied, "there is a good match coming up. Graham has been three down with four to play against Low, but they are now all square with one to play." I rather anticipated that there would be a stampede to see the finish from the balcony, from which coign of vantage you can see every shot played. But not a bit of it! The four golfers proceeded once again to deal the cards, and he who sported the official badge remarked, "I don't take much interest in it now; all my horses are knocked out", apparently referring to the sweepstakes. I said nothing but thought a lot." ...

and doubtless he grieved a little when he had seen the defeat of his clubmate Graham.

Hilton was confident of beating Low over thirty six holes. Whilst Low's local knowledge and his putting prowess gave him a chance, Hilton's superior long game was expected to prevail and that was the way it appeared, as a lead of three holes at lunch had been increased to five when thirteen holes remained to be played. This was when Low's putting came into its own and gradually the lead was reduced. As it dwindled away the St. Andrews crowd factor added to Hilton's problems. When at the sixteenth he missed from three feet for a half and the game was back to all square, there was a rush for the seventeenth tee. One of the crowd barged into him shouting to his friend, "We'll teach these b.....y Englishmen." This was the spur that Hilton needed and he produced two of the finest shots of his career at the next two holes. With his third at the seventeenth he "brought a stupendous shot out of the bag by which he sent his ball, as straight as an arrow onto the green, where, never looking at Scylla on the left or Charybdis on the right, it ran up and over the hole. All felt the moment the shot was played that the fate of that hole, and probably the match, was now settled bar accident." There was no accident as Low was on the Road with his fourth shot and after two further efforts conceded the hole. Then at the eighteenth Hilton, playing his second, "clinched the fight by driving a superb long low shot like a bullet straight for the pin. The ball never deviated a hairbreadth and ran up towards Old Tom who was holding the flag, and stopped about six feet past the hole." Low's valiant effort for a 3 failed and so the champion had retained his title – the first time that this had been achieved since Horace Hutchinson had won his second championship in 1887.

1902

There were several golfing issues that were subject of press speculation during the winter of 1901-1902.

A deputation from Ireland had attempted to propose at the previous delegates' meeting at St. Andrews that an Irish venue be used for the championship. The report in "The Scotsman" at the time was highly critical of their treatment:

"The delegates never allowed the deputation to say a word. They did not show them the door, for the door was all they were allowed to see, and the reason given for this treatment was that the delegates could only entertain a subject which had been given notice of by a delegate three months before the annual meeting. This is surely redtapeism run to seed, and one need not be surprised if a new grievance be added to the already great number inflicted on auld Ireland."

Early in the new year one of the delegate clubs was reported to be supporting the Irish proposition, subject to them discontinuing their own Irish Championship. This proposal was subsequently withdrawn and, though there was no formal proposition for the 1902 meeting at Hoylake, the matter was discusseed and the delegates agreed that it was "not yet expedient to include an Irish green."

There was also much press comment about the new rubber cored Haskell ball, which was sweeping the gutty away in the United States. Though still in short supply here, it was now being tried by a number of amateur players. Ball, Hutchinson and Hilton all favoured it, though the latter described it as having "the habit of playing pranks on the short shots." All were agreed that it outdistanced the gutty by a large margin. Most of the leading professionals were however opposed to it.

The third matter was a decision by the Royal Liverpool to hold an England versus Scotland international match on the Saturday prior to the championship. This had been suggested previously and was a natural development from the Royal Liverpool versus Tantallon match, but the Royal and Ancient had not been prepared to take it on board. Though there was some concern amongst the delegates that the decision had been taken unilaterally, they approved of the selection committees appointed, if not the manner of deciding the contest – by holes rather than matches. Despite an anti-Hoylake feeling it was agreed that this should become an annual fixture.

The match itself generated considerable interest, even if, for the local spectators, the result was not as they had hoped. Scotland, having led by just one hole in the morning, won by an aggregate of six holes over the ten thirty-six hole singles.

By the end of the first day of the championship eight of the twenty players who had represented their countries had gone, mostly falling at the hands of other team members. Darwin and Ellis of England had beaten Balfour Melville and Blackwell of Scotland in the first round, whilst in the second round there were three matches each involving two members of the England team – Darwin beat Ellis, Hutchings beat Hutchinson and Bramston beat Smith. The match that drew the largest crowd, some 1500 spectators, was a repeat of the top match in the International. On the Saturday, Johnny Ball had beaten Robert Maxwell one up over thirty six holes, but in the second round of the championship the latter had his revenge. He needed 4 for 78 which was good enough to gain him a two and one victory.

Hilton, the holder, had an easy passage to the last eight despite being somewhat out of form. He was joined in the quarter-finals by three of the Scottish favourites Robb, Maxwell and Mure Fergusson and it was anticipated that two of these four would contest the final. Hilton and Mure Fergusson however lost in the quarter-final and Maxwell and Robb fell in the semi-final. The former did not play to his normal high standard and lost to Fry. Robb seemed to be in control against Hutchings, especially at the eleventh, where, with Hutchings only a few yards from the pin with his tee shot, he pitched into the hole from sixty yards for a winning 2. That however was the last good shot he played and he lost at the seventeenth.

Charles Hutchings driving at the 8th

Though both were members of the England team, Charles Hutchings versus Sydney Fry was a final that few would have predicted. Hutchings, aged 53, a past captain of the home club and a grandfather, had been a quarter-finalist the previous year. Sydney Fry, aged 33, from the Mid Surrey Club, who was holder of the St.George's Grand Challenge Cup, had a number of things in common with his opponent. Both had come to the game late. Hutchings was over 30 when he started, whereas Fry had only played the game for about six years. Both had a somewhat short and stiff action, and both were high class billiard players, Fry winning the amateur billiard championship eight times. The Haskell ball had helped both of them to the final and John Low wrote, doubtless referring to the semi-final match between Maxwell and Fry, "Players that Mr. Maxwell could formerly overpower with his long hitting can now with the aid of an easy stiff arm shot and the Haskell ball leave the big smiter behind." What he did not say was that their touch at billiards may also have enabled them to handle the livelier ball on the short shots more successfully than their illustrious opponents.

The final was even more dramatic than that of the previous year. In the first round Hutchings, playing superbly, was round in 75 and was eight up after twenty four holes:

"Surely a winning lead," as Guy Farrar wrote, "but holes kept slipping away, some due to his own errors, others owing to those deadly pitch and run shots played by his opponent, until at the Dun his advantage had been reduced to two up with three to play. He reached this green with two magnificent wooden club shots, Mr. Fry, who was short, played a good third over the cross bunker and holed for a 4, leaving Mr. Hutchings, who had been very lazy with his approach putt, an awkward one for the half. This was the crisis of the match. If he failed to hole this putt he would have lost seven out of the last ten holes – six out of ten was bad enough in all conscience. The putt dropped and we breathed again! Mr. Fry, refusing to acknowledge defeat, won the seventeenth in 4; but at the last hole his second was away on the right of the green, his opponent's ball lying about eight yards from the pin. Once again Fry played a beautiful run up with his jigger, leaving himself about four feet from the hole. Could the tired and weary Mr. Hutchings get down in two more? Eight yards can look a long way when, at the end of a championship final, two putts are required for victory. His first effort was a bad one, nothing like dead, but he holed the next amidst a mighty burst of cheering with which the Hoylake supporters relieved their pent up feelings."

It was a great recovery by Sydney Fry, but perhaps it was not surprising that the grandfather's legs were beginning to fail him, as including the international match it was his tenth round in six days. With this in mind some of his friends, confident of his victory, took a chair to the far end of the course to carry their hero home. The bearers with the chair, hot and embarrassed, followed from green to green until their services were required a mere 200 yards from the clubhouse.

Hutchings did not defend his title, through ill health. It was a pity that he did not finish his championship career on this high note, but in 1908 he competed again. By then his time was devoted more to his other sport, salmon fishing, and to tending the beloved roses in his garden in the Cotswolds.

1903

The numbers entering continued to grow. That seventy-nine Scots had entered at Muirfield was not as surprising as the fact that sixty Englishmen had travelled north. The large entry meant that a fifth day was required, with just fourteen matches scheduled for the Monday. This also meant that Tuesday was a very full day. With the sixty-four second round matches starting at 9 a.m. with four minute intervals between games, and the third round starting at 2 p.m., the arrangements were perfectly satisfactory for the early starters but far from it for those at the bottom of the draw. E. A. Lassen for example found himself with a 1.12 start to his first match, which he won at the nineteenth. There was no time for tea as he was due off again at 4.04 and it was no surprise that he lost heavily in the afternoon.

The second round saw a number of upsets with Fry, Hilton, Robb and Laidlay all losing. This left the way open in the second quarter for Robert Maxwell to advance, which he did joining Ball, Hutchinson and Balfour Melville in the quarter-finals. These four looked likely semi-finalists but Balfour Melville succumbed to Herman DeZoete from Royal St. George's despite leading by a hole with only three left. Ball also allowed a lead to slip. He was two up with seven to play against Angus MacDonald from Burgess, but his opponent, having won the twelfth, followed it with three consecutive 3s to take the lead and the last three holes were halved.

In the afternoon MacDonald played Hutchinson, who described the game in "Fifty Years of Golf":

"He was no doubt an immensely strong man. He was so strong and big that he seemed unable to swing round his body, as it were. He was the shortest driver for a player of his ability I ever met; but he was also the longest putter. Time and again, when I thought I had the hole, having arrived on the green a stroke before him, he upset calculations by holing a gigantic putt. He smoked all the time, a long Meerschaum pipe, and had all the air of a man playing the game for pleasure – which is not at all a common aspect for a man to wear when he is playing a championship heat. And after he had been holing these prodigious putts time after time, and I had been following them up by holing humble little things of a yard and a half or so, he fairly petrified me with astonishment by remarking, in a tone of almost pained surprise, "You're putting very well!" I looked at him to see whether he was chaffing, but his face did not show the twinkle of a smile and I had to assume that it was simple honest comment, and that he was accustomed, that he expected, to hole these gigantic putts, but that he did not expect his opponent to hole the little ones after him."

Despite the putting Hutchinson beat him with something to spare.

Maxwell's match against DeZoete was perhaps the match of the championship. The latter, who was playing in his first championship, was a long hitter, longer than Maxwell, but not as straight. By means of some good recoveries and fine putting he stayed with his distinguished opponent, won the eighteenth to square the match and headed for the nineteenth tee. Horace Hutchinson, his contest now over, was amongst the spectators and he watched DeZoete, hitting first, finish just short of the green. Maxwell hooked close to the wall, was a long way from the hole in two and by no means dead in three. Then it was DeZoete's turn.

"It looked as if he had but to do that hole in four to win the match, and it did not look as if he could fail to do it in four. But then, as he told me afterwards for the first time in the whole match nerves got hold of him, and having hold of him they seemed to have taken their hold very hard. He was unable, he said, to see the ball with any distinctness. It looked all in a fog; and, playing at it through this obscuring atmosphere, he sent it about a foot. The end of the hole was that Bobby, by holing his very missable putt, did get a four, and Herman took five and lost the hole."

This was not the result that Hutchinson wanted as Maxwell, formidable wherever he played, seemed better at Muirfield than anywhere else. He knew the difficult greens, and he could gauge the length of his second shots, all the more important in the final as the wind had changed. The match was close for the first thirteen holes, but then Maxwell completing the last five in 3, 4, 5, 4, 4, won four of them. Hutchinson held him to the turn in the afternoon, but Maxwell came again with another burst of low scoring and finished him off by seven and five. No winner at Muirfield could have been more popular. At the age of 26 he had already built a reputation for fine sportsmanship, but was happier playing amongst his friends than in front of a large gallery and was certainly no pot hunter. That was just as well, as for the first time the winner was to receive only a medal. The practice of dividing the balance of entry money amongst the medallists had been discontinued following the delegates' decision at the previous year's meeting. From now on three quarters of any surplus would go to the host club and a quarter to the central championship fund.

Robert Maxwell suffered no reaction when Scotland played England next day. He was in splendid form against Ball, and inflicted an eight and seven defeat on him over thirty-six holes.

1904

As expected the entry at Sandwich was lower than at Muirfield. Only a couple of dozen Scots entered, but there were six Americans. During the previous year the Oxford & Cambridge Golfing Society had toured the United States, the first British team of amateur golfers to cross the Atlantic, and this may have been the catalyst. Amongst them were some who had already made their mark in championships – Low, Bramston, Ellis and Hunter – and the final tour match, a well fought game against an all American team, was their only defeat.

The smaller field meant that the championship could again be completed in four days, which was just as well, as it was preceded by the annual stroke play event for the Grand Challenge Cup, and by the International Match. Arising from these two events Jack Graham established himself as one of the favourites, alongside Robert Maxwell. In an ill balanced draw it was likely that the two of them would meet in the third round. Ball, Hutchinson, Balfour Melville and

Mure Fergusson were all in that quarter as well and it looked likely that whoever won through would meet either Hilton or Robb in the semi-final. There were few of the established players in the top half.

The third round match between Graham and Maxwell duly took place. Graham had been in scintillating form the previous day reaching the turn in 32 against Balfour Melville, whom he beat by seven and six, whilst Maxwell scraped through against W. P. Matthews, a local player, despite having been two down with two to play. Maxwell reeled off the low scores in the match with Graham who continued to strike the ball imperiously, but could not match Maxwell's putting and lost at the fifteenth. With Hutchinson beating Ball in the fourth round, the quarter-final line up brought Maxwell against Hutchinson and Hilton against Travis, an unexpected name at this stage in the championship.

Walter Travis was from Garden City New York. Although Australian by birth, he had been brought up in the United States but had only started playing golf some seven years earlier at the age of 37. He was of small physique, weighing under ten stone – excluding the large cigar which was invariably hanging from his mouth. He was also a short hitter with a style that was said "not to attract the eye." Those that didn't know of him would have given him little chance. Those that did, knew that he had already won the United States Amateur Championship on three occasions, even if this was not yet an event of great significance. They also knew that he was a dour and determined character, made all the more determined by what he deemed to be poor treatment. He had been involved in a dispute in his first match, as to whether a club had been grounded on grass in a hazard. Having won the match he had been given no time to change from his wet clothes prior to going out against James Robb. Furthermore he had been allocated a gormless caddie and his request for a change was ignored by the caddie master. This caddie might indeed have cost him the second match, as when Robb instructed him to "tak it oot", the caddie picked up his master's ball which lay nearly dead. Robb would have been within his rights to claim the hole, but he didn't and lost the match on the last green. Whether it was these incidents or his deep and silent concentration, there was antagonism towards him developing amongst spectators and fellow competitors.

Hilton started badly against Travis and lost the first three holes. The American, reaching the turn in 36, remained three up and, though light and hope flickered briefly for Hilton after the turn, indifferent play, which later he confessed was partly due to the pressure of Travis's accurate second shots, lost him the match by five and four. Meanwhile Hutchinson and Maxwell were having a splendid tussle. All square playing the eighteenth, Maxwell was stymied with his short putt for the half. He bravely lofted it into the hole and then appeared to have the better of the nineteenth. Hutchinson however played a famous recovery from the cross bunker short of the green and Maxwell, having run through the green with his second shot, chipped back six feet past the hole and missed.

Hutchinson, no longer as strong as in his youthful days, was drained by the morning match and failed to reproduce the same form against Travis in the afternoon. Once again the American's straight hitting and accurate putting gave his opponent little chance. He was out in 34 and remained in full control. In the other semi-final Edward Blackwell beat Laidlay by two and one. Blackwell was a fine fluent striker, particularly strong from the tee. His short iron play and his putting were the weaknesses in his armoury. Next day, in the final, Travis again took the lead by winning the first three holes, two due to errors by Blackwell and the other with a long putt. The latter never recovered from these early set backs and the holes drifted away. Improved play in the later part of the afternoon did nothing more than reduce the margin and the two shook hands to lukewarm applause on the fifteenth green. Thus the 1904 Championship did not end on the happiest note.

Certainly Travis was an unexpected winner but not a lucky one. He had by no means an easy passage to the final, having showed his fighting spirit in the third round, recovering from two down with four to play against H. A. Reade a former Irish Champion. His putting was outstanding, with a centre shafted "Schenectady", acquired from a friend a day or so before the championship began. It was however not only the instrument for, as Darwin wrote, "No one kept so still after the putt had been struck." Hilton, one of the best judges of the game, complimented him on his extraordinary powers of concentration and on his technique, saying that he was one of the few to master the science of the game.

At the presentation the new champion did nothing more to endear himself to the crowd. When invited to say a few words, there was a moment's silence and then he said, "I am hopelessly bunkered. I pick up my ball." It was left to Horace Hutchinson to speak on behalf of the medallists and, in congratulating Travis, he said that he hoped that many Americans would keep coming to take part in the championship, "but never again let them win the Cup." Some hope!

1905

It was no surprise that Travis did not come to defend his title at Prestwick; nor were there any of his compatriots. There was however one interesting entry from across the Atlantic, George Lyon of Toronto, who had not only won three Canadian Championships but had become the 1904 Olympic Golf Champion, golf having been included in the Olympic Games for the first time that year. Despite the shortage of overseas players there was a record entry of 148.

The links had been lengthened, which was perhaps just as well, as with the rubber cored ball and the hard dry fairways, which had suffered from a lack of rain, a drying wind and some hot sun, the ball was running huge distances. The greens were said to be "slippery and white," all of which may have accounted for some early surprises. By the time the second day was over Ball, Hilton, Hutchinson, Laidlay and Lyon had all been beaten.

Of the thirty-two players contesting the fourth round, twenty-six were Scots and six were Englishmen. At the end of the day, there were still seven Scots left, as reported in "The Scotsman." In the bottom half of the draw two local players from the home club, Aitken and Whigham, contested one sixth round match, whilst Blackwell, the previous year's runner up, played the Hon. Osmond Scott from Westward Ho!, one of three golfing brothers, with an even more famous golfing sister, Lady Margaret Scott, who a decade ago had won the first three Ladies Championships. In the top half of the draw it seemed to be a question as to whether the other finalist would be Robert Maxwell or Jack Graham. They had won the top two matches for Scotland in the victory over England at the start of the week. The other two, Charles Dick and Gordon Barry, did not appear to have the same golfing pedigree.

It was however the 19 year old St. Andrews University student, Barry, who had the day of a lifetime by beating Maxwell in the morning and Graham in the afternoon. It had begun unpromisingly as his first shot "added to the number of balls which had found a lodgement on the railway line." He soon regained his composure and, out in 37, was a hole ahead of Maxwell, which by the twelfth had been increased to two. A pulled drive at the thirteenth lost him that hole. Another pull at the fifteenth left him with a difficult approach shot which was saved from a sandy fate at the back of the green by hitting a spectator and the hole was halved. A weak pitch at the Alps cost him his lead, and the eighteenth was halved in 4. At the nineteenth, after two fine second shots, Maxwell was at the back of the green and Barry a little nearer. The former, who had been putting tentatively most of the morning hit his approach putt firmly, and the ball trickled on six feet past. Barry putted up to within eighteen inches. Maxwell missed and knocked the ball away with the back of his putter, conceding the match.

Barry's afternoon game with Graham was watched by a crowd of 3000. It began with a half in 3. There were few weak shots by either player and first one and then the other took the lead. Graham squared the game at the Alps and at the eighteenth "neither of them got away a straight ball from the tee. Mr. Barry had the more difficult approach, but he played with great judgement, and lay between four and five yards from the pin. Strong with his run up Mr. Graham laid his third close to the hole, but Mr. Barry ran down the like, amid loud cheers, for a 3 and reached the final."

His opponent for the final was Osmond Scott. There could scarcely be more contrast in their styles. Scott had a beautiful swing and an easy rhythm with no evident hit or rapid acceleration. He propelled the ball considerable distances by sheer timing. Barry also hit a long ball but from a flat and loose back swing he hit vigorously through the ball, swivelling to a low follow through with knees bent and the left foot splayed at right angles to the target. "Fine careless rapture" was Darwin's description of it. He played some wild shots, but his pitching and putting remained sound throughout. This enabled him to reach the halfway stage all square and a strong start to the afternoon round soon put him two ahead – a lead he retained to the sixteenth hole, where another pitch and putt for a 3 clinched the championship.

"Fine careless rapture." Gordon Barry

Gordon Barry had moved to St. Andrews at the age of 13 and stayed there for school and then university. He had no golfing lessons and developed his style from watching and playing with some of the great St. Andrews players, such as Andrew Kirkaldy and Laurie Auchterlonie. The previous year, still only 18, he had become a member of the Royal and Ancient and won the Club Gold Medal with a 75, one stroke off the record. He had however been born in Cornwall of English parents and so "The Scotsman" had to admit that, though he had learnt his golf at St. Andrews, he was not a Scot. It was left to the captain of the club at the presentation to comment that, though an Englishman had won the championship, he had defeated a "Scott" in the final.

1906

Despite a call for the date of the championship to be changed to September, which it was felt would be more popular and would encourage a larger entry, over 160 competitors assembled at Hoylake. The links had been lengthened, and at 6355 yards it was now the longest of the championship tests, twenty yards longer than the Old Course at St. Andrews.

Only a couple of the leading contenders were required to play in Monday's first round matches, one of whom was Gordon Barry, the title holder now at Cambridge University, who had preferred to test his skills against the leading golfers than his knowledge against the University examiners. On the second day however past champions fell thick and fast. Barry lost to Gillies, Hilton and Maxwell were beaten and Ball, having come through a difficult game in the morning, once again lost to Laidlay.

Home hopes now rested with Jack Graham, although one of their lesser known players, F. W. H. Weaver, won an extraordinary fourth round match against one of Scotland's best, Robert Andrew. Andrew was two up with three to play, but putting lapses cost him the sixteenth and seventeenth. At the eighteenth he seemed sure to win as he was on the green for two, with Weaver, over the back for three and still some way away for four, but Andrew "after being slack in the run up, got off the line with his fourth and when asked to hole a putt of two feet he proved unequal to the task." After that Andrew was in no frame of mind to play the nineteenth and Weaver's steady 4 won him the match. Graham meanwhile was setting out against James Robb in the best match of the week. Graham was two under 4s for the first thirteen holes, and yet only one up. He had looked like going three ahead at the eleventh, but Robb holed from ten yards for a 2, whilst Graham missed from much closer. It was the fourteenth that turned the match. Robb was in trouble all the way and eventually holed from four yards for a 6. He had nearly picked the ball up and conceded the hole, as Graham after four good shots was all but dead, less than two feet away. He missed it and the initiative had gone. He lost the fifteenth and seventeenth with more weak putting and, despite carrying the cross bunkers at the last, failed to get the 4 he needed to prolong the match. Both were round in 76.

Robb beat Orr, a fellow member of the Prestwick St. Nicholas Club in the quarter-final and Harry Colt in the semi-final. Colt was Sunningdale Secretary, and two younger members of his club contested the other semi-final, in which C. C. Lingen beat E. A. Smirke.

The weather, which had been rough for most of the week, took a turn for the worse and the two finalists had to contend with gale force winds and squally showers. Robb, having moved from St. Andrews, was now playing his golf on the Ayrshire coast and should have been better equipped for such conditions than

Lingen, who was a recent convert to the game and whose handicap had come rapidly down from a modest 10 in the previous three years. For him it was a new experience. Neither coped adequately with it, but as anticipated Robb fared somewhat better and took a four hole lead by the end of the morning round, which he completed in 86 to 90 by Lingen. Though the weather improved for the second round, the standard of play did not. Robb won another hole, but lost the Telegraph (5th hole) – "and then followed the most extraordinary display ever given in the final of a championship". The Briars measured 365 yards and, played into a strong south westerly wind, had, as it has now, an intimidating drive over the orchard, tempered then by the fact that the out of bounds penalty was only one shot.

"Mr. Lingen drove out of bounds. Mr. Robb got by the side of the fence near the apex of the triangular piece of private ground abutting on the course. The Englishman was called upon to play his third before Mr. Robb had played his second, and Mr. Lingen topped the ball sending it forward only a few yards. Mr. Robb wisely chipped the ball out with his putter from the difficult lie, and then with his next put it into a clump of rushes. In playing out his club turned in his hand and the ball came to rest near the face of a hedge, into which he banged his fifth shot. With his sixth he got away to the right of the green, and Mr. Lingen having reached a bunker nearby in one less now seemed likely to win after all. From that point however the Englishman required four strokes before he holed out and Mr. Robb taking three, putts of two feet being missed by each in turn, the hole was halved in 9. Putts of two feet were again missed by each at the short seventh which was halved in 5. Utterly unnerved first one and then the other missed his ball on the way to the eighth which was halved in 6 and twice foozling with his iron to the ninth Mr. Robb lost the hole in 7 to 5."

Despite having taken 27 shots for four holes Robb was still three up but he lost another one at the twelfth where he drove into a bunker. His tee shot at the thirteenth left him a long putt and he was still five feet away in two. The match was at a crisis point, but he holed and Lingen missed. A winning 4 at the next and a half in 6 at the fifteenth finished the championship.

The standard of play in the final caused Robb to be dubbed a lucky winner. This was unjust. He was still under thirty and in addition to this victory he had gained two silver and two bronze medals in ten years of championship competition. He was now employed at a bank in Ayr and golf was very much a weekend and holiday occupation for him, very different from the days of his youth at St. Andrews. He put the poor play down to fatigue. He had ten gruelling rounds in boisterous conditions and, as all golfers know, it is difficult to retain a smooth swing for a long period in rough weather.

1907

Though a St. Andrews championship was always likely to attract a larger than normal entry, no one expected it to reach 200, which was thought to be unmanageable. The delegates discussed the problem at their mid week meeting but no conclusion was reached. They were asked to report back next year with their views on the two favoured options – applying a handicap limit of scratch, or a stroke play qualifying competition reducing the field to thirty-two for matchplay.

With 72 first round matches played on the Monday and another 96 second and third round matches on the Tuesday, a number of the top players were soon eliminated. One past champion was committed to fall in the very first round, as, yet again, the two Johnnys were drawn together – Ball versus Laidlay. They had played in the first round in 1905 and in the third round in 1906. This was their eighth match in the twenty two years of the championship. The quality of play in this one was probably the best of all and it was one of the lowest scoring matches in the championship. Ball, out in 35, was two up, but Laidlay won them back with a 2 at the eleventh and a 3 at the twelfth. Ball however, after bunkering his tee shot at the thirteenth, recovered with a fine third shot and won that hole in 4 to 5. The next two were halved before Ball holed from fifteen yards for a 3 to go two up with two to play. His drive at the Road hole finished in a cart rut and it looked as though the match might well go all the way, but he recovered well and finished the match with a hard earned half in 5.

The third round saw the defeat of four past winners, Hutchinson, Balfour Melville, Maxwell and Barry as well as Byers the U.S. Amateur Champion. The match of that round was between Jack Graham and Edward Blackwell, and they provided a superb exhibition of striking for a crowd of about 2000. Graham, 35 to the turn, was three up. By the sixteenth Blackwell had squared the match. At the last two holes Graham's putting fallibility recurred and he missed from no more than two feet for the hole at the seventeenth and from four feet for the match at the eighteenth. After two fine drives at the tie hole, Graham played first and the ball landed four yards from the pin "with such cut on it that it remained practically stationary." Blackwell too played a good one and, putting first from eight yards, holed. Graham's effort to stay in the championship slipped agonisingly past the hole.

Next morning Hilton played Robb, the holder, and beat him, just as he had done in the 1900 final, but he lost in the afternoon against Robert Andrew, who was one under 4s for twelve holes and six up, before a couple of errors reduced the margin of defeat to respectability. This left just one former winner in the last eight. Ball was in the bottom half with three Scots – Andrew, Blackwell and Guy Campbell, a youngster of 22, who had been playing excellent golf including a

A fine match. Ted Blackwell (right) beats Jack Graham

win against the much fancied Barker, champion of Ireland and Yorkshire. Whoever emerged from this quartet seemed likely to have little trouble in the final, as Wyatt, Harris, Gillies and Palmer were contesting the other place and none of them had experience of this stage of a championship.

Andrew played as poorly against Ball as he had played well against Hilton and never won a hole, whilst Campbell beat fellow club member Blackwell. His semi-final against Ball in deteriorating weather was full of tension. Campbell took the lead at the tenth, lost the eleventh and then four exciting halves followed as they turned into the wind with rain lashing their faces. At the sixteenth both had driven over the fence into the field (not out of bounds at the time). Campbell played first and pulled it into the pot bunker short of the green. Ball then played a stroke that Harold Hilton described in his report for the 'Morning Leader' as the shot of the championship:

"He pulled his cap just one fraction further down; he looked his favourite cleek up and down, and pressed the head on the turf just to see that it was quite firm and the shaft just right. Then he jumped up again on the wire fencing to take another look at the line. He took just two imaginary shots, and then the cleek did its work – true and as clean a shot as ever that cleek hit, and that cleek is Johnny's best golfing friend. The ball lay snug on the green and looked big and white, when one came up and saw Campbell's lying disconsolately in the sand."....

Ball duly won that hole and the next, clinching his place in the final.

His opponent was Charles Palmer from the Midlands. He, like Ball, was in his 40s but unlike Ball, having come to the game late, had a stiff but workmanlike swing. His success was based largely on his putting, as he had proved in the semi-final match against Harris. Holing putts of awkward length time and again, he played the seventeen holes that he needed in 72 shots, figures that would probably have accounted for Ball as well. Johnny was however a strong favourite to win over thirty six holes, the more so when the curtains were drawn to reveal gales and squally showers. Ball was never behind, but, as the showers turned into a downpour, he finished the first round with a flurry of 6s and 7s and lunched only two ahead. In the afternoon, despite a wrist injury that had been aggravated in the morning round, his superior technique enabled him to draw further ahead. When he won at the fourteenth his main concern was a speedy return to the refuge of the clubhouse, to escape the rain and the ordeal of 'chairing'. He made a dash for it over the ladies putting green and towards the sands, but his retreat was cut off and after all he ended up on the shoulders of his supporters in triumphant march across the first fairway, to celebrate his sixth Championship victory.

1908

The size of the entry and possible new venues were not the only issues filling the golfing columns during that winter. News emerged from Royal St. George's that they had been asked by the British Olympic Committee to manage the golf section for the 1908 Olympic Games. The course was booked, along with Princes and Deal, for the first three days in June, the week following the Amateur Championship. When this became known there were reverberations from Scotland on the grounds that the Olympic movement and golf had little in common and that, if it was to be included, then surely the Royal and Ancient should have been asked to administer the event. This brought the reply that the R & A had indeed been circulated two years earlier about the proposals, but, as no response had been received, it had been assumed they wished to play no part. Regardless of this, the leading amateur players were not prepared to support it, particularly as the dates proposed fell in the busiest part of the season.

This was the explanation for the presence of George Lyon from Canada at Sandwich. For him the championship would be practice for his objective of retaining the Olympic Gold Medal he had won four years earlier. Three rounds in the championship were however the only competitive games he played, as his entry for the Olympic golf was the only one correctly filed and through lack of support it was cancelled. He was asked to accept the Gold Medal, but declined.

Meanwhile there was plenty of action with first the Grand Challenge Cup and then the International match followed by the championship. There were some notable absentees in the entry of just under 200, with neither Robb nor Maxwell travelling from Scotland, and Barry, on this occasion, meeting his obligations to the Cambridge examiners. By the end of the second day a new champion was assured as the six past winners had all been beaten. Hutchinson and Laidlay fell at the first hurdle. Ball, who had played well in the International match and in his first round, lost in the second to Vivian Pollock, a fellow member of the English team. Charles Hutchings making a sentimental reappearance, the first since his victory in 1902, and Balfour Melville also lost in the second round and Hilton fell to E. A. Lassen from Yorkshire on the last green.

The end of the second day was certainly a long time in coming, highlighting one of the problems that the delegates had been addressing. Arthur Lincoln, the winner of the Grand Challenge Cup, set off for his 'morning' match at 2.15. It went to the nineteenth, as a result of which it was well after the advertised starting time of 4.55 when he teed off again and long past 8 p.m. before he completed the eighteen holes that he needed to beat Cuthbert Smith. Even then the day's play was by no means over, for in an earlier game Lionel Munn had lost the eighteenth hole to Charles Palmer and they set off to decide the tie. They halved the next nine holes, and the light was fading fast when Palmer holed for a 4 to win at the twenty-eighth.

No Scottish club was represented in the last eight, although there were the two Scotsman from Royal Liverpool, Jack Graham and Charles Dick. Of the rest, five came from inland clubs near London – Bishop of Wildernesse, Taylor from Richmond, Colt of Sunningdale, Mellin of Beckenham and Darwin from Woking. The Yorkshireman Lassen, who had entered from Lytham, completed the quarter-finalists. Graham beat Bishop in a fine match with the last seven holes all halved. He thus reached the semi–final for the fifth time. Surely against Herbert Taylor, a competent but little known performer, he would at last earn a place in the final and perhaps he would then face his clubmate Dick – shades of 1892 when two other Hoylake stars competed in the final. But it was not to be. Graham, as so often before, missed the crucial putts, four of them in the first nine holes of his semi-final, and then his driving failed him. Taylor won comfortably by four and three. Lassen and Dick were still all square with six to play, but Dick made the crucial mistakes, taking 6s at the thirteenth and fifteenth, and Lassen held on to win by two and one.

Some of the earlier finals had been noted for brilliant golf and pulsating excitement. More recently however they had been disappointing and this one was no exception. The golf over the first nine holes was good and Lassen established a two hole lead. Unaccountably he took 49 shots for the next nine holes, yet Taylor was unable to improve his position and remained two down at the end of the round. When Lassen had won the first two holes in the afternoon the match was as good as over and it finished on the twelfth green.

Every club likes a worthy winner when they host a championship. Ball, Tait and Hilton had been the first three names on the Royal St. George's roll of honour. In 1904 the champion had come from an unexpected quarter and now it had happened again. Lassen had however held his game together over eight competitive rounds and on the way had collected some notable scalps. Educated at Rugby he had been a fine all-round sportsman. It was suggested that he could have played cricket at the highest level, but his job as a Yorkshire wool merchant didn't allow him the time, so he devoted himself to golf. He had won the Yorkshire Championship in 1900 as a self confident young man of 24. Now he tuned his game for championships on the links at Lytham, where he spent many of his weekends supplementing his income by playing for high stakes, part of which went on champagne at lunch time.

As for the problems discussed by the delegates, none of these were resolved and it was simply agreed that a sub-committee should be formed with representatives from each of the five clubs that hosted the championship plus one from Royal Blackheath. There were some rumblings in the press about the unwieldly organisation of the delegates' committee and its lack of progress.

1909

A decision that those entering the championship should have a handicap of scratch or better did have some effect in reducing the size of the entry at Muirfield, which was down to 170. The notice advertising the meeting tells us that the entry fee was still one guinea, unchanged since the first championship. For those travelling from the south by rail, the English railway companies were offering a special deal. The return fare would be one and a quarter times the single fare to Edinburgh, with liberty to break the journey at Drem or Gullane.

When the draw was made the first four names out of the hat raised some eyebrows. By coincidence Hugh Alexander from Dunfermline and Major A. E. Williams (Harewood Downs) were the same names that had been drawn to start the championship in 1905. The second match brought together Lassen, the holder, and Palmer the 1907 runner up. "These two golfers closely resemble each other in style. They are typical examples of the manufactured golfers, and their game is neither pretty nor interesting to watch. There is none of the finesse, none of the delicate touch of the golfer who has been in the habit of swinging a club from youth upwards." Later in the article there were more disparaging remarks about their "customary deliberation." In the event Lassen beat Palmer by two and one, but then lost to Major Williams, who had reversed the result of his 1905 match with Alexander by winning three and two.

The other notable first round loser was a young American Jerome Travers, the U.S. Amateur Champion, who fell to W. A. Henderson of the R & A. The spectators were to remember the match not only for the surprising result, but for the fact that Travers was in shirt sleeves, unheard of at the time, and he wrote afterwards, "I don't think I could bring myself to play in a coat. It is foreign to what I have been used to. This is my sole reason for persevering with what in British eyes is a state of semi 'deshabille'." As for "W. A.", after winning one more match, he found himself with a late starting time against Bernard Darwin, a former University friend, who was staying at his home in Luffness, from where they were driven together to Muirfield by the family chauffeur. Darwin, dormy two down to his host, won the last two holes, and in the dark and wet they set off down the nineteenth, which was halved. At the next, as Darwin describes:

"Our second shots were both well struck, and vanished in the direction of the green. His ball was found beyond it, and mine on the green a little short of the hole. At long last I was left with a putt of a yard for the match. I advanced to the assault and the rain dripped so heavily off my cap that I stood back, shook my cap and began again. Again the same thing happened, and I had once more to stop. This time I took off the cap and holed the putt."

The chauffeur was there to drive them back to Luffness, where they sat down to dine together at 10 p.m. Such are the vagaries of a championship draw.

Defeat of Johnny Ball is always news, and this happened on the morning of the second day (his first match) against P. E. Grant of Dornoch. It had not been his week, as he had once more faced Robert Maxwell in the International match and was four down at lunch with Maxwell round in 75. The latter proceeded to play the next eight holes in 29 shots, thus inflicting on Ball his heaviest defeat – eleven and ten.

Maxwell was clearly the man to beat and, other than a close game with Herbert Fowler, had won all his matches with something to spare, disposing of Laidlay in the fifth round and Balfour Melville in the sixth. In the semi-final he was to play Bernard Darwin, whilst in the top half Captain Cecil Hutchison, a Muirfield member, faced Robert Andrew. In the previous round Andrew had beaten Norman Hunter in a splendid game in which, following the exchange of the first two holes, nine in succession had been halved in figures close to 4s. Andrew was round in 75 winning on the last green. The afternoon match with Cecil Hutchison started with five more halves, but Andrew's play then became ragged and Hutchison won the match at the sixteenth. Maxwell started moderately in his semi-final and, but for a lucky cannon into the hole off Darwin's ball at the fourth and an unlikely scrambled half at the fifth, might well have gone three down. Darwin three putted the seventh to lose his lead and Maxwell slipped into gear and won easily enough, completing the sixteen holes in 65 shots.

Not since 1902 had a championship final gone all the way. This one did. The two Muirfield members, both Old Etonians, played the match almost as a friendly, as they had played so many times before on that great golfing stretch from Gullane to North Berwick. There was no "laborious carefulness", yet the quality of golf was outstanding with long straight driving from each of them and few mistakes. At the ninth in the afternoon Hutchison holed a long putt for a 3 to square the game and, when at the next Maxwell topped his tee shot into a bunker, he went ahead for the first time. Not for long, as Maxwell won back the following hole. With four to play Hutchison was one up again:

"the next two holes were halved in 4 and 5 and amid intense excitement Mr.Maxwell who had hit a tremendous long ball to the seventeenth put his pitch nearly dead. Captain Hutchison who made quite a good one, just failed to hole and Mr. Maxwell made no mistake. All square with one to play. Both had good drives, the Tantallon man having to play the odd pulled slightly, Captain Hutchison on the other hand sliced a little. It took some time to get the crowd, who were in fever heat, steady before the crucial shots were played. The first one that Captain Hutchison played was under the circumstances a great shot, it lay six feet short of the hole. Mr. Maxwell with one of those deft little chips got nearer, but above the hole leaving himself a tricky putt. The first man just missed then came an awful period of suspense. Quite calmly Mr. Maxwell hit the ball. Slowly, slowly it trickled on and on. It got there and no more and so ended a championship which both deserved to win."

Maxwell, from his record in championships and international matches over the preceding ten years was undoubtedly one of the great players of the period. In addition to his Amateur victories, he finished in the top ten in the Open on six occasions. He was a man of formidable physique, but gentle, soft spoken and reserved. There was plenty of body movement in his swing, which Hilton described as peculiar to himself, "and it cannot be termed a style with even an average degree of elegance." For repetition of accurate striking and for the finesse of his half shots and the touch play on and around the green he could in no way be faulted. His very best performances were reserved for his home ground, maybe because he never felt fully at ease in amongst the crowd, the press and all the other trappings of a championship.

1910

There was some criticism of the Hoylake layout for the 1910 Championship. The holes were often cut near to the corners of the large, square greens, making approach shots very difficult. The cross bunkers in front of the Dun and Stand greens also made it virtually impossible to hold the ball down the prevailing wind. The course had been further lengthened and now measured 6455 yards. As it turned out the scoring in the championship belied these comments.

The draw brought the names of Ball and Maxwell close together, the latter having yet again inflicted a heavy defeat on the Englishman in the International match. In the event the anticipated second round clash did not take place, for in the first round Maxwell lost to H. M. Cairnes. This ended the great man's regular appearances for Scotland and in the championships.

There was a remarkable finish that day. Bernard Darwin had come to the eighteenth one down to Horace Hutchinson, who shanked his second and lost the hole. F. Kinloch described the nineteenth in Golf Illustrated:

"Then came a hole which will be historic. Mr. Hutchinson hit a beauty, down the course, while Mr. Darwin lay in one of the grassy hollows to the right, rather badly. From thence he played into the bunker short of the corner of the Race course. Then Mr. Hutchinson forgot all the sage advice he is wont to give – and as a rule acts on. He took his brassie instead of his cleek or iron, and put two balls running out of bounds – his fourth stroke was safe, but wide. At this time he had played two more. It was then Mr. Darwin's turn. He got out of the bunker clear of the course, and then proceeded solemnly to play three balls out of bounds, after which he gave up the hole, having played six shots and presumably exhausted his stock of golf balls. "How to play the nineteenth hole at Hoylake" by Messrs. Hutchinson and Darwin, would be interesting reading."

The Hoylake men were playing well. There were five of them in the last sixteen, of whom Jack Graham had produced some outstanding golf. In an early round in bad weather he reached the turn in 35. After a steady first nine in the fourth round he started for home 4, 3, 3, 2, 4, and another match was bagged. Against Gillies in the afternoon he was out in 33 and followed it with 4, 3, 4, 3, to gain a place in the quarter-final against Hilton, whose golf had been in the wilderness for a year or two, but he was beginning to play his best again. In this match he holed at the first from seven feet. Graham missed from four feet for the half and thereafter both putting and driving deserted him. He was a stroke a hole more than the day before, when Hilton won on the twelfth green.

Meanwhile Ball was coming through the lower half of the draw, but only with some difficulty. Pease, his opponent in the fourth round, was out in 36 and one up, but Johnny turned the game round with four consecutive 3s and when he finished at the sixteenth he needed two 4s for a 71. He had similar difficulty in the next round against Weaver, a sound local player, and only got his nose in front on the sixteenth tee. Three solid halves in par followed. Against Robert Harris in the quarter-final he lost the first three holes. By the thirteenth the game was square again and they halved the last five holes "in a grim dog fight of par figures," as Harris himself wrote. He went on to describe the nineteenth:

"Driving from the tee the balls came to rest within six feet of each other at the corner of the turfed dyke known as the Cop. A strong wind was blowing and a thunderstorm was threatening. Playing my second, I hit a shot with a driving iron and the ball flew low, eight feet or so from the ground into the middle of the green and with satisfaction I registered a thought of relief: "Well I've got the old lad now". Without waiting for my ball to finish its roll, John stepped to his, whisked the same club that he had driven with round his neck, pitched the ball on the green ten feet off and dead straight for the pin to finish eight feet beyond. I then putted three feet to the left, John failed to hole his eight footer and then noisily warned by thunder and lightning that I dare not hole my short putt against the Hoylake hero, tremulously I missed it."

Hilton in practice at Hoylake

With Ball and Hilton in the semi-final it seemed more than a possibility that Hoylake's two favourite sons might meet in the final on their own turf, but Colin Aylmer had other ideas. Aylmer had beaten Lassen in his first match, and apart from a tense struggle against the Scottish International Dr. Scroggie, in which he recovered from two down to win at the nineteenth, he had won his matches with something to spare. His putting against Hilton was as good as it had been all week and he won by four and three. Meanwhile Johnny was playing against Abe Mitchell, a young artisan from the Cantelupe Club in Sussex, who had a reputation for long hitting. He outdrove Ball time and again, but the latter with the advantage of playing his second shots first, put him under continual pressure and won easily.

"Mr. John Ball won his seventh championship by the finest golf he has ever played, and perhaps the finest golf that has ever been played in the championship," was the Golf Illustrated report of the final. Despite two stymies in the morning he was round in 73 and had only to play a further nine holes before he was shaking hands with Aylmer and all the spectators were cheering yet another home victory.

1911

The weather at Prestwick made the championship one to remember. There had been a long dry spell through May and the sun continued to blaze down upon competitors, spectators, greens and fairways. This was to play its part in the final outcome.

In the early matches nobility had a bad time. The Scott family were eliminated, with the Hon. Denys, Osmond and Michael all losing, as did Viscount St. Vincent from York, and the Honourable R. Bethell. The second day saw a thinning out of past champions, as Horace Hutchinson, Johnny Laidlay and Leslie Balfour Melville, all now over 50, lost narrowly to Fry, Darwin and Palmer respectively.

For the first time since 1904 there was a strong international element to the championship, with two leading Americans, one of whom was Chick Evans the U.S. Champion, four from Australia and one each from Singapore and Italy.

One of the best matches of the championship was the fifth round encounter between Evans and 18 year old Bruce Pearce of Hobart, Tasmania, who had come along with his elder brother, a former winner of the Australian Open and Amateur Championships. Evans had been warned about the British climate and customary mode of dress and had come equipped with a fine tweed suit, which despite the heat he had worn for his previous matches. After a blistering spell of eight holes in four under 4s he was three up with five to play against young Pearce. The Australian won back the fourteenth and sixteenth, missed an opportunity by three putting the seventeenth and squared the game with a fine 3 at the eighteenth. After two shots each at the nineteenth Evans was through the back and Pearce in the middle of the green. "Mr. Evans seeing the seriousness of the predicament took off his coat to his shot, and amid laughter and cheers from the crowd, made a good effort but could do no better than 5, and Mr. Pearce laying his putt dead won a popular victory."

Hilton at the top of the draw and Lassen in the bottom half had been working their way through without alarms. Hilton began his campaign with three six and five victories and went as far as the sixteenth hole only once before gaining his place in the final. In the semi-final he had played Gordon Lockhart from the home club who had beaten Pearce, but the locals had no real hope for their man and commented on Hilton, "He's got mair strokes in his bag than Gordon."

The other semi-final was not without incident. L. B. Stevens from Deal, who had surprised everyone by beating Abe Mitchell in the morning, started well against Lassen and was three up after six holes. At the seventh he grounded his club in some rushes, which Lassen queried with the referee. They played on whilst the referee made up his mind and Stevens holed out in one less than Lassen. It was then ruled that there had been an infringement and Stevens was only two up instead of four. Playing the tenth with the score unchanged Stevens sent his caddie forward to mark the line and played before he had moved. This time the referee intervened immediately and awarded another hole to Lassen. The further setback was more than Stevens could withstand, his game became ragged and a shanked mashie at the fourteenth finally swung it in Lassen's favour. "The Times" report on the match commented, "Rules are made to be observed and Mr. Stevens had to pay the penalty of ignorance, but he certainly deserves a full measure of sympathy. He is a fine plucky player possessed of a great strength and a good match playing temperament. He took his mishaps admirably and had he won, his victory would have been exceedingly popular."

Lassen, the tough Yorkshireman, was not the type to be affected by his somewhat fortunate victory, but the events of the previous day may have hardened the crowd against him in the final. It looked as though support for Hilton was unnecessary as he went to three up after nine holes, but with putting problems on the way home, the match was square after eighteen. He missed another short putt at the first hole in the afternoon and went two down when Lassen won the Cardinal (third) with a fine 4, but the latter bunkered his drive at the fourth. Hilton won that and three successive holes from the seventh. With the crisis past he moved confidently to his third championship.

There is no doubt that Hilton mastered the fast running conditions at Prestwick better than anyone else. Although his normal drive was played with draw, here on the Prestwick fairways and greens, a soft landing shot was sometimes needed and he had the technique to achieve this by playing a fade. It was the start of a memorable year for him. This victory was followed by a great Open Championship performance in which he finished third, just a shot behind Vardon and Massy, and then, in September, at Apawamis near New York, he added the U.S. Amateur Championship title to his long list of successes.

1912

After all the discussions over the previous five years there was at last a new venue for the championship. The choice of Westward Ho! was not unanimous. There had been strong support for one of the Irish links but the majority view was that there should be three venues in England and three in Scotland, with

Deal and Westward Ho! as the alternatives. The fact that the 1909 Open had gone to the former created sympathy for the Devon club, and they obtained the vote.

It was no surprise that the entry was well down – just 134, and that included two dozen members of Westward Ho!, almost twice as many as the Scots could muster. Despite this, the International match went ahead prior to the championship, although the format had been changed to foursomes. The Scots, who had to pick anyone with the right accent or birth certificate, won the match yet again. Robert Harris and Norman Hunter were one of the winning Scottish pairs, against Johnny Ball and Abe Mitchell, who were to see more of each other later in the week. Johnny was not in form and admitted that he had only agreed to enter at the last moment under pressure from his Royal Liverpool friends.

Only six first round matches were required and Horace Hutchinson was in

Horace Hutchinson in retirement

the first of these. He will have been delighted that his beloved Westward Ho! had at last been chosen to stage the championship, but less pleased that he was drawn to play another home club member, the Hon. Denys Scott. The latter won by two and one and this was Hutchinson's final game in the Amateur Championship, the end of a long and successful run of twenty three championships in which he had earned himself two gold, two silver and three bronze medals. This was a record that might have been better still but for persistent illness. It was an impending operation that prevented him entering the championship in 1913, and after it he was unable to play golf again. He had however done more than enough to ensure a place of pre-eminence in the amateur game, not just as a player but as a distinguished administrator and prolific writer.

One other competitor was playing in the championship for the last time. The second round match in which Norman Hunter beat William Doleman by seven and six may not have raised many eyebrows. Perhaps it should have done, for Doleman was 74 years old. He was 47 when he played in the first championship at Hoylake in 1885 and in his nineteen appearances he reached the quarter-final twice. He had learnt his golf as a boy at Musselburgh. He might even have played in the Grand Tournament at St. Andrews in 1858 won by Robert Chambers, but for the fact that he was at sea, for at the age of 16 he was aboard a ship bombarding Sebastopol in the Crimean war. He later settled in Glasgow and was a regular competitor in Open Championships from 1865 onwards, finishing leading amateur, sometimes the only one, on no less that nine occasions. As a member of the Glasgow Golf Club he won many of their scratch medals, served on committees and became Assistant Secretary. "Genial and courteous, keen and shrewd, upright and honourable in all his dealings," were the words of the club testimonial at a presentation to him on his 70th birthday in 1908.

William Doleman

Harold Hilton, who had carried all before him the previous year, progressed again reaching the fifth round with one narrow victory against Charles Dick and two more substantial wins, but his run came to an unexpected end against A. V. Hambro from Royal St. George's. There were still a couple of the Royal North Devon players left at the quarter-final stage and so too were Johnny Ball and Abe Mitchell. The latter had not been extended other than in his third round match when he had reversed the previous year's result against L. B. Stevens.

As for the two Royal North Devon members, one was the Hon. Michael Scott, who had played for England in the International match. He faced Charles Macfarlane, a member of the Scottish team, and Scotland beat England again in this match. The other was F. S. Bond who had no previous championship form, yet he found himself five up with seven to play against Ball with a bronze medal seemingly assured. Ball however had not given up. He won back two holes quickly, but was still three down with three to play. A fine tee shot at the short sixteenth to within a few feet of the hole put the pressure back on Bond and, as he teed his ball, he became burdened with the self doubt of one who has seen a long lead disappearing. He bunkered it and lost the hole. Ball followed with three faultless holes and had miraculously escaped again, to earn his place in the semi-final against Hambro. This he duly won, as did Mitchell against Macfarlane.

Friday was a wet and blustery day, but this was no problem to Ball. His experience of such conditions, so he hoped, would counter his opponent's youth and strength. Mitchell also had the support of some locals as Bernard Darwin recounts:

"There trooped out of Bideford a body of spectators who knew very little about golf, but appeared to be imbued with a violent and wholly inappropriate "class" feeling: there was a working man in the final and they had come to see him win. Not content with this reasonable partisanship they fanned themselves into a still warmer flame by imagining Mr. Ball as the typical capitalist, trampling on the honest workman. Their behaviour was at once venomous and absurd."

Their attitude may have done more to unsettle Mitchell than Ball, who became all the more determined. One incident at the fourteenth hole could have helped to defuse that section of the crowd. Mitchell's tee shot seemed to be heading for the edge of the green, but it landed on a spectator's open umbrella and shot at right angles into a bunker. Johnny, true to the spirit in which he played, said, "Wash that one out and drive another ball." Mitchell however politely rejected the offer.

By the end of the first round he led by three holes. This was no lost cause for Ball and he set out in the afternoon with memories of Prestwick and Freddie Tait. Soon he had won back the holes and from there on it was a thrilling match. With three to play it was level again.

"On the sixteenth green Mr. Ball with a putt for a half was layed what looked the deadest stymie that ever was layed, the adversary's ball on the brink of the hole and no apparent way round – no, not a ghost of a one. Mr. Ball looked at his opponent with a smile half quizzical, wholly good natured, and there are not many people who could smile at such a moment. Then he settled down to his putt and with an aluminium putter of all unlikely clubs, played the shot at exactly the dead strength and by some miracle holed it."

So they were still all square with two to play but Ball missed his second shot at the seventeenth and Mitchell took the lead again. At the eighteenth both were over the murky ditch in two, but neither dead for three. Mitchell putted first: "He pushed the ball out to the right of the hole and made a gesture of stifled despair. Mr. Ball rapped his in right at the back of the hole."

They halved the thirty-seventh and the crowd rushed down the fairway of the second hole to see the second shots. One ball arrived down the middle of the course. Then there was a long pause and no second ball appeared. What was happening? The news came down the line of spectators that the match was over. Mitchell had topped into a ditch and the ball had rebounded on to him as he attempted to play his recovery.

So yet again the great man returned to Hoylake with the Cup. His friends, so it is said, gathered as usual at Hoylake Station to do the honours on his return. The train arrived, the fog signals sounded, the crowd cheered, but Johnny was not there. He was walking home along the beach having left the train at the previous station.

1913

"It is particularly unfortunate that in the year when the championship is to be played over it, the famous Course should be in worse condition than it has ever been in the whole course of its history." This was one of the press comments about the Old Course prior to the 1913 championship. Another was more critical of the committee. "In persisting in holding it they are taking an unjustifiable risk and making an inexcusable error of judgement." The 1911 drought had done the damage and belated efforts to restore it with top dressing and new grasses had been only partially successful. Heavy rain during the preceding weeks compounded the problems, leaving the links with lush inland grass in places, bare areas and flooded bunkers.

That was not the only pre-championship controversy. In a preview Harold Hilton, commenting on the ill feeling generated by rumours that Abe Mitchell was to turn professional, wrote:

"Some people feel that he is not quite playing the game to use the championship as a stepping stone towards a subsequent career as a professional, and from an ethical point of view there is probably a degree of justification in the contention. If he does play, it is difficult to name any with a better chance."

There were a number of Americans playing but he thought that there were no likely winners amongst them. Heinrich Schmidt was singled out as the best, "a player full of pluck and good sportsmanship." The editor of Golf Illustrated then added that, in asking Hilton to write the preview:

"We neglected to remember that his natural modesty would prevent him from estimating his own chances. We venture to repair the omission by saying that, in our judgement, there is no player who is more likely to supply the winner than Mr. Hilton himself, and we are sure there is none whose victory would be more universally popular."

The draw was ill balanced. In an entry of 198 the bottom quarter was packed with good players. Mitchell, Hilton, Ball, Lassen and Schmidt were all there. Johnny Ball, for once, was not expected to do well as an unfortunate accident on his motor cycle caused by some "incompetent motorist" had damaged his wrist and there were even doubts as to whether he would play. He did and lost to F. E. Pegler from Sheffield in the first round, but not before he had treated the spectators to one more famous shot. The bunker at the front of the fifteenth green was water-logged and into it he waded. The ball was under about three inches of water, which was lapping over his boots. From there he splashed it out, literally, to eight feet from the flag.

The Water Shot

65

There was a trial of strength in the second round as Edward Blackwell and Abe Mitchell the two longest hitters in the championship were matched together. Each played his second shot first on seven occasions, so it was inconclusive as to which was the longer, but Blackwell was on this occasion the more accurate and, with a score of level 4s, won the match at the sixteenth. It often happens that a player loses tamely after eliminating the favourite and Blackwell did indeed lose that afternoon to Harold Gillies of Woking.

Hilton beat Gillies in the fifth round, whilst Schmidt progressed at the expense of Lassen and Greig. These two now met in the quarter-final, with Schmidt setting the pattern at the first hole by studying his putt for a 3 from all angles and then standing over it for an age before stroking it into the hole. He took an early two hole lead and was still one up at the thirteenth but Hilton squared the game and that was the score as they went to the seventeenth tee. The American took four shots to reach the green and Hilton, putting from the front left, was two shots less. From there, as so many others have done, he took too tight a line and the ball swung wickedly left and down and round and into Road bunker. The silence was broken by an anguished cry from a spectator, "Good God," and Hilton, managing a smile, took out his niblick and recovered bravely to get his half. The eighteenth was also halved and after two fine second shots at the nineteenth it was Hilton who dispatched the ball unerringly for the hole from ten yards for a 3 and the match.

His afternoon game against Aylmer, who had beaten him in the semi-final in 1910, was just as exciting. Aylmer, one up with three to play, lost the sixteenth to a Hilton 3 and then obligingly drove out of bounds at the seventeenth. He repeated it with his second ball and conceded the hole. At the eighteenth Hilton was in a grassy lie through the back of the green with his second. From there he trickled it down not only stone dead but blocking Aylmer's path to the hole and so Hilton was in the final again.

Meanwhile at the top of the draw Robert Harris, a Carnoustie bred Scottish International who was now working in London and had entered from Acton, was coming through without difficulty. His opponent in the semi-final was Edward Kyle, a St. Andrews University student and member of the St. Andrews Club, but for all his knowledge of the Old Course Harris brushed him aside.

The story of the final is quickly told. Harris never did justice to the occasion and was five down at the end of the first round, and eight down with twelve to play. The only question was whether the match would be completed before the impending thunder storm. It wasn't. Hilton lost a couple of holes and, as they hurried to the twelfth tee, "the storm burst with savage fury, as if the Scottish elements were enraged at the disaster which was overwhelming their son. Thunder clap on thunder clap followed flash on flash of vivid fork lightning. The rain came down in thick and merciless torrents." When it had stopped the match could not be resumed, as the hole on the twelfth green was surrounded by casual water and a new one had to be cut. No one could be found with a key to the greenkeeper's shed. When at last they did restart with the players cold and wet, all fluency had disappeared and Harris, despite two tops, won the hole in 6 to 7, but the end came at the next, where Hilton pitched the ball dead for a 4. Harris could not match it and so the prediction of the editor of Golf Illustrated was proved correct.

1914

The 232 entries set a new record. It was as if many sensed that this might be their last chance of success. More significant perhaps was the fact that amongst them was a large overseas contingent. There were ten from U.S.A., three from Australia, a couple from France and one each from Sweden and Manila. Three of them came with sparkling reputations and the real prospect of victory. Ivo Whitton was only 18 when he won the first of his two successive Australian Opens in 1912 and he had come with two other members of the Australian Golf Club in Sydney to try his luck at Sandwich. The second was Jerome D. Travers from Montclair near New York, who was still only in his mid twenties and yet was holder and four times winner of the U.S. Amateur title. Even so, they were not the ones to attract the main interest, for Francis Ouimet, aged 20, from Boston was making his first excursion to Britain after that famous U.S. Open play-off victory over Vardon and Ray. It is doubtful whether any single round of golf can have had such a dramatic effect on the game.

Apart from the overseas entrants it was the familiar names that were suggested as likely winners. Hilton, the holder, was amongst them and so was Jack Graham, who, having missed the previous two championships, was now back to his best form and had won the Grand Challenge Cup, which as usual preceded a Sandwich championship. His fine score of 146 for the thirty-six holes prompted the comment that, had the championship been by stroke play, he would surely have won it.

The first round saw Travers lose to Charles Palmer on the last green and another, though unsung, champion Mr. Anderssen from Sweden went out to H. Stevens, "a cheery porter from Surbiton." It was not until the third day that other crowned heads began to roll. Ball, who as was his wont, had come from four down in the previous round to win by a hole, lost to Hambro and the two bright young stars Ouimet and Whitton were dimmed. Hilton, of the past champions remained, but only after a narrow victory in a replay of the previous year's final against Harris.

The most dramatic golf of the championship was played by Charles McFarlane, the 1912 semi-finalist, who was drawn against Chick Evans in the fourth round. Francis Ouimet, now a spectator, wrote:

"Chick Evans hit a fine long ball well across the famous undulation known as the "Kitchen". McFarlane was in the "Kitchen", from where he hit a long iron straight for the pin. Evans followed with a high pitch that seemed to hit the flag. When the green was reached the two balls were close to the hole, one about two feet away the other four. The one nearest the hole was McFarlane's and it was dead in the way of Evans. Chick failed to negotiate the stymie, and then those of us watching the match were treated to one of the most bizarre stretches of golf we had ever seen. On the tough, windswept Sandwich course, with a 6 on the fourth McFarlane was out in 31 and stood five up. He holed several long putts, two chip shots, and could do nothing wrong. Evans played well enough to beat anybody in the field, but could not match such golf."

That game apart the best golf was coming from Graham, who beat Harold Gillies in the fourth round and then Ellis at the nineteenth for a place in the quarter-final, at which point he seemed the most likely winner, especially as both Hilton and Blackwell had now been eliminated.

This was the year that Golf Illustrated ran a competition inviting their readers to nominate the last eight in the championship. A prize of twenty-five guineas was offered. That results had not gone according to the form book was evident from the fact that, out of several thousand entries, only thirteen people could pick as many as three of them and they, John Low amongst them, shared the prize, winning £1.17.6 each.

In the quarter-final Graham played Everard Martin Smith, a member of Royal St.George's and no mean player, having represented England in the International matches on four occasions. They turned all square with both of them out in 34, but it was Graham who faded over the second nine, and yet again the fact that he had been established as championship favourite proved the kiss of death.

Two little known youngsters in their early 20s contested the first semi- final, Charles Hezlet from Portrush winning by a hole against R. P. Humphreys, a Cambridge Blue from Kidderminster. Laurence Jenkins from Troon won the other place in the second semi-final. This was no surprise as he had fine credentials, having reached the sixth round twice and fifth round once in the preceding three years. He won by two and one against Martin Smith, though by now the golf was being played before a "rapidly diminishing crowd, who, as their various favourites fell by the way, like the Boojum silently melted away."

In the final Hezlet took an early lead, but Jenkins, round in 76, was three up at the end of the morning's play. The Irishman was out in 35 in the afternoon and won back two of the holes. The tenth and eleventh were turning points. At the tenth Jenkins' second shot was hit on a dangerous left-hand line and looked like falling off the plateau green, but it didn't. At the next he played three poor shots to the back of the green but holed from fifteen yards, and as everyone knows in golf three poor shots and a long putt beats three good shots and a missed putt. Hezlet was now three down again and that was the margin of his defeat.

Jenkins played a careful and thoughtful game winning all his matches before the eighteenth. He had what some described as a spirit of optimism whilst others called it "extreme self confidence," or simply "cocky." Whatever his demeanour, he had the deserved honour of taking the championship cup home to the west coast of Scotland, where it was to remain for six dark years.

Three months later the country was at war. The R & A minute book stated tersely that the meeting of Amateur Championship delegates scheduled for the end of October had been postponed indefinitely. There was far more at stake than the winning and losing of golf matches.

This championship was the thirtieth to be played. Four of those who had entered at Hoylake in 1885 competed at Sandwich. Ball had played in all of them bar the two when he was away fighting the Boers. Laidlay played in one less, Balfour Melville in twenty-four and Mure Fergusson eighteen. If you add to these the names of Hilton, who played twenty-seven times, Hutchinson twenty-three, Maxwell eleven and Tait eight, one has accounted for nearly three quarters of the Gold medals awarded, not to mention another thirty-three assorted Silver and Bronze ones. It was indeed the end of an era in amateur golf, as although some of these great players would compete again, they would not have a realistic chance of adding to their medal tally.

Amateur Champions in Hoylake clubroom. Standing: Mr. W. J. Travis, Mr. John Ball, Mr. Robert Maxwell. Seated round table: Mr. Leslie M. Balfour Melville, Mr. A. G. Barry, Mr. Horace G. Hutchinson, Mr. Peter Anderson, Mr. J. E. Laidlay, Mr. C. Hutchings, Mr. James Robb, Mr. H. H. Hilton

CHAPTER THREE

Between The Wars

1920

Norman Boase, Chairman of the Royal and Ancient Green Committee, addressed the Annual General Meeting on the 23rd September 1919 and stated that:

"There was a movement on foot which would probably result in the Club being asked to undertake the entire management of the Open and Amateur Championships, and that the Green Committee presumed that it would be the wish of the Club that it should accept the offer when and if it be made, leaving all details to be fixed by a General Meeting of the Club."

The delegates committee had been unwieldy and ineffective in running the championships, as had been demonstrated over the failure to agree on how to limit the size of entry and on the choice of venues. There was a rigidity to their system in that motions had to be precirculated and the self interest of individual clubs tended to dominate discussions at many of the meetings. Furthermore as a body it was no longer representative of the wider geographical spread of the game.

As envisaged a meeting of delegates was held in early December with Robert Maxwell in the chair, at which it was agreed that the best interests of the game would be served by having a supreme ruling authority for the management and control of the game and, on that basis, they should take over the running of the Open and Amateur Championships. The R & A accepted this at an Extraordinary General Meeting on 21st February 1920 at which the formation of a Championship Committee was approved.

Seven of the fifteen nominated members met next month with the R & A Captain, who handled the first item on the Agenda, the election of Norman Boase as chairman. The nominated members, including representatives from the clubs that had staged the championship, were formally elected and the meeting dealt with the Amateur Championship issues by approving the definition of an amateur golfer, agreeing to a handicap limit of scratch, an increase in entrance fee to two guineas and the abandonment of press lunches. There was one controversial matter. It had been suggested that the entry should be limited to 128 and, if exceeded, there should be qualifying rounds on different courses at the end of the preceding week. In the event the committee at Muirfield which had been chosen to stage the championship agreed to extend the date by one day to accommodate the full entry, which had reached 165, including a number of members of the USGA Rules Committee who were in Scotland for discussions with the R & A.

Many of the names from the past were in the draw including six of the last seven winners. Only Johnny Ball was missing. Sadly there was one other name missing. Jack Graham had been killed in action with the Liverpool Scottish at Hooge in 1915. His record in championships was outstanding and five bronze medals are on display in the Royal Liverpool clubhouse to prove it. In the sixteen championships in which he played he reached the last eight on a further four occasions. Add to this his record for Scotland in the International matches and his performances in the Open Championship – he was leading amateur on four occasions including a fourth place behind only Braid, Vardon and Taylor in 1906 – and one could claim for him the distinction of being the greatest amateur golfer never to win an Amateur Championship. For some reason he was unable to sustain the high quality of his game over so many rounds. It was often fallibility with the short putts that had cost him his chances and it was suggested that he lacked some

Jack Graham

mental toughness. Whether that was so or not, he was a man of quiet charm and left, as Bernard Darwin wrote, "an unforgettable and pleasant memory".

With fewer than twenty matches to be decided on the first day, and no surprises, it was the caddies who grabbed the headlines. Owing to a shortage, some were demanding contracts for the week at a pound per day whether their employer was still in the championship or not. It was even suggested that some of the players might be seen carrying their own clubs. If the first day was a short one, particularly for the unfortunate American F. S. Wheeler who succumbed by ten and eight to Captain Carter of Portrush, the second was not. Play commenced at 8.30 and finished thirteen hours later. At the end of it only Jenkins, Barry and Hilton of the past champions remained. Robert Maxwell, who had given little hope of a third consecutive Muirfield championship win in his play the previous day, improved but not sufficiently to beat Gordon Simpson of Scotscraig, to whom he lost at the eighteenth. Another game that went all the way was the one between two of the longest hitters, in which Cyril Tolley from Rye and Oxford University beat Bobby Cruikshank, a local player who within a couple of years was to make his mark on the American professional scene.

The third day was a bitter sweet one for Bernard Wragg from Sheffield, playing in his first championship. He was two down with two to play against Jenkins, but squared it with a brassie shot, "the best I ever hit," at the eighteenth and showed no nerves in beating him at the nineteenth. In the afternoon against W. I. Hunter, son of the Deal professional, he was six up after eight holes. The lead began to slip away, but he was still two up with three to play. Here his cool temperament deserted him. He topped his second into a bunker at the sixteenth, saw Hunter hole a tricky putt at the seventeenth and then went from bunker to bunker at the eighteenth to lose the match.

An Englishman and an American came through the penultimate day to reach the final. Tolley had beaten Simpson in the quarter-final and then G. L. Mellin. Though aged 24 he was in his first year at Oxford, having won an MC in the Tank Corps before spending thirteen months as a prisoner of war in Germany. Apart from his prowess in the Oxford team, he was little known as a golfer, but with a fine physique and a long rounded swing, he hit the ball great distances, although at Muirfield he was mostly using his spoon from the tee. There was one other aspect that caught the attention. "Not even Ted Ray could be a more consistent devotee of the pipe on the links." It was said that in his match against Simpson he smoked a cigarette on the first two holes, lost them both, and, switching to his pipe, won the match without losing another hole.

The American, in his early 30s, was Robert Gardner. Not only had he won the U.S. Amateur Championship in 1909 and lost a final in 1916 but he had excelled in other sports. He held the world record at pole vaulting and was the national doubles champion at racquets. He earned his place in the final with a two and one victory over the Hon. Michael Scott. Despite weak putting in that match he was a firm favourite to beat the inexperienced Tolley.

The final seemed to be going according to the form book when the American lunched two up. Tolley won the second hole in the afternoon and from that point he retained the honour to the fifteenth tee, where he was three up with four to play. After a fine drive he was left with a pitch of sixty yards to the green, with his opponent only on the edge for two. Whether it was a trifle thin or just over hit does not matter. It ran to the back of the green and trickled on into a bunker and the hole was the lost, as was the next at which he three putted. He saved his half at the seventeenth, having watched Gardner hole from seven yards, by following him in from half the distance, but a wild drive and bunkered second at the eighteenth enabled Gardner to square the match. The American was now seemingly in control. A smooth clean strike from the tee found the green some 200 yards away, though a little to the left of the hole. This was the moment for the shot of the championship. Tolley plumped the ball down by the pin no more than ten feet away and, after Gardner had putted dead, walked up and stroked it straight into the hole.

Tolley was later to recount that there were two crucial factors in his victory. One was meeting Roger Wethered in an Oxford street the day the entries were due to close. His mind was more on cricket at the time, but Wethered persuaded him to play and the entry was wired to the Royal and Ancient. The other was an April match at Hoylake, in which he had been soundly beaten by Charles Dick. After the match Dick gave him a lesson on his putting and loaned him a steel bladed putter that he had made himself. This was the weapon with which he putted all week and holed those vital ones at the end of the final.

1921

It had been agreed that the International match should be restarted on the Saturday prior to the championship at Hoylake, but a subsequent approach by the USGA for a match between an American and British team, "which it would show lack of courtesy to refuse," caused the deferment of the England v Scotland match. Anticipation of this new match overshadowed all else as Hoylake prepared for the championship.

Naturally it was presumed that the home team would win, even though the Americans included four players with a high reputation. Francis Ouimet and Chick Evans had appeared in the championship before the war. The other two were Jesse Guilford in his mid 20s, known as the "seige gun" because of his enormous hitting, and a 19 year old who had reached the final of the U. S. Amateur Championship two years earlier and who had made a highly favourable impression on Vardon with whom he had played in the U. S. Open. His name was Bobby Jones. The Americans hoped that by pairing these four players in the foursomes they would be able to share the points with the British team in this unfamiliar part of the contest. In the event, they won all four foursomes. Only Tolley restored some pride by beating Evans in the top single.

The American victory was as humbling as it was surprising and raised expectations, or, to be more correct, fears, of an American victory in the championship. The first day was a quiet one although an out of form Wethered lost to Pegler from Sheffield, but by the end of the second day three of the

American stars had been eliminated. Tolley had beaten Guilford by two and one, Evans had lost to a fellow American team member Fownes and Ouimet to Charles Hodgson of Baildon. It looked as though Jones would join them on the sidelines, as he was two down with five to play in his second round match against E. A. Hamlet of Wrexham and ill at ease with himself. He banged his club head on the ground after hooking his second shot at the fourteenth and showed further annoyance at missing a putt for the hole. But Hamlet's mistakes let him back into the game and he won it at the last, although his score for the round was no better than 85. There were adverse comments about his temperament – "Mr. Jones has a boyish habit of gesture which takes the crowd fully into his confidence as to how he feels about things," was one of the kinder ones. Jones improved in the afternoon beating Robert Harris by six and five, whilst the two immediate past champions, Tolley and Jenkins, were battling together. They were level 4s to the turn and little separated them on the way home. Jenkins was one up on the seventeenth tee. Here he thinned a pitch onto the road and was unable to match Tolley's fine second shot at the last. Thus Tolley, with two narrow victories against strong opponents, confirmed the excellent form he had displayed in the afternoon of the International match.

The high hopes for him were short lived, as he lost next morning to a comparatively unknown player, J. B. Beddard from Penn. There was however one even more surprising result. This was the defeat of Bobby Jones by Allan Graham, younger brother of the illustrious Jack. Graham was three up after four, lost a hole at the seventh, which was followed by an amazing half at the next. Jones had hooked his second close to the boundary fence. He turned away from the hole and hit it firmly into the fence from where it rebounded to the far side of the green. Graham, on in two, was unnerved by this and took three putts, but a 3 at the ninth set him going again and he won by six and five.

At the end of the day there were just two survivors from the International teams – Ernest Holderness and Fred Wright, a deliberate young American, who beat Johnny Ball in the fifth round. A great cheer had gone up in the morning when Johnny, in his 60th year, holed for a 3 at the nineteenth to win against another American, Douglas, but it was a hot and windless day, which was not what Johnny wanted if he was to progress further, and Wright closed him out at the fifteenth.

With Jones and Tolley beaten, the top half of the draw was wide open and Allan Graham faced H. S. Tubbs from Sunningdale in the semi-final. The gun metal putter, which had behaved so well earlier in the week, was failing him, just as if no Graham was ever destined to reach a final. But Allan, one down with three to play, changed to a putting cleek borrowed from Charles Dick and won two of the three remaining holes. In the lower half Willie Hunter came through with relative ease. Hunter had reached the previous year's quarter-final and had been leading amateur in the Open at Deal, the club at which his father was professional. He beat Holderness in the quarter-final and then Bernard Darwin, who had been one of the championship's heroes having put to the sword the last two of the American team. The New York Tribune referred to this, saying that their national vanity had been bruised, but that the responsibility for this untoward occurrence could be attributed to the beastly British climate.

Whatever the British climate had been like in the early part of the week, the final day dawned with heavy rain falling to the extent that the greens were flooded and the start of the final was delayed for an hour. It was not only the weather that cast a pall of gloom over the proceedings. Graham's father was lying critically ill, which had even caused Allan to consider withdrawing from the final. He played, but whether his mind was not fully on the job, or whether it was simply Hunter's crisp and accurate striking, the holes slipped away. Hunter was out in 35 and six up. Graham won back the eleventh and thirteenth, but fell irreparably behind by losing the final five holes of the morning round. A huge crowd of about 7000 came to see their local man in the afternoon, but they had only a short walk. The end came at the Dowie and, as Graham was walking to the eighth tee, the referee quietly pointed out that the match was over.

The cup had arrived at Hoylake in a damaged condition, as confirmed by the minute, "the secretary was instructed to have the cup repaired and the account rendered to Rye Golf Club," but one doubts whether this detracted from Hunter's elation as it was presented to him.

1922

Willie Hunter and Cyril Tolley, the last two winners, were the favourites for the 1922 championship at Prestwick, but it was not just these two who provided the golfing scribes and readers with their first round stories. Whilst Hunter was winning easily against Viscount Maidstone of Royal St. George's and Sam Robinson from Southport & Ainsdale was narrowly defeating Tolley, two lesser known competitors captured the headlines. One was James Ingram, who set off from Ayr station in good time for his match against J. J. Murray. Indeed he was within a few yards of the first tee with nearly an hour to spare, but was moving fast at the time. That was when he realised he had boarded the Glasgow express instead of a local stopping train. There was only one thing to be done, so he pulled the communication cord. By the time the train had come to a standstill it was near Irvine. It then became a race against time and Ingram ran off to find a taxi. He might still have made it to the first tee and avoided disqualification but for the vehicle he requisitioned bursting a tyre.

Eccentric putting – W. Preston Hornby

The other was W. Preston Hornby, a 49 year old from Devon, who had only taken up the game a few years earlier. He carried only five clubs and started and finished his first match with a putter. His opponent, Sam Runcie, had driven two balls over the railway at the opening hole, so Hornby used the putter for safety. His golf was clearly eccentric, for when on the green he stood square to the hole and, holding the putter in one hand with the back of the hand to the hole, swung it between his legs. With this method he holed a number of useful putts including one on the eighteenth to win that first round match, but it wasn't surprising that he made no further progress.

With no serious American challenge things proceeded smoothly and without undue upset to the penultimate day. Four Scots, three Englishmen and an Irishman had reached the last eight. As a result of the quarter-final matches a final between an Englishman and a Scot was ensured. Willie Hunter playing with great confidence beat the Irishman Ernest Carter from Portrush and faced Ernest Holderness in the first semi-final. In the lower half Robert Scott from Glasgow, having surprised Wethered in the morning, lost narrowly to John Caven from Cochrane Castle in the afternoon. Ahead the two Englishmen were locked together. With four holes left to play Holderness was one up, but he hit his approach putt four feet past the hole at the fifteenth. Hunter putted to within two feet and Holderness missed leaving his putt on the lip. He reported afterwards that he was about to concede the hole, when Hunter stepped quickly up to his ball and "hit his ridiculously easy putt so hard that it turned at a tangent from the hole and lay behind the other ball, and stymied the champion even out of a half." Two down with three to play instead of all square was a terrible blow and he was unable to recover from it.

So the final was between Ernest Holderness and John Caven. The former, a pre war Oxford Blue now aged 32, was a member of the Bar and Principal Secretary at the Home Office and very much an establishment figure. He had played in the British team at Hoylake and had reached the quarter-finals of that championship. John Caven was a clerk in an engineering firm in Johnstone on the outskirts of Glasgow and could afford to enter championships only if they were played nearby. The fact that it was another final between the two old enemies meant that there was a huge crowd, "a tense heaving phalanx of humanity," estimated at 20,000. It was a fine match with Holderness round in 76 taking the lead in the morning by driving the eighteenth green, a shot of some 300 yards. It was equally close in the afternoon with the Englishman twice losing a two hole lead. He regained it at the thirteenth after his second shot bounded from the head of a spectator into an awkward lie below the narrow green. He played a high pitch to perfection and won the hole. Though he lost the next, another delicate pitch at the sixteenth put him two up again. So to the Alps. Here Caven's putt from ten feet for a win was greeted with a mighty burst of partisan cheering, which rumbled on as they walked to the final tee.

"It seemed an eternity before the players drove off, for the whole 20,000 people stampeded down the course to see the last act of the drama played out... In England golf is a dignified game in which emotions are severely repressed, in Scotland the masses are inclined to lose their heads... Mr. Caven lashed with unaccustomed savagery, but there was a slight hook on the shot and the ball finished in the closely cropped rough pin high. Mr. Holderness undismayed which rather surprised some people, drove slap onto the green, about fifteen yards short of the flag. Mr. Caven chipped out, but the ball ran away five and a half yards from the hole. Mr. Holderness putted, and ran three and a half yards past the pin, and for the first time during the day gave a distinct sign of annoyance; he banged his foot on the ground as if to say "stop you infamous wretch." Down went Mr. Caven's putt for a 3 and instantly, even before the ball had reached the hole a wild exultant yell wrent the air, it must have been heard on the battleship lying under the shadow of Ailsa Craig far out to sea. Here was a desperate situation. The consequence of Mr. Holderness's first putt looked more ominous than ever. To hole a three and a half yards putt for a Championship after the other fellow has bolted one of five yards may be simple enough and charming enough in our dreams, but in reality it must be one of the most agonising, most harrowing moments of one's life. Deathly pale, but as cold as an ice block, Mr. Holderness struck the putt pleasantly and truly. The ball trickled slowly on its way, went up to the hole, hovered on the very brink – I held my breath – and then toppled in."

It was not the outcome the Scots had wanted. None the less they applauded, but it was Caven at the presentation who modestly and sportingly summed up by suggesting that justice had been served. "It would have been a shame if Holderness hadn't won, as he is so much better a golfer than I am."

1923

The Walker Cup, now firmly established, was to be played at St. Andrews at the end of the week following the championship at Deal. With the American team present and the British team to be chosen at the end of the week, the interest was intense. The entry exceeded 200 for the third successive year, which proved that the days were gone when a championship in the corner of Kent failed to attract a good field.

The draw gave the holder a tough first round match against John Wilson, a studious looking bespectacled schoolmaster, who was reigning Scottish Champion. He had beaten Tolley in the International match two days earlier and Holderness had lost in that match to Harris, so the omens were not good for him. Wilson was one down at the turn and had a series of opportunities on the way home, but failed to take them and lost at the eighteenth. Robert Gardner and Jess Sweetser two of the American team also lost. Had they played earlier in the day, the result might have been different, for at midday the wind strengthened, blowing hard and cold from the sea and making the links totally different from the one they had experienced in practice.

By the end of the third day only three of the American team remained. They were all in the top half of the draw, which also included Tolley and Wethered. The lower half looked easier once Holderness had gone, beaten by Douglas Grant, an American, though not one of the team. He had won championships in California years earlier, but was now settled in Kent and a member of nearby Royal St. George's.

Next day one of the national daily papers sported a sensational headline "Wethered beaten." Roger however was still in the championship and due to play Bernard Drew from Stoke Poges. It was his sister Joyce who had lost

Roger Wethered playing from the rough at the 15th

unexpectedly, beaten in the semi-final of the Ladies Championship which was being played at Burnham in Somerset. If the male Wethered could win his quarter-final he would face Tolley or Ouimet. Wethered did win, but only after surrendering four holes of a five hole lead and allowing Drew to take him to the home hole. Tolley meanwhile had held Ouimet for nine holes, but then the American had played superbly with a run of 4s and 3s and finished him off at the fifteenth. There was still a question mark about Wethered's match play ability. His performance in tying for the 1921 Open had given him the reputation of being a stroke play specialist and, with Ouimet in such fine form against Tolley, expectations for the semi-final were not high. As it turned out Ouimet's putting deserted him and in horrid, squally weather he was nearer to 5s than 4s when he reached the turn two down. Wethered added to his lead and, four up with five to play, was on the fourteenth green with his tee shot and Ouimet was not. A five and four victory seemed likely, but the American chipped dead and Wethered took three putts. At the fifteenth Ouimet went one better and holed his chip and Wethered was back to two up with thoughts of the morning's finish on his mind. Fortune however came to his rescue at the sixteenth, where a half stymie caused Ouimet to miss a holeable putt for yet another win, and Wethered making no mistake at the seventeenth got the necessary half.

Meanwhile Robert Harris, who had beaten his fellow Scottish International, Walter Mackenzie, in the quarter-final, was winning easily against Douglas Grant to reach the final as he had ten years earlier at St. Andrews. His play then did not measure up to the occasion nor maintain the high standard he had set in earlier rounds. This time it did but Wethered played better and, despite the wind and one violent hailstorm, was round in 73 in the morning and four up. In the afternoon a 3 at the second and a 2 at the fourth put him out of reach of Harris and he won by seven and six. Harris had no complaints. "I couldn't have beaten him. He was too powerful from the tee and too good on the putting green."

The strongest part of Wethered's game had always been his iron play and his pitching. If there was a weakness it was in his driving which, though long, was not always straight. This week however he had found a perfect tempo to his swing and that enabled him to drive with greater consistency than ever before. Some recent advice from his sister had also charmed his putter. Harris was right

The final. Harris putting on the 3rd green with Wethered watching

in his assessment. It was never in Wethered's style to speak of his own play, other than in self-deprecating tones. Had he been asked and prepared to answer truthfully he would probably have agreed that was the best he ever played.

1924

An Amateur at St. Andrews always produces a large entry though on this occasion, at just over 200, it was below the record field at Prestwick two years earlier. One alteration that benefited competitors was in the starting times – now set at six minute intervals. The championship was played over six days, Monday to Saturday, with a more leisurely start than in recent years. Some competitors, those with byes to the second round in the lower half of the draw, did not play their first match until the Wednesday morning. The favourite, Roger Wethered, did however play on each of the first two days, although not many holes. He was five under 4s in beating Lassen in the first round by eight and seven and nearly as good next day when he needed a hole more to beat D. R. Cox of Royal St. David's.

Harold Gillies made the news on the first day. He was a London surgeon who played at Woking and had entered regularly for the championship before the war, having represented England in 1908 (as he was to do again in the late 1920s). He was however a great theorist with some odd ideas. His latest experiment involved a tee made of a wooden pin and some hosing nearly a foot in length and a driver with a face three to four inches deep. These were what he used for the first round of the championship against J. B. Pease of Alnmouth. Nothing was said when he drove from the first tee, but the facts were reported to the committee and by the time he returned to the clubhouse there was a notice posted. It read:

"The Rules of Golf Committee hope that golfers, before making use of abnormal implements, will earnestly consider whether they are acting in conformity with the spirit of the Rules of Golf and in particular with the spirit of the Regulations covering the form and make of golf clubs. The Committee considers that it is much to be deplored that players, instead of trying to master the use of golf clubs, should endeavour to overcome the difficulties of the game by using implements which have never been associated with it."

Gillies took the hint and was beaten in the next round, but as his opponent was T. M. Burnell, the Scottish Champion, he might have lost it regardless of the height of his tee.

Tolley, Wethered and Holderness, the three most recent champions in the field, all reached the fifth round without undue drama. Tolley then played Denys Kyle, the younger of two St. Andrews born golfing brothers. Kyle had won a dramatic match that morning with Harry Braid, son of James, against whom he had been five up with six to play. He had lost them all and extra holes were necessary. In the afternoon, with the tension gone, he was out in 34 against Tolley and held on to win.

Kyle, Caven and Harris, the Scottish hopes were all eliminated in the quarter-finals and an all English final became a certainty, with Wethered versus Holderness the likely one. Eustace Storey, the Cambridge Captain, was playing in his first championship and had beaten John Caven with the aid of a local engine driver, who sounded his whistle whilst Caven was at the top of his back swing on the sixteenth tee, causing him a stone cold top of fifty yards. Storey was not to be overawed by the holder in the semi-final. In truth, Wethered played one of those inexplicably sloppy rounds that he was guilty of from time to time. The game was full of errors. All square at the turn, Storey visited two of St. Andrews most feared bunkers, Strath at the eleventh and Hell at the fourteenth, and Wethered went ahead. Two putts from not so far at the next would have put him two up with three to play, but he failed and then drove out of bounds at the sixteenth. At the seventeenth Storey played the shot of the championship. From forty yards short with the pin hard behind Road bunker, he pitched it high and stopped it a yard away. That was one up and Wethered was never in sight of winning the last.

The atmosphere was sombre next day. It was raining and the St. Andreans prefer to watch their golf if there is some Scottish flavour to it. Neither Holderness nor Storey was noted for dramatic striking and, with Storey in his light blue tie, it was perhaps a match more suited to the Oxford and Cambridge Golfing Society's President's Putter. Doubtless Holderness would have won there. He normally did at Rye. His only loss, after four consecutive Putter victories had been earlier that year to O. C. Bristowe, against whom he had got his revenge on Thursday. Here in the final his play was not as tight as usual and Storey, taking his chances, was four up after eleven holes. Had he not missed from eighteen inches at the sixteenth, he might well have held a useful lead at lunch. As it was, he was only one up. Holderness went ahead early in the afternoon, but the match was square again at the eleventh. From that point Storey's putting deserted him and soon Holderness had joined the select band who have won the championship twice.

The three Oxonians had now won four of the five championships since the war. Tolley and Wethered, from the post-war Oxford school, were close friends and each, in his own way, was an exciting player with some special flair and charisma. Holderness could boast a better record over the five year period. In the championship, in addition to winning it twice, he had also reached the fifth and sixth rounds – twenty six matches and only three defeats.

Why then did he not receive the same public approbation as the two younger men? Perhaps it was because he never seemed to be enjoying the combat; he showed no emotion, was dour and unsmiling. His genius, it was said, was in that infinite capacity for taking pains. He combined application with reasoning, and this highly professional approach extended to hours of putting practice – even on the drawing room carpet at home – and to physical fitness. Of his style Henry Longhurst said, "He had that simple, in the best sense, elementary sort of style that enables man to leave his clubs in the attic, and on retrieving them to play from memory." When one allows for the fact that, as a heavily occupied civil servant, he had little time for golf other than at weekends and during holidays, his performance was truly remarkable and he must be rated as one of the great champions.

1925

The inaccessibility of Westward Ho! resulted in the lowest entry since 1912 – the last time it had been played there. Once again there were only a few Scots. This time the English took advantage of it in the pre-championship International, in which there was one significant result. In the top single Robert Harris beat Ernest Holderness by four and two.

The first day was to confirm the fact that the holder was not fully in practice, and he had no opportunity of playing himself in with an easy first round match. He was drawn against John Cruikshank, a 30 year old Scot who had learnt his golf at Cruden Bay but was now working in a Buenos Aires bank and was champion of Argentina. Cruikshank with some fine strong hitting was out in 38 and became four up with six to play. The holder was not however giving up his title without a fight and, having won back the next three holes, he might also have won the sixteenth but for a stymie. He holed a missable putt to save the match at the next and kept the pressure going with a fine spoon shot to the eighteenth green. Cruikshank followed with an even better iron shot, good enough to ensure a half and the match.

Another player from overseas also made the news. This was Herr Hans Samek, runner up in the previous year's German Championship. Forgive and forget was the attitude towards most Germans, but not to Herr Samek. He could be forgiven for entering but, because of his style and dress, certainly not forgotten. He stood to the ball with it well outside his left foot, lurching forward on his down swing and, as for his dress, he looked bizarre in a blue, white and yellow pullover, baggy plus-fours and white spats. His performance on the course was less noticeable and Tolley, not at his best, won by four and three.

Both Wethered and Tolley were eliminated next day, and with no former winners left, a new champion was assured, although it was some time before the aspirants could put their claims to the test. Heavy overnight rain continued in the early part of the morning and the intended 9.30 starting time for the fourth round was delayed until noon. Even then "to walk the fairways was like treading a sponge." By the time the fifth round matches had left the tee in the early evening Westward Ho! was basking again in glorious sunshine and there was still some excitement to come, with a disappointment for the local spectators. Michael Scott, a home club member, was three up with three to play against Harry Tubbs. With Scott assured of his 3 and entertaining thoughts of his dinner, Tubbs holed across the green for a 2. Scott was short with his pitch and his putt at the next and with the initiative gone he missed another opportunity at the eighteenth. He lost the match at the third extra hole and his dinner would not have tasted so sweet.

There were some surprising names in the last eight. Few would have suggested any of the four in the lower half of the draw. It was Kenneth Fradgley, entered from Warren but also a member of Royal North Devon, who won a place in the final by beating Robert Hardman from Southport. In the top half Cruikshank played Noel Layton and Robert Harris met Tubbs. Cruikshank, after his first round win, had continued to demonstrate his powerful game and pleasant personality. In his quarter-final match he was never behind until the nineteenth, where he had looked likely to win the hole and match. Layton was short of the green for three and chipped ten feet past, with Cruikshank only just outside him in a shot fewer. From there he putted not quite dead and, when Layton holed, stepped hurriedly up to his little putt and missed it. Layton looked like repeating his "Houdini" act against Harris in the afternoon. He was down all the way, until he squared the match with two to play. The seventeenth was halved in 5 and then Layton, going for a long drive so that he could be sure of carrying the murky ditch in front of the green with his second, skied it. None the less he attempted the impossible and a low hooking brassie jumped the ditch and ran on into an open drain some forty yards to the left of the green. Harris played his second, which hit the green but rolled off down a slope, also on the left. He describes the next few moments in his autobiography, "Sixty Years of Golf":

"Contentedly and complacently I crossed the bridge with the spectators and stood behind the hole to watch Layton's shot, folded my arms,...... calculating that a 5 by me would again put me in the final. Layton, I judged, must surely take 6 after dropping from the drain, under penalty of a stroke. Noel appeared to top his shot. My spirits rose. Suddenly the ball appeared up the bank rolling towards the green; it reached the green and trickled slowly on. I thought, well, it must stop now. On came the ball towards the hole, on and on and on in tense and terrifying exasperation. Four inches short it looked as surely as anything it was going in. Either a bristle in the grass or the ball being a foul ball made it turn to the left round the hole and come to rest three inches beyond. From serene complacency I saw a lifetime of endeavour almost frustrated in two minutes....

When I reached my ball I observed that I had to guide the ball, to start with, through a series of hoofmarks made by wild ponies which gallop over Westward Ho!...... Three or four feet up a bank of hoofmarks I had to putt, and had I not seen Layton's shot and learnt the pace of the green I could not have accomplished it. My ball missed the hoofmarks, reached the green and sidled down a slight right to left slope to rest some fifteen inches short, going beyond it would have meant a stymie. I don't think I would have missed this putt, but to my surprise Noel Layton conceded it by picking up my ball. He should not have done that – never give a putt for the match."

The final was even more one-sided than at Hoylake in 1921. Harris took six of the first seven holes and marched steadily and inevitably on towards the biggest recorded victory – thirteen and twelve. He simply played as well as was needed against an opponent who could do no better than level 5s for the twenty-five holes played. Fradgley had moved down to Devon some years earlier for health reasons. He was a good player and had won the Devon Championship, but now, aged 40, he played only occasional golf, no more than a dozen rounds a year. He was keener on fishing. It was not surprising that by the end of the week he was exhausted and, whether through nervousness or illness, he did not sleep before the final and could manage only a glass of milk and a biscuit for breakfast.

Whilst the anti-climax of the final may have detracted from the credence of Harris as champion, all were agreed that he richly deserved a championship for his many fine performances. He had played eighteen times and was to continue playing for another ten years. But for the Great War his tally of medals would surely have exceeded the gold, two silver and one bronze he had won. Whilst in his later days he was much respected as an elder statesman of the game, he retained his youthful spirit and the free yet compact and uncomplicated style he had developed as a boy at Carnoustie – this despite the fact that he was forever working on new theories. His great joy was trying out new clubs, changing them or tinkering with those which had served him so faithfully in the past. He was one of golf's great enthusiasts.

1926

There was a large international entry at Muirfield. Entrants came from clubs in Australia, New Zealand, India, Switzerland, Holland and France, as well as about two dozen from U.S.A. This was not surprising, as 1926 was another home Walker Cup year, with the match to be played at St. Andrews the week following the championship. The American team looked more formidable than ever. Bobby Jones was now a fully established star with two U.S. Amateur titles and one Open title to his credit. It might have been two U.S. Opens, as the previous year he had tied and tied again in the play off, before losing a second play off by a stroke. There were several other young players with high reputations, George von Elm, Watts Gunn, Jess Sweetser and the youngest and most powerful, Roland Mackenzie, a 19 year old.

The championship committee had decided for the first time to make a charge for spectators, hoping that this would reduce numbers and ease the crowd control problems associated with Scottish venues. There was no great value for the half-crown they paid for the first day's golf, although local spirits were raised with a couple of the better known Americans, Fownes and Gardner both losing to Scots. Tolley, in lackadaisical form, also lost.

The home hopes were further depleted with Wethered and Holderness losing in the second round, the latter to a 17 year old, Robert Peattie, the Boys Champion for the last two years. Two more of the American team were certain to lose before the fourth round, as Ouimet, Watts Gunn and Sweetser were together in the draw. In the event Ouimet beat Gunn, but then lost on the last green to Sweetser, who had been two down at the turn. There might have been another American casualty as Jones was not demonstrating his best play. "His play would, five years ago, as the impetuous youth, have provoked him to demonstration. Today he was the more mature golfer master of himself all through, who could show his amusement at some of the odd effects his clubs were producing."

Next day, however, Jones needed only twenty-four holes to win his two matches. In the afternoon he beat Robert Harris, the holder, by means of some sensational golf described in "The Scotsman":

"Mr. Jones in this match, which he won by eight and six, and which quite eclipsed everything else in a day packed with links drama, held the biggest crowd of the week spellbound. It was a great scene and the youth, who is the idol of American golf, by play and personality dominated it from first to last. Framed in that great three sided square formed by the spectators and open only to the hole, Mr. Jones played drives that went away with a crack and the straightness of a gun shot, hit iron strokes that flew right onto the pin as if from a machine, and when we had closed the great square at the greens simply left us gasping with the uncanny touch and precision of his short game. What he gave us was a specimen of American "birdie" golf, in which he was time and again putting to break the par of the hole, and which showed us the amazing skill that has given him a record in the American Open Championship that the professionals, even Walter Hagen, cannot rival. Cool, calculating, completely master of himself, he was, in cap and white shirt which picked him out against the mass of the spectators, a figure to remember. Altogether it was great golf, and a fine picture worthy of the occasion, the course, and the day."

The quarter-final line up included an Englishman, the Hon. William Brownlow, two Americans, Jones and Sweetser, and five Scots. Two of them had represented their country, Bill Murray and Robert Scott junior, but they failed to reach the semi-final, leaving the honours to two of their lesser known compatriots Alex Simpson and Andrew Jamieson. The latter caused the sensation of the round. Jones started as he had left off the day before with two fine shots to the first green. Unaccountably he three putted and that set the pattern for the match. Jamieson, out-driven time and again but with some masterly pitching and putting, was level 4s for the fifteen holes needed to account for the American Champion. Jones, in his own language, "had shot his wad yesterday."

The other American, Jess Sweetser who had won the U.S. Amateur Championship in 1922 at the age of 20, came through two difficult games. He was not at his best in the morning. Robert Scott had missed a short putt to go four up at the eighth hole and later, when all square at the seventeenth, addressing his ball on the green, he saw it move. These two mishaps were the margin of his defeat. The American played better in the afternoon against Brownlow from Addington, the 24 year old son of Lord Lurgan, who, up to then, had attracted attention for his aristocratic golfing attire. He wore a small peak cap, a long coat and black silk gloves. In this match he played some fine golf but came to the seventeenth two down. He holed for his 4 from twelve yards and from eight yards at the eighteenth, with Sweetser missing for the match from inside him at each hole. At the first extra hole Sweetser bunkered his second shot and Brownlow was just off the edge of the green. Another major surprise seemed imminent, but Brownlow putted well past the hole and failed with the return. Another half followed and he lost at the twenty-first.

Sweetser was a firm favourite to win the final against Alex Simpson, a good club player from Lothianburn, who had caught Jamieson on the rebound in the other semi-final. The greatest excitement came before the final began. Simpson, a civil engineer who lived and worked in Edinburgh, was travelling from home each day. A friend had offered to drive him over but failed to arrive as arranged, and a taxi had to be summoned. When a flock of sheep impeded their progress on the road to Gullane, it became a race against time and the Scot arrived breathless on the tee with shoelaces still untied. Perhaps this may have helped to allay pre-match nerves for he started well, holding the American for eleven holes. Sweetser then won four of the next seven holes and completed the morning round in 75. He was heading for a similar score in the afternoon when the match ended six and five.

It became known later that Sweetser had been unwell throughout the week. He had contracted what was thought to be influenza on the voyage over and was near to withdrawing from his first round match, when news broke that his opponent had scratched, leaving him with another day to recover. Thereafter he was said to have "dragged himself to the tee" for every match. Although Sweetser himself admitted to feeling stronger each day, he was clearly battling with illness, as, on his return home after the Walker Cup, he was carried from the ship on a stretcher, and spent several weeks recuperating from a serious chest infection.

1927

The fact that the championship was back at Hoylake in 1927 resulted in two notable entries from the home club. Johnny Ball, now 65, and Harold Hilton in his late 50s were making their final bow. Both were in sight of winning their hundredth championship match. The latter lost on the first day to Norman Sutton, a 19 year old from the West Cheshire Artisans, later to become a successful professional. Ball had a bye into the second round in which he faced Jack Abercrombie, a fellow Hoylake member. He too lost, but only after some memorable shots. Bernard Darwin described how he went out to watch him for the last time and saw him play the Cop (fourth hole) with a strong west wind sweeping the shots of lesser mortals away to the left of the green. Johnny took his cleek and hit it straight through the wind – eight or nine yards past the pin. His putting had however deserted him and for the second time he missed a short one, but the stroke to the green was one to remember. Later, when dormy five down, he had two more great shots at the Field (490 yards) to the middle of the green. He won that and the next as well, but a long putt by his opponent brought an end to thoughts of another great recovery and to his long, illustrious championship career.

Hilton had played 124 matches in thirty-three championships, three more than Ball. This is not the moment to draw comparisons between them. Both, in their different ways, were outstanding. In an article in "Golfing" about the great amateurs of the 1920s Captain Carter, having argued that there can be no comparisons between players of different generations because of changes in playing conditions and equipment, went on to say:

"If Mr. Hilton and Mr. Ball by some marvellous dispensation of the Almighty were to shed some twenty five years, and on our improved courses with our improved implements, and playing amongst our larger and better fields, to play once more for championship honours, they would stand out again even as they have done in the past, and show that there is a difference between mere ability and genius."

There was plenty of ability in the field of just under 200 at Hoylake, although in a non-Walker Cup year, there were few Americans. The names that stood out were Tolley, Wethered, Jamieson and Harris together with one formidable overseas player – Len Nettlefold a left hander from Australia. By the fifth round only three of the twenty players that had contested the pre-championship International match remained in the field. Tolley had lost unexpectedly to a long hitting American student, E. H. Haley, and Jamieson had fallen to Dr. J. D. MacCormack, one of Ireland's top players. Jamieson had looked like winning but his second shot at the final hole hit the top of the cross bunker from which he emerged two strokes later and lost the hole to a 5. The hardest defeat to bear was that of Froes Ellison from Hoylake, another of the England players. In his third round match he had a five foot putt to beat Aylmer on the home green. The latter's ball was lying on the lip, which appeared to widen the hole rather than narrow it. He took the wrong line and shaved the far side of Aylmer's ball which fell into the hole.

Two of the Internationals reached the last eight, Wethered and Gillies, and they were playing each other. The winner would play Nettlefold or a doctor from Stourbridge, Bill Tweddell, who had been playing steady golf in the early part of the week and brilliant golf to dispose of Aylmer in the previous round, taking a mere 33 shots to the turn. At the bottom of the draw there was a young Scot who had been involved in the quarter-final the previous year – but only as the caddie for Andrew Jamieson in his match with Bobby Jones. This time the roles were reversed and Jamieson was carrying for his 19 year old protege, Andrew McNair, but he lost at the last to Eustace Landale, who had recently joined Royal Liverpool following a business posting. Both Landale and his semi-final opponent Captain Robert Jobson had played for Oxford before the war. The latter, aged 35 and the younger by a few years, had beaten five internationals on the way, but in the penultimate round he bowed to local knowledge.

The day belonged to Tweddell. He played superbly to beat the Australian challenge in the morning, being one under 4s for fifteen holes. He started in the afternoon as he had left off and was quickly in the lead against Wethered. The latter had failed to play his best golf all week and that was what he would have needed if he was to make a match of it, for Tweddell started with five 4s and two 3s and was five up after seven holes. Wethered won the ninth and tenth but these were his only successes and Tweddell won again by four and three. The Doctor, as he became known, first played golf in Yorkshire, but acquired his reputation whilst studying medicine at Aberdeen University and built on it once he had settled into practice in the Midlands. With his upright back swing and arched wrists he did not have the most elegant style. He had the reputation for being a painstaking player and his concentration and his serene temperament were fundamental to his success. He was considered a better stroke player than match player, even though he had on two previous occasions reached the fifth round of the championship.

The final was a disappointing affair. After Landale had won the first hole and halved the second Tweddell found his best form, winning six of the next seven holes. His round of 76 was not quite as sharp as in earlier rounds, but good enough for a lead of eight holes against Landale whose form had become increasingly ragged as the round progressed. The doctor was out in 39 in the afternoon to add a further hole to his lead. At this stage that doyen of golf writers Leslie Edwards, working then as a young reporter for the Liverpool Echo, slipped away to 'phone through the result of the championship in time to

Some Impressions of the Players.

catch the last edition. The Doctor, disturbed by the Pathe News cameraman trying to film the winning putt, lost the next two holes and with poor stewarding of a crowd of about 10,000 it took an age to play them. Over an hour had elapsed by the time the match ended on the twelfth green and the crowds, streaming back to the clubhouse, were greeted with shouts of "Echo – final" and the paper displayed the headline – "Tweddell's victory." Smart work!

Tweddell with his friendly personality and his relentless golf was a popular and worthy champion who was to make his mark in later years, not only in Championships, but as Walker Cup Captain and Captain of the Royal and Ancient.

1928

With the championship back at Prestwick, it was not a good year for the Scots - not that Prestwick had been a happy hunting ground for them in previous championships. The International match had been a debacle with the Scottish team winning only one and halving two of the fifteen matches. At the end of the week two Englishmen were to contest the final, but it was the crowd control arrangements that they found most upsetting. They were required to pay half a crown to watch, when, in places, they were kept off the course. A temporary bridge had been built over the Pow burn to take spectators onto the waste ground to the right of the third from where they could not see the green. Confined by rope fences and spectator direction signs, they had lost the freedom to roam where they pleased. Despite this the gate money was over £600, suggesting about 5000 paying customers. The Open Championship at Sandwich later in the year could only generate £350.

The entry was over 200 again, though there were a large number of scratchings. One was from Silas Newton, a good American, who had come to Scotland, practised under the eye of Tommy Armour and apparently taken a dislike to the bone dry fast running fairways. He "folded up his tent" and headed for home before the championship began, though whether it was the state of the course or the fact that he had drawn another young American, John McHugh, the Amateur Champion of California, one will never know. If it was the state of the course, he made a mistake, for torrential rain on the Saturday night turned it soft and green again. Another American, Joshua Crane, caught the eye on the first day, but it was for his equipment rather than his golf. He used a midget putter – about the same length as the tees used by his opponent, Harold Gillies, so it was suggested. Putting one handed he holed a number of good ones, to keep Gillies at bay until the sixteenth. The latter had the stronger armoury in every sense, for he carried "several woods, a dozen irons and a number of fancy extra clubs including a running up putter."

Things came to life during the second day, with an outstanding match between the holder and the Irish Champion, Major Charles Hezlet, a larger than life figure, conspicuous for his size, dress, stance and long hitting, if not always for his accuracy. On this occasion he was in superb form and was two up at the turn. The best ball was 30 and Dr. Tweddell's score for those nine holes was 35. When Hezlet holed for his three at the 505 yard twelfth to go three up, there was no way back for the champion, who bowed out with nothing but gracious comments for his opponent. If one Midlands doctor had failed, it was a better day for another one. Dr. MacCallum of South Staffs beat Cyril Tolley. Tolley was clearly annoyed at his own topped second into the Cardinal bunker at the third which was followed by an unsuccessful left handed attempt at a recovery. He then allowed MacCallum's slow play to irritate him. "Though he does not hold up the course, he takes his time in weighing up every stroke, long or short, and gave the impression he was not going to be hurried or flurried with an important piece of business like this on his hands." Tolley went to the other extreme, walking up to the ball and lashing it away, and pitching and putting without due care and attention. Having taken 42 to the turn he was never in the match and lost it at the fourteenth.

The performance of Monty Pease of Alnmouth in reaching the last eight was one of the highlights. Aged 59, he had been in the quarter-final twice before, but that was more than twenty five years earlier (1900 and 1903). As Chairman of Lloyds Bank, he was a well known city figure and a member of the championship committee. Amongst his victims were Sir Ernest Holderness in the third round and Froes Ellison in the fifth round. Against Holderness, Pease won five of the first six holes and was still three up with four to play, but with a lucky bounce from a spectator the former champion got his three at the sixteenth, won the seventeenth and looked certain to take the match to extra holes after a poor drive and a fluffed second by Pease. The veteran was still twelve yards away in three, but he holed it to win a famous victory. Against Ellison, a member of the successful English team, he was four down with four to play, but a pushed drive, a missed putt, a visit to the whin bushes and then a bunker and the match was squared. They halved the nineteenth and with Pease two yards from the pin with his tee shot at the twentieth Ellison thinned one across the green from a bunker and the match was over. This brought Pease against Wethered who, without playing at his best, had moved comfortably through his section of the draw. Although the golf was not of the highest quality, there was plenty of excitement. As in his match against Holderness, Pease came to the last one up. Again he played the hole badly and this time failed to get his 4. After two further halves his second shot at the third extra hole caught the top of the sleepers at the far side of the Cardinal bunker and that was that. Wethered played E. B. Tipping from Royal Ashdown Forest, an ever present contestant at the Amateur, who had played each year from 1920 and would continue to do so until 1939. Wethered was too good for him and reached his second final.

The other semi-final was a Scotland-England affair between William Tulloch from Glasgow, a Scottish International, and Philip Perkins, a 23 year old salesman from Castle Bromwich, who was the form player. Earlier that month he had been runner-up in the English Championship, a brave effort at retaining the title he had won the previous year. He had also finished as leading amateur in the last two Open Championships. Though he had come through a relatively soft part of the draw without scares, his play was improving as the week progressed. In the semi-final against Tulloch his golf was immaculate and he beat him six and five.

The Final. Roger Wethered driving from the first tee

That Perkins was favourite to win the final was as much a tribute to his golfing performance over the previous twelve months as it was a recognition of Wethered's inconsistent form. The Midlander was always ahead and went three up at the twelfth. Wethered won his first hole of the day at the next but could make no further inroad before lunch. Perkins was three up again after nine holes in the afternoon and went further ahead at the eleventh when Wethered, seeing his ball move in the rough after address, penalised himself. Three holes later Wethered chipped past the hole from light rough at the back of the green, missed the return and walked over to congratulate Perkins. The fourteenth is a good place to finish at Prestwick.

Perkins had an intriguing background. At the age of 14, following an accident, he had been forbidden to participate in vigorous sports and turned to golf. He became a member of the West Bromwich Golf Club and during his school holidays he was out practising for up to ten hours a day. At the age of 16 he became Warwickshire Amateur Champion and he had won it each year since then, but had never until 1927 tested himself in national championships. He did that year when the English Championship came to nearby Little Aston and he won it. With his wide hornrimmed glasses and tall slim build he did not look like a successful sportsman. He lit as many cigarettes in a round as did Harold Hilton in his heyday. Like Hilton he had a fast rhythm to his swing, but the same crispness of striking particularly on the short irons and pitch shots. He also came as near as anyone to emulating Hilton's 1911 performance by reaching the final of the U.S. Amateur Championship, following the Walker Cup match, but he lost to Bobby Jones.

Philip Perkins putting on the Alps green

1929

Through the second half of the 1920's the championship committee were facing up to two problems, defining an amateur golfer and controlling the size of the entry by handicap without a uniform handicapping system. The committee did not want to be involved with all the detailed work that would be necessary in establishing pars and scratch scores throughout Britain and this was delegated to a Joint Advisory Committee with representatives from each of the

Home Unions. They were invited to formulate a scheme for approval by the championship committee. Friction however had developed between the two bodies, with the Advisory Committee feeling that they should also be consulted on matters relating to the rules, equipment and the dates of championships. They also believed that they were entitled to a share of the gate money accruing from the International matches. As to their proposed handicapping system, the R & A Committee "were not agreed that the system was satisfactory or any better than the one it followed." Amateur status issues also took a great deal of committee time with decisions required on those that earned a living on the fringe of golf, writing, selling or teaching, and on reinstatement of those that had spent some time in the professional ranks. The simple early code no longer resolved these problems and the rules, as they now are, began to take shape.

The championship was back at Royal St. George's for the first time since the war. With the entry near to 256, only three players received byes to the second round. One of several scratchings resulted in a walkover for John Dawson of Chicago, the strongest American in the field. As his next game would not have been until the Wednesday, he was given special permission to play a practice round between championship matches and he was joined by John de Forest an early loser. A "dead" match therefore took a few hundred spectators, one of the largest galleries of the day, though modest by Scottish standards.

A notable second round clash took place between Willie Sutton, the West Cheshire artisan, and Cyril Tolley. They had met in the semi-final of the English Championship a few weeks earlier, which Sutton had won, and both were members of the England team. The match was square after the fourteenth, but Tolley's second at the long two shot fifteenth was one to savour, as it fell lifeless by the pin, and he was one up again. The next two holes were halved. At the final hole Sutton played the better second but it ran over the back of the green, whilst Tolley, fortunate to miss the bunker, was not so lucky as the ball stuck in thick grass on the down slope. Sutton chipped back three yards short, and Tolley did well to get it inside him. Sutton holed bravely, but so did Tolley, to win a splendid match.

Excitement on the third day was caused for the wrong reason. Philip Perkins, the holder and favourite for the title, was playing Captain Stroyan from Sunningdale. Since his championship victory the previous year, Perkins had become an even more deliberate player. In the match immediately behind there was a local member who was no doubt more accustomed to a two hour foursome. As a gap opened ahead, he sent his caddie forward with a request that they be allowed to pass. This was ignored. A little later a further message was sent drawing to the attention of the champion that if there was more than a clear hole they had a duty to wave through the following game. It was irrelevant, as Perkins finished his match at the fourteenth, but an official warning on the first tee in the afternoon put him in an ill humour for his match with C.

Shankland. He found himself two down with five to play against some moderate golf, but fought back to take the match to extra holes and, after an uncharacteristic miss from short range at the twenty first, he thinned his pitch at the next. It struck the pin and this time he holed it for a fortunate win. That was not the end of his problems. Returning to the clubhouse, he was denied access because he had left his competitor's badge in his coat, hanging in the locker room. Next day after losing a close match to Andrew McNair, he confided that he had gone to the tee with a heavy heart following the previous day's incidents, and this had contributed to his poor play. Perhaps it was as well he lost, as his next opponent would have been none other than A. J. Evans, the instigator of the slow play warning. Evans, a good club golfer, was better noted for his cricketing skill. He had captained Kent and played once for England against the Australians and his fine matchplay temperament, perhaps with a sprinkling of gamesmanship, took him through to the last eight where he lost to the American John Dawson. As for Perkins, that was the end of his amateur competitive play. Later that year he emigrated to the United States, where, after becoming a victim of the Wall Street crash, he turned to professional golf.

Meanwhile Tolley was advancing with some good golf and some narrow escapes. Watched by the Prince of Wales, he had beaten Douglas Grant with some magnificent figures in the third round. He followed this by eliminating two Oxonians in consecutive rounds – Oppenheimer and then Baugh. Against Keith Thorburn in the quarter-final he found himself one down with three to play and in danger of losing the short sixteenth, where he had missed the green and Thorburn had found it. Unaccountably the latter took 4 more to hole out, and Tolley's crisis was past. Rex Hartley also hounded Tolley to the home hole in the semi-final.

It appeared that Tolley, as in the 1920 final, would be attempting to uphold British honour against a strong American. Dawson was playing against John Nelson Smith, a Scottish artisan from Earlsferry in Fife, who, at the age of 36, was making his first trip south of the border. He would not have played but for the fact that he had been selected for the Scottish team. He was a quiet modest man "with a masklike expression that gave not a clue as to whether things were going well or ill." A solid 4 at the fifteenth had put Dawson three up with three to play, but he bunkered his tee shot at the sixteenth, thinned it over the green into thick rough and from there put it back in the same bunker. He found another bunker from the tee at the seventeenth and took 4 to reach the green to lose that hole as well. Even then, with the Scotsman six yards from the pin in three at the eighteenth and the American certain of his 5 it looked as though the match was over, but the Scot holed. At the nineteenth both were just a yard away in 3. The American putted and there was a great gasp as it slipped by – followed shortly by a cheer as Smith holed for an unexpected place in the final.

In a high wind next day a crowd of a thousand followed the fortunes of the two in almost complete silence. How different it would have been at Prestwick or St. Andrews – Scotland against England. Both were round in about 80 in the morning and the game was square. It remained that way for three holes in the afternoon and then suddenly the rhythm of Smith's swing disappeared and nothing would go right. He lost five holes in a row. Though he recovered some of the lost ground, Tolley was playing steadily, heading for a round in the mid 70s, when he won by four and three to add his name to those that had won a second championship.

1930

The unparalleled achievement of Bobby Jones eclipsed all other golfing events in 1930 and one makes no apology for concentrating on the story of how, at St. Andrews, he came to win the first of his four championships. Another strong American Walker Cup team had administered a severe drubbing on the British at Sandwich – one point in the foursomes and one in the singles were all they could manage. The nine and eight defeat of Wethered at the hands of Jones was no major surprise, for the latter had added a third U.S. Open Championship to his four Amateur titles and wherever he went he was the centre of attraction, not only for the quality of his golf, but because of his personality. He set off at 3 p.m. on Monday 26th May accompanied by as large a crowd as had ever been seen on the first day of a championship. They were immediately rewarded. His start of 3,4,3 was followed at the fourth hole by a sensational second shot, from a bunker 140 yards from the green, into the hole. He needed this brilliant start as his artisan opponent, Syd Roper, began with four solid 4s. The three holes he lost were the margin of his defeat and he was one under 4s for the sixteen holes.

Jones was not in an easy part of the draw and his route to the quarter-final was barred by the British and U.S. Amateur champions. The match against Tolley in the fourth round was a classic. There were many fine shots, plenty of excitement and some mistakes as well. At the eleventh, Tolley was short of Strath with his tee shot and Jones was over the back. Tolley fluffed his pitch and Jones, looking up, hardly moved the ball. Tolley mishit again, and in Jones' words he won the hole by one head up to two. They were still all square with two to play, enthralling a crowd of over 10,000. After the drives both of them were in range of the green but with difficult second shots from the left of the fairway. Jones after much deliberation signalled for the crowd to be cleared from the eighteenth tee. That appeared to be the safest shot and he played it as intended. Tolley, attempting to hook one into the green, overdid it and left himself with an apparently impossible shot over Road bunker with only a few yards to stop it by the pin. Somehow he played it – stone dead – and Jones was struggling for a half, but he holed bravely. Neither was close to a winning 3 at the home hole and the crowds swarmed back down the first. Jones played the better second, missed his putt for the hole but achieved the next best result – a stymie, which left Tolley still a few feet away with no chance to save the match.

Next morning Jones had an easy victory in preparation for his test against Harrison Johnston the U.S. Champion. Another comfortable win seemed likely and the crowd were drifting away as Jones came off the thirteenth green four up, but a 4 by Johnston at the next and a missed putt by Jones at the fifteenth kept the match going. Jones got his half at the sixteenth, but, playing safe at the Road hole, allowed Johnston another win in 4. At the eighteenth both were well past the pin with their second shots. Johnston played first to within a yard; Jones, misjudging the pace of his putt, left it short and faced a downhill left to right eight footer to avoid extra holes. A four hole lead slipping away would have reduced an ordinary golfer to far from positive thoughts, but there was nothing ordinary about Jones and he stroked the ball into the hole for a place in the quarter-final.

After a four and three victory against Eric Fiddian, another fine Midlands player, Jones faced George Voigt, a fellow member of the U.S. Walker Cup team, in the semi-final. It was another tense struggle and Jones again missed a short putt on the fifteenth green to go one down, but Voigt drove into the "Principal's Nose" and the match was square again. At the seventeenth Voigt was sure of his 4 and Jones was left with a five yard putt for the half. The Sports Editor of "The Scotsman" in his review of the Championship, wrote:

"If I was asked to name the stroke which was the most vital to Mr. Jones's victory, I should at once select, not some spectacular pitch, not even the amazing "two getter" from the sand, but his seventeenth hole putt against Mr. George Voigt. That stroke, five yards in length, wanted, in the most pressing crisis of the week, touch judgement and courage. That it went down to keep the match even was an eloquent glimpse of will to win that places Mr. Jones in a class of his own."

At the last Voigt underhit his second and Jones watched with relief as the ball subsided into the "Valley of Sin". The report continued:

"The big chance was now undoubtedly his. He had his man at his mercy, and what a stroke he pulled out for the occasion. For a moment he stood under the strained gaze of thousands of eyes; there was a practice swing, then the stroke itself. Mr. Jones was in an instant swallowed up in the human wave that swept past him in the rush to the green, the ball sailing through the clear sunny air, dropping on the green and pulling up five feet to the right of the flag. That is one of the biggest thrills I remember in the game."

The fact that Jones missed it was not relevant as Voigt, doing as so many others have done from a similar position, failed to make his 4.

The final between Jones and Wethered, who had beaten W. L. Hartley, brother of Rex, in the other semi-final, ensured another massive crowd. Whilst Jones may well have been vulnerable in the one round sprints, there were few that could see him losing over thirty-six holes, especially with the memory of the match at Sandwich still fresh in his mind. This view was correct. Jones, four up at lunch, continued untroubled to the twelfth green at which point, two under 4s for the day, he won by seven and six.

At the presentation Jones said, "I felt that St. Andrews had been good to me when I was lucky enough to win the Open Championship. I wish to say now - that the winning of the Amateur Championship Cup has made me feel happier than the winning of any other Cup in the past." That Jones went on to win the Open at Hoylake and then the two American Championships at Interlachen and Merion needs no further comment here. He had played in only three Amateurs, which, because of the vagaries of the eighteen hole match, he felt was the hardest of all to win. In each of those appearances, at Hoylake, Muirfield and St. Andrews, he left special memories, but the greatest were left to the townsfolk of St. Andrews.

1931

The atmosphere of a championship at Westward Ho! could scarcely have been more different from that of St. Andrews in a Walker Cup year with Bobby Jones playing. There was however one similarity. At St. Andrews no charge could then be made for spectators and at Westward Ho!, because of the grazing rights on the links, the same was so, not that many were expected. The tranquillity was however disturbed by one American entry – that of Douglas Fairbanks better known "as a romantic champion of the screen." The crowd that turned out were largely inquisitive youngsters and doting nursemaids with their prams, which they pushed over Northam Burrows to have a glimpse of the Hollywood star. It also gave the golfing press an opportunity to deviate from their normal literary style, hence:

"Fairbanks was less romantically costumed than usual; plus fours and pullover, swarthy skin, glossy black hair glistening in the sun, and incidentally one down at the third. Before him, as he takes the fourth tee, lies that immense bunker which some here claim as the biggest bunker in creation. Here was the real cinema country for the screen stuff. The flappers and the other fans felt that the moment had come; the children were popeyed with excitement, ... but Fairbanks failed with the carry from the tee and was deep in the sand below the sleepers. This was disappointing. Give him a fiery pony, and, with a salute to the ladies, he would go over that sand with a streak leaving a whirl of dust behind him. But golf is different. ..... the children who had possibly seen him outwitting a gang of gunmen, capturing a whole pirate fleet himself, and performing other everyday trifles of a cinema hero's life, did not lose faith. Oh dear no! when he banged his ball against the sleepers and rebounded some forty yards into the turf behind, they were satisfied. It was immaterial to them that he lost the hole and was two down. ....."

But back to golf. The article continued:

"Fairbanks hit some first rate strokes, such as that to the short fifth, swung like a man who knows how, and religiously kept his head down at the putt."

He was playing Jack Abercrombie, a useful player from Hoylake, who was three up with six to play, but Fairbanks recovered to square the match with a long putt at the seventeenth. At the eighteenth he could neither carry the ditch in two, nor pitch near to the hole, and his opponent, whose second shot was on the green, putted up, just far enough away to allow Fairbanks the opportunity for a final graceful gesture – conceding a putt for the match, which against other opponents Abercrombie might have been required to hole.

There was one other American of note in the field. George Voigt, who had so nearly deprived Jones of his St. Andrews crown, was, along with Wethered and Tolley, a favourite for the title, but all three of them lost in the fifth round. Voigt seemed to have control of his match against Syd Roper the former miner from Nottingham, another of Jones's victims at St. Andrews, but his lead of two disappeared with shots into the giant rushes at the eleventh and twelfth. He went one up again, but Roper squared at the short sixteenth, halved the next and hit a great second shot to the home green. Voigt followed it with a weak slice into the murky water of the ditch. Wethered had come storming back from four down with six to play although his win at the sixteenth to reduce the lead to a single hole was fortuitous. Standing at the side of the green, he saw his opponent William Tulloch, with a yard putt to stay two up, stoop and pick up the ball. It had moved after address, but justice was done and Tulloch won at the last.

The quarter-final brought together some relatively inexperienced players though Tulloch had reached the semi-final in 1928 and Dr. John D. McCormack, now over 40, had remarkably been one of Ireland's strongest players since the mid 20's. Following a war injury from which he had not been expected to survive, he had spent five years paralysed from the waist down. Such was his determination and strength of character, that, having learned to walk again and defying pain, he went back to the game he loved. Within 12 months he had won the Irish Championship and he won it twice more in the next four years. He would also have made a Walker Cup appearance but for unsympathetic employers refusing him the necessary leave. J.D., as he was known, and Tulloch got through in the morning and were paired with two young Englishmen in the semi-finals – Tulloch against 24 year old John de Forest of Addington, the Surrey champion, and J.D. against a Cambridge blue

Eric Martin Smith of Royal St. George's, son of Everard, a former English International. Once again the afternoon play went against the form book and the two young men each won by a single hole.

This set up an unlikely final and the press were not alone in expressing surprise, for one of Martin Smith's Cambridge friends sent a telegram – "Ridiculous but keep it up."

"If they were perhaps conscious that no-one had expected to see them in the final," wrote Darwin, "they put such thoughts away from them and gave a show worthy to rank in memory with the great match of 1912." Maybe he was being unduly generous, for the spectacle was somewhat spoiled by de Forest's stuttering style. Lengthy waggling preceded a swing with a distinct pause, which extended also to his putting action. This contrasted with Martin Smith's uncomplicated method. The match was certainly exciting. All square after ten holes, Martin Smith won the next two, but missed chances at each of the last three holes to extend his lead. Playing the second and third poorly in the afternoon, de Forest lost the former and failed to win the latter, where his opponent took four putts. Martin Smith with a 3 at the fourth then went four ahead, but de Forest played the next twelve holes in two under 4s and squared the match with two to play.

The seventeenth and eighteenth were into a stiff breeze, with the former requiring three of the best, which Martin Smith achieved whilst de Forest bunkered his second. So the Cambridge man had restored his lead as they came to the last hole. Both played short of the ditch with their second shots. Both pitched to within six or seven yards. Martin Smith putted dead and then de Forest ran his ball firmly at the hole, but it missed and the match was over, with Eric Martin Smith at 22 becoming the youngest and most unexpected champion since Gordon Barry had achieved his success at Prestwick in 1905.

1932

Despite a new National Handicap system and the limit being set at 4, there was another huge entry at Muirfield. It was in excess of 240, although only five of them had come from the United States. Two were Martins, L. Martin from Apawamis and D. Martin from California, and they created the first round shock waves. The former played Eric Martin Smith who began his match with a number of shots of a quality appropriate to a champion intent on retaining his title, but, as the match progressed, the holes slipped away and his putting became tentative, which allowed the American to catch him and win on the last green. The other Martin beat Leonard Crawley, the previous year's English champion, also at the eighteenth, but by the end of the third day all the American aspirants had been eliminated.

Competitors still playing on the Thursday morning had to face the severest of storms. The first match was near to finishing when the storm broke and McCallum from Troon and Forbes from Leven came to the eighteenth tee all square. In the blinding downpour Forbes, with the club slipping on his downswing, missed the ball and knocked up some turf behind it. Without thinking he trod it down. The hole could have been claimed but McCallum preferred to ignore the infringement, and win on merit, which he did with a stroke or two to spare.

At the end of the day there were four Scots, two Irishmen and two from England left to contest the quarter-finals, so the home crowd were optimistic of retaining a patriotic interest to the end. Eric McRuvie, also from Leven, a former Boys champion, now in his early 20s played the best golf next morning, but had burnt himself out and played a disappointing game in the afternoon semi-final against Eric Fiddian, the current English Champion. Any chance of survival ended at the last, where he topped his second and could not reach the green in three. The Scottish interest was gone, as Sam McKinlay and William Tulloch had also lost in the quarter-final, the former despite a round of 73 losing to Lionel Munn.

Munn seemed certain to become the second Irishman to win a place in the final, which, bearing in mind that his championship successes in Ireland had come twenty years earlier and he was now in his mid 40s, would have been a remarkable achievement. One up on the eighteenth tee, he drove into the rough but then watched his opponent John de Forest hook his tee shot into a bunker. Munn would surely win now... but from the rough he topped into the cross bunker and lost the hole to a 5. De Forest scrambled a half at the nineteenth, where Munn three putted, and again all seemed lost for him at the twentieth as he hooked his second against the wall. After endless delay, determining how to play the shot and with what club, he knocked it only a yard and could do no better than 5. Munn three putted once more and paid the penalty for his indulgent actions at the next.

Fiddian against de Forest was not the final that locals had hoped to watch. It was a match that would be remembered for the wrong reasons. Covering the first nine holes in 34, excellent golf in a stiffish breeze, de Forest became seven up after ten holes, but the quality of his golf was marred by an unfortunate bout of "staggers", as he described it. He waggled endlessly and was unable to start his back swing. Even his putting was affected; the ball it was said seemed to hypnotise him. It was not surprising that this had an adverse effect on his opponent, as well as the spectators enjoyment, yet Fiddian pulling his game together, won back three holes by lunch time. He looked like reducing the lead further at the third, fourth and fifth holes but each time de Forest saved himself with brave putts. The latter was still three up at the turn, but two more holes dribbled away and Fiddian needed two putts at the short thirteenth to square the match. The pin was placed precariously at the front of the top plateau. In the crowd behind him he heard a stage whisper, "If he's not careful, he'll knock it to the bottom level." He left it short and missed his chance. Two more halves followed before de Forest won the sixteenth to become two up again.

Many years later John recalled his feeling of relief as he saw Fiddian top his second into the cross bunker and hit his third shot into the face. Though in the edge of the rough himself he took a putter for his third shot, put it safely on the green and clinched the championship. Six and a half hours to play 35 holes does not sound serious by today's standards, but in contrast with the famous four hour final between Maxwell and Hutchinson in 1909 it was much too long. The Times report of the match summed it up – "Unfortunately the greatest drama is spoilt if it is played at too slow a pace, and so this match, which might have gone down in history amongst the great finishes, gave an impression of drabness and weariness."

1933

With steel shafts replacing hickory and the quest for length amongst ball manufacturers some of the championship links were in danger of becoming outdated. Hoylake's answer was to create new tees to meet the demands of the equipment and at 6855 yards it was now the longest. Surely a strong hitter would come to the fore.

Two overseas competitors to catch the eye in practice were George Dunlap, a small, quiet and unassuming American, who had played for the U.S. Walker Cup team, and Ross Somerville four times Canadian Champion and holder of the United States Amateur title. McLean, the young Scottish champion, was a new emerging star, whilst some of the fading English stars, Tolley, Wethered and Dr. Tweddell, were still among the favourites. Any thoughts that last year's finalists would challenge for medals were quickly dissipated. Fiddian was beaten by Ivor Thomas from Formby and de Forest lost, though not without a fight, to G. D. Hannay of Woking.

Steel shafts caused another problem on the second day when a thunderstorm late in the afternoon threatened to disrupt play. Several players appealed for a postponement due to lightning, but the course remained playable and the committee who had not recognised the danger ordered that play should proceed. Fortunately there were no mishaps.

The fourth day brought together some of the likely winners. Wethered played Tweddell in the morning, in a repeat of their 1927 semi-final. It was closer this time, though there were erratic shots from both players, none more so than

Wethered's wild hook from the eighteenth tee with the match all square. His ball was amongst the parked cars. There were no rules defining cars as "temporary immovable obstructions", such as the one that was to benefit Ballesteros at Lytham, and four stewards aided by spectators manhandled the cars out of the way. This done, Wethered played his shot to the green and got his half. It was to no avail, as he cut his second shot into the bunker bounding the cop at the nineteenth and failed to match Tweddell's 4. The doctor lost that afternoon to Michael Scott. The two Transatlantic stars also battled it out, Dunlap versus Somerville. The latter seemed to have won the initiative when Dunlap knocked the Canadian's ball into the hole at the twelfth in a vain attempt to negotiate a stymie. They were all square again at the sixteenth and here a fine second from the rough by the American unnerved his opponent. Even then he looked to have saved the hole with another stymie, but this time Dunlap successfully lofted it into the hole for a 4 and followed it with a good putt for a winning 3 and the match at the seventeenth.

Dunlap, Tolley and Dale Bourn, recent runner up in the English Championship, which he had won in 1930, seemed the strongest players in the quarter-final. They were joined by three locals, Schunck and Holden from Cheshire clubs and Hardman from Birkdale. The other two were in the veteran category. Michael Scott had been a regular competitor in the championship since his return from Australia in 1911 and was now aged 53, whilst Douglas Grant, the American from Royal St. George's, had played most years since 1920. Both had reached this stage on three previous occasions and they had each earned a bronze medal. The morning matches went according to form and Scott faced Dunlap in the first semi-final, whilst Tolley played Bourn in the other. Scott failed with his putter on a couple of occasions and was two down after six holes, but from there, with immaculate play, he holed the next nine holes in 34 shots to win six of them and leave Dunlap to earn the reputation of a sporting loser, as he congratulated Scott on his wonderfully steady play.

The other game was full of drama. At the ninth Tolley's ball ran up the bank amongst the spectators at the back of the green and lodged under a macintosh. He was required to play it and on his hands and knees felt for the position of the ball. Then taking a putter he hit the offending garment in the right place and the ball ran down onto the green for him to get his half. From there holes were exchanged with Bourn losing a lead of a single hole on three occasions. They came to the last all square, both about a yard away from the hole in 3. Bourn putted first and missed. He must surely have reconciled himself to defeat – but Tolley too failed with his putt. There were further errors at the nineteenth which was halved despite Bourn going out of bounds (loss of distance only at Hoylake then). The final rites were delayed at the twentieth by swallows, trapped by the crowd encircling the green, swooping around the flagstick. When all was still again Bourn holed for victory.

The macintosh incident

Dale Bourn was in his early thirties and combined his golfing skill with an amiable temperament and an extrovert personality. Under normal circumstances he would have been the crowd's favourite, but it was "the old un" that the 4000 strong gallery wanted to win and they applauded warmly his straight driving, neat pitching and solid putting, which in the morning round of 76 put him five holes ahead. Bourn won the first two holes in the afternoon and looked like winning another back at the seventh, where his tee shot was on the green and Scott's was not, but he putted short and missed. He was also well placed to win the eighth, but fluffed his pitch and a fine recovery from a bunker by Scott meant that Bourn lost the hole to go four down again, from which position there was no escape.

The first person to congratulate Scott on his victory was "the father of the championship", Johnny Ball. "Thank you Johnny," Scott had replied, "but I've seven more to win before I draw level with you." "Well, you've plenty of time before you," was Johnny's response. It was a remarkable victory and none were more pleased than the members of this distinguished golfing family. His brothers, Osmond and Denys, were there to see it and his sister Lady Margaret shared their delight.

1934

It was another home Walker Cup year. The British captain was Michael Scott, and the Walker Cup match ruined his chance of defending the title. Not only did he lose heavily in the top single to Johnny Goodman, the U.S. Open Champion, but thereafter, in the abortive task of trying to encourage his team, he contracted a chill which developed into a severe cold and he withdrew from the championship.

Michael Scott

The main interest on the first day at Prestwick related to the fortunes of the all conquering American team. Three of them lost and two of them might well have done. Of the three that lost, one was in the first match of the day, an all American affair in which Moreland and Ouimet raced round in little more than two hours, the former beating his captain on the last green. Marston and Egan were the other two losers, the former to Ham Martin from Kent and the latter to a local artisan from Troon, James Wallace. Of the two that might have lost, one was Westland who was one down to Robert Harris with four to play; Harris lost the fifteenth but battled bravely until, at the twenty first, he hit his drive into thick rough and required four more to reach the green. The other was George Dunlap and his was one of the great escapes in the history of the championship, as described in "The Scotsman":–

"George Dunlap's escape was one of the most amazing things I've seen in the championship. Never have I seen anybody bear a more charmed life even among the chops, chances and changes of the eighteen hole drama. .... Pakenham Walsh, three times between the thirteenth where he was five up and the eighteenth, was left with the mere formality of signing the American's death warrant but the crisis was on and he could not clinch one of them. I have seldom heard a crowd gasp as that one did. He had only to put down any one of three putts of about a yard to four feet and the glory was his. At the seventeenth he did not hit the putt the length. .... Dunlap must have shaken his opponent badly at the eighteenth for after he was still in the rough with two played, Walsh on the green in two, the American as nearly as maybe holed his third, the ball finishing right on the lip of the hole. That was a wonderful effort in the face of extinction. Walsh was that yard or so short with his first putt from about eight yards, and then missed his next, and so his whole commanding lead of five holes was gone, and if ever a man breathed again it was Dunlap. I think I saw him tug himself to see whether it was all real."

It took a few more holes to resolve it. Pakenham Walsh began to hole the putts that he had been missing to save himself, but at the fourth extra hole he sliced his second shot over the crowds and into the Pow Burn.

A couple of rounds later there was another Dunlap escape. He was one down with four to play against Wethered and it required two good putts from him at the fifteenth and sixteenth and two short ones missed by Wethered at the seventeenth and eighteenth to achieve it.

As the championship progressed it became increasingly likely that there would be an all American final between Dunlap and a senior at Stanford University, Lawson Little. He was a sturdily built young man with the broadest of shoulders, who had beaten Tolley with ease in the Walker Cup, outdriving him by twenty yards or so. Only Dale Bourn of the six British players remaining looked capable of preventing it. As it turned out Bourn lost to Little in the quarter-final and it was left to another long hitting youngster from Addington, Leslie Garnett, who had disposed of Johnny Goodman in the fifth round with a flurry of 3s in the closing holes, to give Little his severest test. Both were round in about 74 with Garnett holing a long curling putt on the eighteenth to take the match on, but the American won his place in the final after all.

Dunlap did reach his second semi-final where his opponent was James Wallace, who had not only beaten the American on the first day, but had followed it by eliminating three British Walker Cup players in consecutive rounds – Tolley, Fiddian and Jack McLean. The locals were vociferous in their support of the Ayr artisan, who worked in a local sawmill, and this may have contributed to McLean's defeat. In the semi-final Dunlap was two up after six holes and still one up at the turn. Wallace squared the match at the tenth and, gaining in confidence, he peppered the pin all the way home. A 3 at the fourteenth and another at the seventeenth, where he holed an eight yard putt, were each greeted with mighty roars, the second one acclaiming another famous Scottish victory. He would have required a 4 at the eighteenth for a round of 69.

Lawson Little's place in the final created one problem. The American team were due to return by liner from the Mersey on the evening of the final. A flight to Liverpool would have solved the problem, but Little had promised his parents that he would not travel by aeroplane, so arrangements were made for the final to be rescheduled with the rounds commencing at 9 a.m. and 1.30 and for the sailing of the liner to be delayed until midnight. This would leave time for him to make the journey by rail.

Some of the crowd, who came to watch the afternoon round of the final without knowing the revised timings, were in for a disappointment. All they saw were the competitors walking in from the fifth green. A combination of Little's immense power and brilliant touch around the greens, and the nervous tension created by the occasion had overwhelmed poor Wallace. Little's figures for the match were:–

First nine   : 4 3 3 4 3 3 5 4 4 = 33
Second nine : 4 3 5 4 3 4 3 4 3 = 33 = 66

Afternoon   : 3 3 4 3 3

Wallace had done the last ten holes of the match in three under 4s but had lost four of them. So Little caught an early train, and Wallace was left to ponder the doubtful privilege of being the recipient of the championship's heaviest defeat – fourteen and thirteen. It did not however discourage him from turning professional soon after the championship.

1935

A new venue had been chosen for the 1935 Championship. It had taken fifty years from the inception of the championship for a second club in the north west of England to be selected. Royal Lytham and St. Annes was an obvious choice. It had staged the 1926 Open Championship, famous for the second shot by Bobby Jones at the seventeenth hole in the final round, and several other professional events. The English Close Championship in 1928 had been the only major amateur event to be held there. Pym Williamson, their long-standing secretary, had ardently hoped for this ultimate acknowledgement of the links. It was sad that they were not displaying their lovely velvet green carpets, the hallmark of Lytham, as the leatherjackets had been busy in the early part of the year. An advertisement in the programme by the Board of Greenkeeping Research (forerunners of the S.T.R.I.) proclaimed that the St.Ives Leatherjacket Exterminator had been used exclusively on the putting greens of the Royal Lytham and St. Annes Golf Club.

The first round saw some surprises with two of the best Scottish players, Jack McLean and Hector Thomson, both losing, as did the Canadian Ross Somerville. One other major upset had looked possible, as the holder, Lawson Little, now Amateur Champion of the United States as well, was below his best form against a local player T. H. Parker from Fairhaven. A round of 80 enabled him to snatch a last hole victory.

Of six former champions playing, only Dr. William Tweddell remained to contest the quarter-finals where he was to meet his fellow club member and finalist in 1932, Eric Fiddian. The winner would play Tony Torrance, whose best golf seemed to be reserved for Walker Cup matches (he won three out of four singles), or another Scot, young Morton Dykes, better known as a rugby player having been picked twice as reserve for Scotland.

In the bottom half, Lawson Little, who was still not playing at his best, continued to survive precariously. In the second round he had been one down with five to play against Hugh McCallum, who obligingly three-putted at the fourteenth and fifteenth, and in the fourth round against J. L. Black, the Welsh Champion, he suffered the indignity of an airshot in a bunker at the sixteenth, before winning at the last. The draw had however been kind to him, with none of those remaining in his half a likely threat, and Little came through, beating Robert Sweeny in the semi-final despite taking 40 to the turn.

The excitement on the penultimate day came in the top half of the draw with both quarter-finals going all the way. Tweddell beat his clubmate, whilst Tony Torrance won the battle of the Scots despite two self inflicted stymies, the second of which at the eighteenth left Dykes with a four foot putt for the match. He missed it and Torrance's 3 at the first extra hole gained him his semi-final place, but he played tired golf in the afternoon against Tweddell and lost by two and one.

The final was truly memorable. Little started as though he had a boat to catch, and Tweddell was quickly three down, but the Doctor was not deterred, and despite being constantly out driven, sometimes by as much as eighty yards,

The final. View of the 8th hole

he maintained his concentration and his slow rhythm. He went to four down at the fifteenth but improved his appetite for lunch with a winning 3 at the final hole. Little had returned to his hotel for lunch and, arriving back late and flustered, lost the first two holes. By the sixth however he had regained his lead of three.

Peter Lawless in the "Morning Post" takes up the story:

"That period of intense excitement started at the eighth in the afternoon. Tweddell holed a six foot putt to win the ninth in 2 and reduce a three hole deficit. He halved the tenth in 4, then hit the most glorious shot out of short rough to the left of the eleventh about five feet from the pin and holed the putt for a winning 3. A roar of approbation from the crowd, pell mell to the next teeing ground, Tweddell the imperturbable wiping his hands on a handkerchief, the sudden hush as he took his stance, then another roar as his spoon shot soared against the blue sky to finish on the green. Little pulled his iron shot badly and followed with one of the few weak chips he had played all the week. Tweddell ran his putt up stone dead, and each man deafened his neighbour with a spontaneous bellow – "square" – before breaking into a gallop towards the thirteenth, with the blue flags of the stewards bobbing overhead."

Tweddell had another chance at the thirteenth, but his nine footer to take the lead was not quite firm enough, and then he missed at the next from five feet for a half in 4. That was one down again. The next two holes turned on two bunker shots. Tweddell at the fifteenth, hitting the sand too far behind the ball, only just reached the front of the green in 3 and could not match the American's 4. At the sixteenth Little, having dragged his second into a greenside bunker, exploded out just inside Tweddell's fine second and holed for the half. It didn't break Tweddell for at the next he played a shot of "indomitable courage" from the bunker to the right of the seventeenth green: ...

"...... he again took his mashie and played a delicate flick off the sand. To a thousand "Oo's" the ball rolled straight over the hole, to stop four feet past. Little who had cut his second, was twelve feet past with his approach and missed the next.
All the windows of the clubhouse and the balconies were packed with spectators, a crowd ten deep .... round the back of the green, and now the moving gallery looped the whole fairway. Both had good drives, Tweddell was about ten yards short of the pin with his second, and Little about the same distance past. He putted first, and any hopes of three putts faded as his ball rolled to rest near the hole. Tweddell made his last great bid. The ball was firmly struck, but gradually slipped off the line to finish a few inches to the right."

Thus Little became the ninth golfer to win the championship more than once and the third to do it in consecutive years. He followed this win by finishing fourth in the Open at Muirfield and after returning home he had a second victory in the United States Amateur. This set a record of consecutive wins in both championships, an achievement unlikely to be emulated by any other golfer and almost worthy of comparison with that of Bobby Jones in 1930. Little turned professional next year but, though he won the 1940 United States Open, his record never matched the expectation generated by his play as an amateur in 1934 and 1935.

1936

The Walker Cup team to play at Pine Valley was to be finalised after the championship at St. Andrews. Who would win the final two places? Amongst those already picked were three young men – Langley, aged 18, the current Boys Champion, and two former ones, Laddie Lucas, 21, and Hector Thomson, 22, the Scottish Champion. These were not the only young men who attracted attention, as two outstanding overseas players had entered. A.D.Locke, aged 18, had won the previous year's South African Amateur and Open Championships in the space of eight days and was now making his first appearance in Britain, as was the 21 year old Jim Ferrier, Australian Amateur Champion. Another good young player, and the best of the Americans, was Dick Chapman from Greenwich, who had reached the fifth round at Lytham, but interest for him ended in the second round against Cyril Tolley, who finished him off with two perfect shots at the Road hole.

One of the notable matches on the first day was that between Jimmy Mitchell from Prestwick and Lionel Munn. Twenty eight years earlier, at Royal St. Georges, Munn had created a record by going ten extra holes with Charles Palmer. It looked as though that record might be surpassed, until, after five hours in the grey mist, he took three putts at the short hole out (the twenty sixth) to lose. Munn must surely have played more extra holes, all to no avail, than anyone else in the history of the championship, for in addition to those eighteen holes, he had succumbed at the twenty first against John de Forest in the 1932 semi-final.

Locke versus Dykes, the popular Scot who had been in the quarter-final at Lytham, was one of the matches to draw the crowds on the second day. They were all square after fourteen holes. The tall slim Locke was described as "very quick to the ball with every stroke, with a marked economy of preliminaries", (how times change!). On the fifteenth green, with a short putt for the half, he played without apparently studying the line and missed it. He was bunkered at the sixteenth and lost that as well. Although he saved the match with a fine 4 at the next, Dykes putted dead for his 4 and victory at the home hole.

The last eight included three Scotsmen, three Englishmen, an Irishman and an Australian. The Scotsmen, all current International players, were Thomson, Peters and Dykes. Hector Thomson had been playing best of all. He had been out in 32 against another Scot from Whitecraig, Ian Mitchell, but the latter having benefited from a tip by Thomson's father, a professional, matched his score to the turn. Thomson continued in the same rich vein and was five under 4s when he won at the sixteenth. In the next round, against Colin Brown of Pollok, he was 33 to the turn and won by six and four. Yet another Scot from Pollok, Andrew Jamieson, barred his path to the quarter- final. This time Thomson relapsed to a mere 37 to the turn and was all square. The match turned in Thomson's favour at the fourteenth where Jamieson's mammoth drive, more than 300 yards, ran out of fairway and into the Kitchen bunker just short of Hell. Thomson won the hole and held his lead to the end. In the quarter-final he faced his fifth consecutive Scottish opponent, Gordon Peters, whom he beat at the seventeenth.

Meanwhile two of the Englishmen, Cyril Tolley and Alec Hill, were having an exhilarating match. Tolley took an early lead, but Hill, doing eight holes from the seventh to the fourteenth in 25 strokes, was three up with four to play. Tolley came again and when Hill missed from five feet at the eighteenth the match was square, but Tolley stymied himself at the nineteenth allowing Hill to win a semi-final place against Ferrier, who had beaten Dykes in the previous round.

It was not surprising that Thomson, the Scot, took most of the crowd of about 5000 in his semi-final match against Cecil Ewing. Again he played solid golf to the turn, level 4s, and that was good enough for him to take a winning lead. Ferrier for the fourth time in six rounds had to go all the way before beating Hill to join Thomson in the final.

The final going to the 15th green

Of the two finalists Thomson had the more elegant and grooved swing. Ferrier, 6'2" and 14 stone, with an untidy leg action, was the longer hitter, which gave Thomson the opportunity of putting him under constant pressure with accurate second shots. The morning round was not without error. Thomson started with three putts and did the same a couple more times in the middle of the round. The turning point came at the Long Hole In where Ferrier, three up, cut his tee shot over the wall and out of bounds. From there Thomson took the initiative and had recovered all three holes by lunchtime. In the afternoon he resumed the accurate golf that he had been displaying earlier in the week, and well though Ferrier stuck to him by excellent chipping and approach putting, he came to the seventeenth tee two down. Thomson played for a 5, leaving Ferrier to go boldly for the plateau of the green with his second shot. He found it and made his 4. At the Home hole Ferrier from the left played his second first, a good shot over the Valley of Sin but well past the pin. Surely Thomson only needed a four for the championship. From the right of the fairway he played a low pitch which looked good enough as it ran up onto the green. On and on it came and finished within six inches of the hole. "Ferrier, the giant Australian, shook his head, and laughed, before picking up his opponent's ball handing it to him and congratulating him warmly on his success." The cheering that greeted a Scottish victory on Scottish soil, the first since Robert Maxwell's at Muirfield in 1909, echoed through the St. Andrews streets and alleys.

1937

Hector Thomson

There were two talking points prior to the start of the championship at Sandwich. One was the weather, as torrential rain during the previous weeks had left water logged bunkers and acres of casual water. The sodden fairways were uncharacteristic of links golf and the rough was fierce. Discussion had taken place on possible relief for plugged balls, but this was rejected by the committee. In the event threatening skies gave way to heatwave conditions, casual water was forgotten and the cries were for other types of liquid.

The other was the scratching of Hector Thomson, the holder. There was no clear reason given. He had been preparing for the championship, though mostly on the practice ground rather than in competitive events. The Scottish press may have elevated the significance of his 1936 title to the extent that wearing the crown was imposing a strain on him and blunting his enthusiasm for the game. His absence was however soon forgotten, because more sensational news broke – the resignation of the Prime Minister.

The weather caused another, though less momentous absence. Brigadier General Critchley was due to play Lieut-Colonel Moore Brabazon in what would have been a needle match, but the Brigadier, returning by sea from America, had waited fog-bound for twelve hours outside Southampton. When at last he disembarked the only chance of making his starting time was to fly and an aircraft was duly arranged. He circled the clubhouse to announce his arrival, but alas it was too late and the flyover simply became a prelude to a walk over.

After a quiet first day there was an interesting second round match between Dick Chapman, the American, and James Bruen, an Irish prodigy, who was the holder of the Boys Championship. The Irish youngster, clearly displeased with his form, was one down playing the fourteenth where Chapman hooked into a wet area. Bruen was reluctant to agree a drop from casual water and Chapman pointedly rolled up his white trousers which would have been splashed with mud had he played it. After some comments from spectators, Bruen agreed that he could take relief, but then a further argument ensued as to where he should drop. The hole was eventually halved and Bruen unaffected by the incident won the fifteenth to square the match, but it had hardened Chapman's determination and the game ended quickly with a 2 by the American at the sixteenth and Bruen driving into thick rough at the seventeenth, from where he could only move the ball a couple of yards.

Pennink, the English Champion, who had beaten Tolley, moved forward to the quarter-final and although there were no dominant personalities amongst those last eight, Gordon Peters and Chapman were there as well. There was another American, Wilfrid Wehrle, who had been lucky to win his fourth round match against that good home club player A. J. Evans. Evans had a four yard putt to beat him at the last, but he missed it and, worse still, the ball had moved at address. So he lost the match, despite Wehrle's protestations that he should disregard it.

Those four seemed the most likely semi-finalists, but as so often happens, not one of them gained a medal. Chapman was out of sorts and was in the rough at each of the first eight holes. Even so he only lost to Count Alaric de Bendern (de Forest – John's elder brother) at the nineteenth. The other American, Wehrle, faced Robert Sweeny who was out in 34 and, maintaining his fine form, held on to win by three and two. In the afternoon Sweeny was better still, 32 to the turn against Charlie Stowe and so the 25 year old reached the final. There was some confusion as to his nationality. He was an American citizen by birth, had been brought up in France and had graduated at Oxford University, staying in England thereafter and playing much of his golf over the fence at Princes.

The extra hole specialist. Lionel Munn complete with Paddy hat

His opponent in the final was Lionel Munn, who had beaten Pennink narrowly and de Bendern more easily. Munn had won a handful of Irish Championships before Sweeny was born. He had however given the game up until the late 1920s, when, having moved to Kent, he became a member of Royal St. George's. Despite the local interest and the delightful sunny day there was only a sprinkling of spectators. Sweeny, elegant in dress, demeanour and style, was the longer hitter, though not by much. Munn, with his drab fawn pullover and shapeless paddy hat, which contrasted with Sweeny's mauve shirt and white slacks, had throughout the week benefited from his local knowledge on the greens and the quality of his approach putting had removed the strain of holing out the awkward ones. Sweeny started fast with a 4 at the first, a putt for an eagle 2 at the third and another long putt at the fourth to win a hole he had looked like losing and become three up. Munn continued steadily and despite the fact that his opponent had reached the turn in 34 he was only one down and that was how the morning round ended with Sweeny round in 73 and Munn 74. By the fifth in the afternoon the Irishman had taken the lead, but with the honour he failed to find the green with his tee shot at the Maiden and lost it to a 3. Sweeny won the next as well and never lost his lead. Munn began to play a few tired shots, which at the age of 50 he was entitled to do, and a long putt by Sweeny for a 2 at the sixteenth finished him off.

Sweeny who had first played in the 1929 Championship was to continue playing for a further four decades, his final appearance being in 1974, but for Munn it was a last attempt.

1938

The Walker Cup was to be played at St. Andrews following the championship at Troon. This new venue, like its neighbour Prestwick, was one of the shorter tests, but with three new tees at the tenth, sixteenth and eighteenth holes the links now measured near 6600 yards and, if the wind was from the north, it was a long long way home.

In addition to the American team players there was a visiting squad from Australia including four former champions. The draw had been unkind to the Americans. Five of them were close together in the second quarter and in the third quarter Johnny Fischer played Charlie Yates in the first match on the second day, so some early fratricide was preordained.

Yates from Atlanta, a great admirer and friend of Bobby Jones, was making his first trip to Britain and Jones, warning him of the likely climatic conditions in Scotland, had armed him with some bright red flannel underwear. He played near perfect golf for the first nine holes against Fischer, but from four up after ten holes he struggled on the way home, with the wind over his left shoulder, and the match was square after eighteen holes. With Fischer twelve feet away with his second at the nineteenth and Yates inside him, the former putted up and slipped a couple of feet past. Charlie's attempt for the match lipped the hole and laid a dead stymie, which Fischer failed to negotiate. Yates, writing about it more than fifty years later, remembered telling Fischer after the game, that things had a way of evening out. In the 1936 U.S. Amateur final at Garden City, he had laid Jack McLean a stymie on the thirty-fifth hole, which saved the match for him. "You live by the sword and die by the sword," Charlie told him.

Two of the Australians, Hattersley and Ryan defeated members of the previous British Walker Cup team, Hill and Lucas in the first round, and there was some nostalgia in another match in which the two most recent Scottish winners of the championship played each other – Thomson against Jenkins. The 1914 champion was a member of the home club and now in his mid 50s was a respected member of the championship committee. There was no surprise result.

Bobby Fischer "died by the sword" with Charlie Yates

115

By the time the field had been reduced to eight, three overseas competitors remained – Yates, Somerville of Canada and Hattersley. They were joined by three of the British team, Hector Thomson, Leonard Crawley and Cecil Ewing plus Tolley and a good local player J. B. Stevenson. There is no doubt that Friday's play produced the drama of the week, with three of the four morning games and both semi-finals going to the eighteenth or beyond. The one that didn't was full of incident as well, for in the Yates versus Tolley match the former holed his second shot with a 5 iron at the second hole, which made Tolley, seventy-five yards ahead from the tee, jump a couple of feet in the air from the seat of his shooting stick. He soon levelled the game, but Yates had further 2s at the eighth and fourteenth and was two under 4s when he won by three and two.

Stevenson had in the preceding round knocked out Kocsis, an American who, to use the words of Darwin, had a "swing like a heavenly machine", and he looked like prolonging the local interest when, against the Irishman Ewing, he was all square playing the last and in the middle of the green, which Ewing had missed. The latter chipped up and holed for a 4 leaving Stevenson with a tiddler to take the game to extra holes. He missed it.

Crawley and Thomson had a superb contest with the former winning the eighteenth with a 3 to square the match. They were round in 70 and 71 respectively. Crawley might have had another 3 at the first extra hole but for a stymie. At the second however he missed from four feet to give Thomson an afternoon match against Yates. The game between the colonials, Hattersley and Somerville, went all the way and it was the stylish Canadian who won.

Both semi-finals were charged with excitement. Ewing took advantage of Somerville's early mistakes and was four up after five holes, but the Canadian resumed normal service and by the fourteenth had taken the lead, which he looked like increasing at the next. Ewing however scrambled his 4 and Somerville took three putts and the initiative swung back to Ewing. He won the long sixteenth with two fine shots, kept it going with a half in 4 at the seventeenth and laid a long putt dead for another 4 at the eighteenth, with Somerville taking 5.

The pattern was similar in the other game. Yates again played brilliant golf for nine holes, reaching the turn in 33 for a three hole lead, but was less sure on the homeward nine, and Thomson, who had battled to the eighteenth and beyond in every match bar his first, did it again. He had squared the match by the fifteenth and was one up playing the last, but, to the disappointment of the Scottish supporters, he drove into the left rough and dragged his second left again, into a greenside bunker. Yates was near the pin in two and certain of his 4, which Thomson failed to match. At the nineteenth the American played his second to ten feet and knocked it in for a place in the final.

After the drama of the previous day the final was something of an anti-climax. With his two escapes, the lucky red underwear and further encouragement of a cable from Bobby Jones, it seemed that fate had decreed that Yates would win. Ewing played fine golf, but Yates matched him through the green and outputted him. He finished the job with a niblick and an eight foot putt for a 4 at the 566 yard thirty fourth hole.

If an American was to win, none could be more popular than the youthful Atlantan. His cheerful and easy going personality ensured friendships wherever he went and this was reaffirmed after the Walker Cup match, when Charlie led the singing on the steps of the clubhouse at St. Andrews to celebrate the first British victory.

Not long after came the sad news that Norman Boase had died. He had joined the delegates committee as the R & A representative in 1908, had been elected chairman of the newly formed committee in 1920 and had held that office until his death. The minutes of the November meeting referred to him as a man who was

"keen to uphold the best spirit and traditions of the game, and through his combined gifts of energy, knowledge and patience had brought to the service of the committee advice and guidance which gave his work a special value. The intimate and pleasant relations which existed between him and the members of the committee enabled all who worked under his presidency to understand and value his great gift."

That the status of the championship had been enhanced under his stewardship is without question and the Amateur had become a truly international event. The composition of the committee brought added respect as well as a wealth of golfing experience at the highest level. Four former Champions – Jenkins, Harris, Tolley and Tweddell were all members of it. Lord Wardington was elected as the new chairman at the November meeting. As Monty Beaumont Pease he had been an ever present competitor since 1893, having played in 34 championships, so his election to the chair was wholly appropriate.

1939

   Jimmy Bruen was the strong favourite at Hoylake in 1939. This was not just because he came to the championship as a member of the previous year's winning Walker Cup team, and as holder of both the Irish Amateur titles – Open and National – but because his form in practice was outstanding. He had broken 70 each time on a course now measuring 7048 yards. Bruen was still only 20, and had more or less eradicated a kink from his swing. Now, with a more orthodox style, he generated awesome club head speed. Henry Cotton thought that he was the best amateur in the world – "I would sooner play Locke for £500 than Bruen," and Henry Longhurst in his review of the championship wrote "I shall not be in the least surprised if he wins the Open". (He finished thirteenth equal, tied with Henry Cotton and two strokes behind Locke).

A late hit. Bruen practising

Bruen's first match was against Leonard Crawley, another Walker Cup player. Before the match Crawley looked nervous and strained. He had been out on the course as far as the Dowie testing the pace of the greens and then back to the practice ground. Meanwhile Bruen was enjoying a game on the club's bowling green. He carried his enjoyment with him onto the course and Crawley was beaten at the fifteenth. He then advanced with a series of comfortable victories to the quarter-final. His fifth round opponent was John Graham, with whom he had been staying. Graham, a Walker Cup trialist, was from the next generation of Hoylake's famous family. By the ninth tee the 2000, who had set off to

118

watch their local hero, had evaporated. Graham was seven down and no one was there to see him pitch in for a 3 at that hole, and follow it with another 3 and then a 2 at the Alps to bring the margin of defeat down to respectability.

Alex Kyle, a Scot now playing from Sand Moor in Yorkshire and another of the 1938 Walker Cup heroes, played Bruen for a place in the semi-final and this was the match of the week both in anticipation and in retrospect. Bruen was out of bounds at the first. He had not been down in any match up to that point. Perhaps this unsettled him, or perhaps it was Kyle's recovery shots, but he was not quite at his best. None the less it seemed that he was in charge until Kyle, left with a blind pitch at the twelfth following a badly hooked second shot, pitched it stone dead and won a hole he might have lost. When Bruen took 6 at the Field (fourteenth) the match was all square again. Kyle followed with 4s at the next three holes, the one at the sixteenth with another great recovery shot, and Bruen could match only two of them. So Kyle came to the home hole one up. "Here he layed the ball with a thump into the cross bunker in front of the green. With Bruen safely on in 2 a nineteenth hole seemed a certainty, and as Kyle descended to the bunker, the blue jerseyed stalwarts who manned the ropes were proceeding in advance to the first fairway. Their trouble was in vain." Kyle played one more gallant bunker shot nearly dead and, worse for Bruen, a stymie – no just reward for his splendid second shot to within five yards of the pin. He could not negotiate it and a few moments later Kyle had holed and the favourite had fallen.

The final was notable for a number of reasons not least that the first round took less than two and a half hours. The contestants, Kyle and Tony Duncan, Oxford Captain of 1936 and the reigning Welsh Champion, had beaten off the American challenge, with Kyle eliminating William Holt in the semi-final and Duncan too steady in the quarter-final for Dick Chapman. The light breeze and sunshine of the earlier days had given way to a stiff westerly wind, and Hoylake was at its meanest. There were mistakes and the innocent cops marking the boundaries at a number of the holes took their toll, but there were many fine shots as the holes were exchanged with first Kyle taking a two hole lead and then Duncan. In the second round Kyle went ahead again with a two at the thirteenth only to lose the fourteenth. Duncan was on the fifteenth green in two fine shots and Kyle well short, so Duncan's chances looked good again, but Kyle ran his approach to six feet and holed. All square. The match would surely go all the way or beyond, but it did not. It ended quickly and tamely with Duncan three putting the sixteenth and then pushing his second onto Stanley Road at the next.

It was a stymie that clinched Kyle's victory against Bruen. A stymie, or the fear of one, may have decided the final. Fifty years after the match Tony Duncan clearly remembers that fateful three putt. "There was a crucial decision on the sixteenth green, where in the like we each lay some six yards from the hole –

Alex short, me past. I thought the referee should have paced it out, but as is his privilege, he looked once and decided it was Alex to putt. He made a good effort but was inches short. For me, this left the ball behind the hole and I could not afford to be past for fear of laying myself a stymie. I had to putt defensively. Alas, I left it two foot six short and missed."

The final words of the last championship before the war are those of Bernard Darwin in his description of the finalists. "They were perfect alike in demeanour and pace. This was as somebody said a "gentleman's final", with no pottering and posing and stomachy tomfoolery. It was a true joy to look at, and ought to be a moral lesson to many people."

Alex Kyle and Tony Duncan

CHAPTER FOUR

American Domination

1946

After six dark years an inquiry from the USGA about the R & A's intentions prompted Lord Wardington to send a letter in September 1945 to canvass the views of the committee on the resumption of the championships, and where they should be held. Birkdale had been selected as the 1940 Open Championship venue and Muirfield for the Amateur. The decision was taken to restart in 1946 with the latter at Birkdale and the Open at St.Andrews.

As the contestants gathered, much had changed. Post-war austerity, particularly the rationing of food and petrol, created its problems, but one at least had been overcome by the club, as it was reported that there was a plentiful supply of whisky for both members and visitors. One thing that had not changed was the composition of the entry. Many of those that had played their part at Sandwich, Troon and Hoylake before the war were back again, and Bruen, now 26, was favourite for the title, as he had been seven years earlier. Lack of competition meant that there was no recent form on which to make an assessment, but Bruen's play in practice showed that he had lost neither his ability at shot making, nor his prodigious length. Kyle, now fully recovered from the broken arm he had sustained on RAF service, was also playing well. Crawley, Stowe and Peters of the 1938 winning Walker Cup team were present, but there were only two Americans. One was Chick Evans, a regular and popular visitor, now aged 55. The other was the son of a millionaire and a more likely contender for the title. Frank Stranahan had been testing himself against the American professionals and had played in more than twenty tournaments since leaving the American army. He rated himself about fifth of those on the circuit, behind Nelson and Hogan.

The first clash of giants came on the second day when Crawley and Kyle met. Crawley had shown good form in his first round match, reaching the turn in 34 before winning out in the country, and had then dispatched Ian Patey, the

English champion, by five and four. Kyle had also won his first two matches with ease. At the very first hole Crawley hit the flagstick with his second shot, a portent of things to come. The match was close throughout and when at the sixteenth Crawley took three putts it was square again and Kyle won the seventeenth. Crawley saved himself with a bunker shot and a four yard putt at the eighteenth and they halved the nineteenth in 4. With Kyle's second ten yards from the pin at the twentieth, Crawley hooked into the hills. He found the ball on a grassy downhill lie, from where he hit it thin but straight. It struck the pin amidships, stopping close to the hole instead of finishing over the green. "The pin had been left unguarded which was an error Kyle had cause to regret," the match report read. The rules at the time would have permitted the opponent or his caddie to hold the pin and doubtless the oversight was on Kyle's mind when he putted past and missed the one back. His seven year reign as champion was over.

There was another match that day in which interpretation of the rules played a part. Ken Gordon has two unusual distinctions. First, he has served, as an Englishman, on the USGA committee and second he plays all his golf shots with pipe in mouth. Ken tells of his match in the second round.

"I had been smoking a pipe since I was 17 and when I teed up my ball I would place it alongside the ball so that I would remember to pick it up when retrieving the tee. On the second hole I went through my usual drill and was about to hit the drive when my opponent asked "Are you allowed to do that?" He accused me of lining up my shot with the pipe (a five inch Dunhill). As I had always done this and no-one had complained I presumed that I was not violating any rule. Anyway on the next hole I put my pipe behind me, hit my tee shot, walked down the fairway to my ball before realising that I had left my pipe on the tee. I had to send my caddie back to get it, (no claim for playing without undue delay!). I decided then that if Ted Ray could play well with a pipe in his mouth then perhaps I could and so that is how I have played every shot since that day."

Next day Stranahan played another newcomer to the championship, Ronnie White. He was a Birkdale member and had excelled at junior level before the war, captaining the England Boys team. The unthinkable nearly happened as White had a possible putt to go two up with five to play. Instead he missed it and the next one, and was back to all square. Stranahan went on to win the match at the eighteenth, but, despite the fine play, it was a match that Bernard Darwin described, because it had taken three hours and forty minutes to play, as "monstrous and farcical."

Stranahan's challenge failed the following afternoon against Gerald Micklem who was undisturbed by a fracas between the American and his caddie which resulted in the latter abandoning the bag. Micklem went on to reach the semi-final where he lost to Robert Sweeny the 1937 champion. Sweeny had struggled with his golf at the beginning of the week and needed his fine temperament and experience to carry him through a series of close, if scrappy matches, but by the semi-final his classical swing was fully oiled and he beat Micklem by five and four.

In the top half of the draw the favourite was making progress. He had a close call against Pressley from Fraserburgh and a closer one against Charlie Stowe. On the eighteenth green Stowe was one up and a yard away from the hole in 3, with Bruen at the back in 2, just off the green. It appeared that he needed to hole it to save the match, but he chipped it a few inches short, leaving a stymie. Stowe tried to loft it without success and, with three putts at the nineteenth, he was out of the championship.

Despite Bruen's driving which found "places it would be odds of a stack of ration books to a tram ticket that the opponent might pick up a hole", his powers of recovery from the thickest of rough carried him through a quarter-final against Bill Tweddell and a semi-final against H. E. Walker.

The first round of the final was played in a boisterous wind and Bruen's wild driving, great recoveries and fine putting contrasted with Sweeny's smooth and steady play. There was scant justice in the fact that Bruen was round in 74 and two up. In the afternoon however he harnessed his power to better effect and soon took a commanding lead. At the 517 yard fourteenth (now the fifteenth) he hit a drive and spoon shot into the wind and rain and was on the green. This put him four up with four to play and he finished the match at the next.

Hector Thomson had progressed from Boys Champion in 1931 to Amateur Champion in 1936. That year Bruen won the Boys Championship and now he had achieved the same double, winning both titles on the same links. Birkdale doubtless had special memories for him.

1947

The chance of a British win in the 1947 championship at Carnoustie was diminished by the absence of the holder and of the two most successful home players in the Walker Cup match, held a week earlier. Bruen had injured his wrist, probably through excessive practice aggravating an earlier accident with some paving stones in his garden. Trials for the British team had taken place a fortnight before the match and the selected team stayed on for practice. This meant that Joe Carr and Ronnie White could not take further time away from work.

The American team was however there in force and it seemed unnecessary to look elsewhere for the likely winner, although the draw had not been kind to them, in that five were together in the top quarter. Another American made the news in the first round. This was Eddie Lowery, better known as the young caddie of Francis Ouimet in his 1913 U.S. Open triumph, than for his own golfing successes. On this occasion he beat the Frenchman Henri de Lamaze, saving the match at the nineteenth in unusual fashion, by pitching a stymie onto the top of his opponent's ball from where it fell forward into the hole, and then sinking a long putt at the twentieth.

The second day saw a repeat of the previous year's U.S. Amateur Championship final, which Stanley Bishop had won as a result of Smiley Quick missing a short putt at the extra hole. At Carnoustie Quick played the better golf on the outward nine, but Bishop holed from everywhere on the way home and, three under 4s, converted a one hole deficit into a three and two victory. Quick, unhappy at his own errant putting, which, so he felt, had caused this second defeat at the hands of Bishop, stormed away and broke his putter across his knee. As someone in the crowd suggested, it might have been better if he'd broken Bishop's putter an hour or so earlier.

Frank Stranahan made the news on the third day, sadly for the wrong reason. At the very first hole George Morgan, a local member, raked Stranahan's ball into the hole in the act of conceding a putt for the half. Stranahan would not continue until a ruling had been obtained and the spectators, thinking that he was trying to claim the hole, were incensed during the delay. In due course it was agreed that the hole had been halved and Stranahan, after winning the match by one hole, explained that he did not have any intention of claiming the hole but was simply wanting to ensure that he would not be disqualified for waiving the rules. More bad press came the following afternoon when he lost to Willie Turnesa, this time as a result of the pace of play.

With three Americans left in the last eight and only J. C. Wilson (Cawder) of the British team, an all American final became an increasing possibility. John Campbell and Sam McKinlay, who had beaten Wilson in the quarter-final, joined Turnesa and Dick Chapman in the semi-final. Turnesa had won through the difficult top quarter, where there had been four American Walker Cup players in the last sixteen. Having beaten Stranahan on the seventeenth he did the same to Bud Ward. Dick Chapman, with a somewhat easier draw, had reached the semi-final without playing the last two holes. His match against McKinlay was played in heavy rain and neither player came to terms with the sodden greens. Turnesa, having won the first semi-final against Campbell at the sixteenth, headed back to give support to his team mate, and saw him edge anxiously home on the last green.

Willie Turnesa was the youngest son of a greenkeeper. All his brothers had turned professional and one of them, Joe, had come within a shot of winning the 1926 U.S. Open, deprived by Bobby Jones completing the last nine holes in level par. Willie, a shy unassuming man of 33, had gone to college through the generosity of his elder brother and had repaid him the by winning the 1938 U.S. Amateur Championship (which he was to win again ten years later). The basis of his success was his short game, particularly his bunker play which had earned him the nickname of "Willie the Wedge". Dick Chapman, a more extrovert character from a wealthy family, was a couple of years older and had won the U.S. Amateur in 1940.

A typical grey Carnoustie morning with a chill haar greeted the two Americans, the first time a final of the Amateur Championship had been played without a British player. This and the weather factor meant that there were only a few hundred spectators to see the excitement. Chapman, holing a couple of long putts and a chip, raced to the turn in 34 and was four up. He looked certain to win another at "South America", the famous tenth hole with its burn guarding the green. Turnesa's second seemed destined for the water, but somehow it skipped into the bank and onto the edge of the green and Chapman, unsettled, hooked into a greenside bunker, from which he failed to recover. Turnesa, now with the initiative, played the next four holes in 4, 4, 2, 4, and that was all square again, which was still the position at lunchtime. News had reached the locals that the morning's play had been of the highest quality and by the afternoon the crowd had swelled to 3000. They witnessed some more fine play. Turnesa was out in 36 and one hole ahead, a position he maintained for fourteen holes. He won the fifteenth with a good putt, and the match finished unexpectedly at the next, where Turnesa, having missed the green, pitched to eight feet and holed, whilst Chapman from an easier place failed to make his 3. Both Americans were warmly applauded. It was Turnesa's outstanding short game that had enabled him to prevail and he had needed two 4s for a round of 70 that afternoon.

1948

The championship went back to Kent, but to Sandwich, not the original choice of Deal, which had been ravaged by sea-water flooding. The entry was spearheaded by Turnesa, Chapman and Stranahan, so no-one could suggest that the overseas challenge was inconsequential, especially as one other attracted attention. Mario Gonzales from Brazil had won the Royal St. George's Grand Challenge Cup during the weekend prior to the championship, beating Turnesa by a stroke. He was wafer thin, only nine stone despite being about six feet tall, and he introduced himself to the press with the comment, "If I turn sideways, my opponent doesn't know I'm here." As it turned out a number of opponents became well aware of his presence.

With Scrutton and Carr, two of the best British players, losing in consecutive rounds to Chapman, Stranahan taking his revenge on Micklem and Turnesa and Gonzales easing their way into the last sixteen, a second consecutive year without a home representative in the final looked a distinct possibility. There was however one overseas casualty in the fifth round. On Thursday morning Chapman played the first nine holes in 29 strokes, seven 3s and two 4s with only two putts of any length, everything else being by the pin. Hamilton McInally was the unfortunate victim who shook hands on the eleventh green. That afternoon he was to play Charles Lawrie, who had entered from the Honourable Company, but now farmed in Anglesey and was playing little golf. He was comforted before the match by another American who told him, "Chapman only does that sort of thing once a day." Sure enough, in the afternoon, he took ten shots more to the turn, was four down and went five down with six to play. Lawrie lost the next two holes but managed a half at the fifteenth. At the sixteenth he was in three bunkers and he missed from five feet for the match at both the seventeenth and eighteenth, so it seemed that the American would win after all. Unaccountably however Chapman drove into the rough from where he found a horrid lie in a bunker and could do no better than a six, leaving Lawrie to take his place in the quarter-final.

Stranahan was still there and he beat Gonzales at the sixteenth and Ham Martin from the home club at the seventeenth in the semi-final. Turnesa, the holder, reached the semi-final without a close call, all his matches finishing at the fifteenth or earlier. His opponent was Charlie Stowe, who had gained bronze medals twice before the war and had been beaten in the final of the English Championship in 1947. He had played excellent golf in the morning, reaching the turn in 31 in his six and five victory over Lawrie. Against Turnesa he maintained this form and was three up after twelve holes. Turnesa, with a difficult shot to the thirteenth green, took his time, changing his club several times, before hitting a fine iron shot to the middle of the green. He won that hole and Stowe, perhaps unsettled, drove out of bounds at the Canal hole. Turnesa's wedge play came to the rescue at the next two holes and at the seventeenth for the third time he missed the green and pitched close. It was no surprise when Stowe, on for two, took three more and the match was all square. At the eighteenth yet again Turnesa was in long grass short and to the right of the green and yet again he pitched well to within a couple of yards of the pin. This time he missed and Stowe holed for his 4 and had beaten the holder with a round of 72.

The millionaire's son, Stranahan, with his meticulous approach to every shot was not the ideal opponent for Stowe, a bluff character from the Midlands with a working class background, who liked to get on with the game and wasn't afraid to say so. The conditions compounded the problems for him as, in the gusting winds and unrelenting rain, Stranahan was for ever throwing grass in the air and wiping his hands. Despite this Stowe held him for the first eighteen holes, although in the vile conditions neither player was much below 80. In the afternoon the American won the first two holes. It looked as though Stowe might win one back at the fourth, but somehow he took four shots from the

Stranahan and Blair on the 7th tee, fifth round

bank above the green and Stranahan won it with a 5, and the next two holes as well. Out in 35 he was four up and went on to clinch the match with a fine 4 at the Canal hole.

Stranahan had not endeared himself to the amateur golf scene in his first two attempts to win the championship. He seemed incident prone. There was jealousy too, as he never had to work for a living, for his father felt that his golfing ability would benefit the business (Champion Sparking Plugs) in terms of public relations and paid him accordingly. This gave him the "spoilt boy" image which his individualism and bearing did little to dispel. Health he believed was fundamental to sporting success and this meant no smoking or alcohol, a strict diet and rigorous exercise. "You need length to be a winner," he said, so weight lifting apparatus was always a part of his championship baggage.

Whatever people thought of his personality, he had earned the respect of the golfing world at Hoylake by his brave finish, which failed by only a few inches to deprive Fred Daly of his Open Championship, and his victory at Sandwich added to this. By his failure to win the U.S. Amateur title he had acquired the reputation of a stroke player. It was suggested that he was too intense to withstand the vagaries of fortune in an eighteen hole match, but on this occasion singleminded determination overcome the intensity.

1949

As Patrick Campbell pointed out, 1949 was the first occasion when British competitors had to show their passports before being permitted to play in their own championship. There had been much discussion about Portmarnock and whether to change the venue both because of political pressures and because of opposition from some committee members on grounds of expense for competitors. An impassioned plea by 'J.D.' McCormack at the November meeting of the committee decided the issue and, because of the speculation a press release was issued to the effect that there would be no change of venue.

In the event, Portmarnock was outstanding for the quality of the links, the Irish hospitality and the large galleries. The deputation of 1901 would have been proud to see the long overdue result of their initiative. The first championship in Ireland will always be remembered for the performance of two Irish competitors – the winner and the aforesaid Patrick Campbell. His chapter, "The Big Big Time" from "How to become a Scratch Golfer", gives a classic account of his match with Willie O'Sullivan and his progress to the fifth round. There is however one story from his first round match that is not included in the book. Campbell was playing a frail, elderly American, Udo Reinach, who had come to the championship each year with Willie Turnesa, acting as friend, adviser and road manager. Back home, as a prominent business man, he had set up Turnesa as President of one of his companies. Reinach had no pretensions about his game and as Campbell said, they were both heading for a round in the mid 80s when the match ended. At the penultimate hole Reinach had knifed his second shot into the face of a bunker short of the green, where it had plugged. Campbell ambled over to see for himself and, stuttering as ever, offered some sympathetic words, "B-b-b-bad luck, it j-j-j-just t-t-t-trickled in!"

Reinach was not the only senior American playing. Ouimet and Lowery were competing again and another Stranahan, the holder's father, who had come with Frank's sister to watch him defend his title. Frank's first match with Brigadier Critchley was a scrappy affair, but he won it at the sixteenth and hurried forward in time to see his 63 year old father take his match to extra holes and win at the twentieth.

There had been some other surprises on the first day, not least of which was the withdrawal of Bruen. It was not connected with the injury that had prevented him defending his 1946 title, but a gastric disorder. Irish hopes received a further setback when Ewing, who had been up on McInally most of the way, hooked into impenetrable rough at the eighteenth and lost the match.

The third day produced one of the classic championship encounters, between two of the best British players, Ronnie White and Laddy Lucas. The latter played the first nine holes with nine consecutive 4s and White with one 5 and one 3 was square. The next six holes were halved in strict par before the sixteenth and seventeenth were exchanged with birdies. At the eighteenth White bunkered his second, but splashed out to two feet for the half. Both were round in 71. It was cruel for Lucas to lose, but he did, to a 3 at the twentieth. Another fine round of 73 by White next day was not good enough, as Ernest Millward pipped him at the last.

At the quarter-final stage, the champions of 1947 and 1948, Turnesa and Stranahan, looked likely to meet in the final. Turnesa had not yet played the seventeenth and eighteenth holes and Stranahan with seven and five and eight and seven victories on the previous day seemed to be running into his best form. Unexpectedly, in the next round he found himself three down with four to play to a 31 year old Ulsterman, Max McCready, who had been a wartime pilot and was the post-war R.A.F. Golf Champion. Although he had been a Walker Cup trialist, he had not previously played in the championship. It looked as though a fight back might begin at the fifteenth where the American's fine tee shot left him with a five yard putt, while McCready was off the green. Instead the match ended there with the Irishman chipping close and Stranahan leaving his putt halfway to the hole and missing the next.

The first semi-final saw Turnesa, outclassed by Millward in the long game, save himself again and again with ruthless wedge play to win on the last green. Meanwhile, McCready was playing Ken Thom, an England International, in a

Max McCready

desperately close match. All square at the eighteenth, Thom suffered the indignity of fluffing a little pitch into a greenside bunker in front of his nose, but he recovered bravely to take the match to extra holes. McCready was lucky to salvage a half from a wayward drive at the nineteenth and at the twentieth he was left with a six yard putt for victory, with Thom's ball apparently in the way. Tony Duncan, a spectator at the time, remembers seeing McCready's putt pass Thom's ball on the opposite side to the one anticipated and, with some Irish magic, veer back into the hole.

In the final McCready played like a man inspired, as he probably was by a huge and vocal Irish crowd, who had taken the burly extrovert Ulsterman to their heart, despite the fact that he now lived near London and played at Sunningdale. He was round in 70 shots in the morning and four holes ahead. As heavy clouds built up during the afternoon, McCready's lead began to evaporate and the crowd's passion began to wane. By the eleventh the sky was black and the match back to all square. When the storm burst the Irishman was one down with four to play. All was gloom and the only noise was the torrential rain beating on thousands of umbrellas, but McCready had not lost his self-belief and in the deluge he scrambled two pars, which Turnesa could not match, and so took the lead again. By the time he had holed for a winning 4 at the seventeenth the sun was shining again both literally and metaphorically.

Although McCready played in the Walker Cup later that year and again in 1951, his championship appearances were limited by overseas postings.

1950

Whether it was the success of their compatriots or simply the attraction of St. Andrews, there were thirty Americans amongst a total entry that exceeded 300 for the first time. Apart from Turnesa, Stranahan and Chapman there were others with a real chance, notably Jim McHale, who had played in the 1949 Walker Cup match, Bill Campbell, a tall and amiable Virginian in his mid 20s, and a short, square Californian, Bill Goodloe, known as "Dynamite" for his explosive hitting. Goodloe set the locals buzzing early, not just for his green trousers, red jacket and tam-o-shanter, which brightened a grey morning, but for his play at the very first hole. The news spread that he had driven the first green and holed for a 2. It was only partially true, for in the second match of the day his opponent, Jack Cradock-Hartopp, had played his second to within a few feet of the pin, and stood back with a warm glow of satisfaction only to watch Goodloe hole his pitch over the burn.

It was another American who caused the crowds to line three deep from tee down to burn. Bing Crosby had emerged from the clubhouse a few moments earlier, debonair and smiling, to face first a battery of cameramen and then J. K. Wilson a useful local player. Crosby was playing the Old Course for the first time, although he had practised on the Eden, as far as had been possible bearing in mind the huge and uncontrolled mob that had come to watch. The match started in poor visibility but it did not prevent Crosby from pitching his second shot dead at the first, holing from eight feet for another 3 at the second and winning the third with a four. There was evidence of a neat and efficient golf swing, but the greens found him out and by the eleventh he had lost his lead and more holes slipped away until, with three from the edge of the sixteenth green, the match was lost. He played the last two holes, finishing as he had begun with a 3 to give the gallery full value for their five shillings admission fee.

Another celebrated singer made a first round exit – Donald Peers. He ended a long day standing on a coal cart near the R & A clubhouse, singing "By a Babbling Brook", not inappropriate, if one can describe the Swilcan Burn as "a Babbling Brook", for he had lost on the nineteenth.

It was a relief to revert to pure golf on the second day, when matches largely went according to form. The third and fourth rounds, 96 matches, were scheduled for the third day with five minute intervals between starting times. It was not surprising that they lasted for nearly fourteen hours. At 9.50 p.m. with the street lamps alight, Bill Campbell won at the Road hole to eliminate Turnesa. It had been a fine match, but too late for Bernard Darwin to report in detail, "full of great things," and the result was all that appeared in "The Times" next day. What was more surprising was that the two of them had survived the morning, for Turnesa had won from three down with seven to play, and Campbell had lived more dangerously. He had driven into the burn by the old stone bridge at the nineteenth in his match against J. Orr from Hayston. This went beyond misfortune, as he had done the same driving from the first tee at the start of the match. Campbell chose to trudge back to the tee, instead of dropping out. This may have worked to his advantage because it gave Orr too long to contemplate the second shot and, when the time came, he plopped it into the burn, the hole was halved and Campbell won at the twentieth.

Six of the best Americans were evenly spaced through the draw for the fifth round. If anyone was to prevent an American victory, it looked as though the Irish might do it. McCready, Carr and O'Sullivan were still there and a couple of others. In the event, only Carr survived to the quarter-finals, beating Bill Campbell after more than four hours on the course. He had two putts for it at the seventeenth, but took three and needed a 3 at the nineteenth to clinch it.

There were two unexpected quarter finalists. Cyril Tolley at the age of 54, thirty years after winning his first championship, had used all his knowledge of the Old Course to work his way through a relatively easy part of the draw. The other was Peter Tait, son of J.G. who had won a bronze medal in 1887 and nephew of the great Freddie. He was home on leave from Kenya and, despite the American McHale looking a class above him, he hounded him all the way to the last green. Tolley went one better against Carr. After losing the first three holes he played the next fourteen without a blemish and came to the eighteenth one up. He three putted it but the fates forgave him and he won at the twentieth, to become the sole British survivor in the semi-final. Tolley held Stranahan for ten holes, but three putts at the eleventh and a 3 at the twelfth by the American from a drive that might have been in the gorse put the match beyond him. Chapman beat McHale in the other semi-final, despite the latter's superior striking, but that is often the way in match play golf, not least on the Old Course.

The final started at 10 a.m. Poor weather and an all American final kept down the crowds. Stranahan was three up at lunch, round in 77, not a bad score in the difficult conditions, but it had taken so long that the starting time of 2.15 had to be delayed by half an hour. The game finished tamely on the twelfth green with Stranahan winning by eight and six. The fact that it was a disappointing final should take nothing away from Stranahan's achievement in winning a second championship.

The final, 5th green

There was criticism levelled against some of the Americans, not Stranahan this time, for their speed of play. One of those that had suffered the castigations of the press was Bill Campbell and he had answered it perfectly by saying that, "he was somewhat prejudiced against hasty golf after taking the time and trouble to play 3500 miles from home. It is hard to conceive a more unfortunate situation than seeing the roll on one of those complicated St. Andrews greens – after the putt had been missed!" He also said some nice things about the Old Course, the caddies, the galleries, St. Andrews and its traditions. This was reported by Henry Longhurst in one of his Sunday specials and he concluded his article by saying that, "We hope that Campbell himself will come and see us again." He did – again and again.

1951

The championship committee broke new ground again. This year it was a first for Wales and Porthcawl, a delightful links course of full championship length with the early holes hugging the coastline and those on the higher ground played through acres of gorse. At every hole the Bristol Channel was in view and that meant that there was little protection from the westerly gales.

The Walker Cup had been played at Birkdale a fortnight earlier, so a strong American entry was assured. Once again, however, a diversion from proper golf was caused by one American entry, Bob Hope. Far from starting with two 3s, as Crosby had done at St. Andrews, he played some poor shots, below his normal form. He took four to reach the green at the second, missed his drive at the third and was over the wall at the fifth. His opponent, C. Fox from Brough was the perfect straight man to Hope's cabaret act. "What's your handicap, Mr. Fox?" "I'm 3, what's yours?" "Mine's my wooden shafts." Despite all the media attention Fox played well enough to win at the seventeenth, but Darwin was not amused – "I cannot help thinking we have had enough of these exhibitions."

There were plenty of other Americans in the draw and the Walker Cup men were spread evenly through it, so that the American domination of the championship looked set to continue, the more so because half of the British Walker Cup team had either withdrawn or failed to enter. The absence of Ronnie White was particularly regrettable as he, with Joe Carr, had been unbeaten in the match at Birkdale.

Seven Americans, six of them team members, won through to contest the fourth round. The only British victory to cheer was that of young David Reid, a former Scottish Boys champion, who won at the twentieth against Turnesa by means of a stymie, which two weeks earlier the USGA and R & A Rules Committee had agreed to abolish, but not until the revised rules became operative at the end of the year. In commenting about Turnesa's misfortune, the press overlooked the fact that he had only gone ahead at the fourteenth by means of a similar stymie.

There was more to cheer on the fourth day as Carr beat Stranahan, a repeat of his Walker Cup singles victory, and Albert Evans, a stocky Welshman with weatherbeaten face and bristling eyebrows, beat two more Americans, Winninger and Campbell. His win against the former was largely the result of inspired putting, though he clinched the match at the twenty first without having to hole out, for Winninger having missed his putt for a 4, picked his ball up and stood back to watch Evans hole for the match. The latter had to explain that by lifting his ball he had conceded the hole and match. Evans used his ancient aluminium putter to good effect again in the afternoon and Bill Campbell succumbed at the sixteenth. Evans and Carr continued the good work next morning, with the former beating Joe Gent from Bradford and the Irishman winning against John de Bendern to reach the semi-final. The best of the quarter-final matches had been between two Americans, Charlie Coe and Sam Urzetta, won by the former who had reached the turn in 32 to lead by a single hole. The semi-finals were disappointing for the home players. Coe was out in 33 and too good for Evans, though he fought bravely to the sixteenth, and Carr, of whom there were great hopes, seemed poised, two down with six to play, to mount a challenge against Dick Chapman. Instead he lost the next two holes and the match by four and three.

Both Americans had played outstanding golf on the penultimate day. Coe was five under 4s for his two matches and Chapman two strokes better. The former had won the U.S. Amateur championship in 1949 and at the age of 28, twelve years younger than his opponent, had the more elegant style, but, tall and thin, there was a questionmark about his stamina. Victory had eluded Chapman in his two previous finals, but he was not short on experience. His job in real estate did not prevent him from finding both time and money to play in championships throughout North America and Europe. As well as winning the 1940 U.S. Amateur title he had been champion of Canada, France and Italy. The final was full of good golf, with Chapman round in 70 to Coe's 73 in the morning. After twenty seven holes Coe was back to just one down, but, if Chapman had anxieties about losing a third final, he soon dispelled them by playing faultless golf for the next five holes. 3, 2, 4, 4, 3 was good enough for him to win four of them and clinch the title by five and four. His win was well earned as, in addition to those two previous finals, he had reached the quarter-final on four other occasions in his ten appearances.

1952

The decision to take the championship back to Prestwick did not meet with approval from all quarters. There was a school of thought, voiced both by members of the championship committee and the press, that the links were too short, there were too many blind shots and they were unsuited to large galleries. What's more, cold winds and sunshine had dried the greens to the extent that, in the words of Leslie Edwards, "a feather tied to a matchstick would be the only club delicate enough to start the ball on its course downhill and downwind." They were tricky to the extreme and surely this would favour the home players.

There were however two highly regarded competitors amongst the new crop of Americans, Billy Maxwell, 22 year old holder of the U.S. Amateur Championship, and Harvie Ward a smooth swinging young stockbroker from Atlanta. Chapman, Stranahan and McHale had all come again.

Several of the best British players were again missing. The golfing calendar had placed the Home Internationals a couple of weeks after the Amateur and it was not surprising that some of those selected for international duty, Ronnie White included, could not afford the time or money to play in both. This was one reason for the poor home performance and not, as suggested by one newspaper, the fact that the Americans were taking it all too seriously, to the point of contravening the amateur spirit!

It was a true amateur who gained the headlines after the fourth day. There were twenty one Scots, seven Americans, only two Englishmen, a solitary Irishman and an Australian in the last thirty two and it was one of the Scots, Major David Blair, who had a day to remember, beating both British and American champions in successive rounds. Blair, aged 34, was a fine sportsman as much at home with gun or rod, as with clubs. He was a former officer in the Seaforths and now a partner in a whisky firm, but had been involved in a horrifying road accident the previous December, leaving him with a cracked spine, five broken ribs and depressing thoughts whilst he lay in plastercast for two months, that he might never play golf again. He had been Scottish Boys champion before the war and had given further notice of his ability by winning the 1947 Army Championship and qualifying for the final day of the 1950 Open. Miraculously his fine golf swing came out of the casing undamaged and on this special day not only did he hit every shot from the centre of the club, but he followed it up with splendid putting. He beat Dick Chapman by three and two and Billy Maxwell at the fifteenth.

There were still three Americans and an Australian left to fight out the quarter-finals with three Scots and Joe Carr. Carr beat Blair who could not reproduce his play of the previous day. Harvie Ward, playing brilliantly, beat his compatriot McHale with something to spare and at the bottom of the draw Stranahan came through against Carlow. The surprise of the round was Robin Cater from Williamwood, a partner in the same firm as Blair and another genuine amateur, who had won the West of Scotland championship the previous year. He beat Keppler Enderby, the Australian challenger, to win a place in the semi-final, in which he was one up on Stranahan with four to play, but the American holed the putts when it mattered for 3s at the fifteenth and eighteenth. In the other match Harvie Ward gave Carr little chance and the latter fell for the second time running at the penultimate hurdle.

View from the Himalayas

So for the third consecutive year there was a final between two Americans. Despite the fact that Stranahan had won it twice before, Harvie Ward was favourite, justified by the quality of his golf through the week. Only in the second round, when he needed 4 for an 83, did his form desert him. He had learnt the demands of the ground conditions and from off the green was playing the pitch and runs, as though he had been weaned on links golf. By contrast Stranahan had scrambled through several matches, with wild driving causing the problems. It was suggested that a change to his grip was the reason for the trouble. Despite this, or more accurately because of some short putts missed by Ward, Stranahan took an early lead in the final and was still two up after thirteen holes. The course of the match changed in the next five holes as Ward won four of them. The seventeenth was perhaps the critical one, for Stranahan's near perfect drive took a fearful bounce from the fairway into a bush. Once he was ahead Ward relaxed and with powerful and accurate play swept on to a six and five victory.

A pleasant gesture by Stranahan won him more friends. In the sixth round he had played Jimmy Walker, a member of the local police force. After the match they had sat together discussing at length the mechanics of the swing and golf equipment. Stranahan expounded the theory that Walker needed a heavier driver and a few weeks later a matched set of appropriately weighted woods arrived – a gift from the American.

1953

The start of the 1953 championship at Hoylake coincided with the Whit holiday weekend, which, as often happens, provided an unpleasant afternoon for holidaymakers and golfers alike. The early starters were fortunate. As their matches ended dark clouds were building up and distant rumbles of thunder could be heard. Torrential rain soon followed and it became almost black, with the streaks of lightning overhead providing the only illumination for competitors. Within minutes the course was flooded and unplayable. The championship committee's efforts to communicate a suspension of play, through the radio and by runner, were not immediately successful and some matches continued for a while in farcical conditions. Players found what shelter they could on the course and others returned to the sanctuary of the clubhouse. Miraculously within about ninety minutes the pools had disappeared and play could be resumed, although two competitors, Michael Pearson and Ernest Arend, were not required to conclude their matches, as their drenched opponents, assuming play would be washed out for the day, had returned to their hotels.

There was more gloom on the second day, but this was due to the elimination of a number of the British hopefuls. Micklem, Blair and Langley all lost narrowly. No-one however will have suffered quite the same agony in defeat as Ken Gordon, the man with the pipe. Gordon was playing in his third championship and had been beaten at extra holes in the first two of them. Now he came to the eighteenth one up against Schofield of Mere. He played his second to within six feet of the pin, whilst Schofield's ball bounded over the back of the green. As they searched for it Gordon allowed himself the luxury of a glance back to the match behind to identify who his second round opponent might be. Then Schofield's ball was found, in a horrid lie, and he gave it a sharp hack with his wedge. It hopped out onto the green and trickled slowly on and into the hole. Gordon missed, of course, and lost the nineteenth, thus departing the championship scene with an unusual record.

The weather improved and so did British hopes, in that only one American remained in the last eight. Admittedly he was the holder, Harvie Ward, who, but for a close and high quality match with Frank Stranahan in the fourth round, had been winning all his games with ease. Of the others, Joe Carr and the talented and youthful Arthur Perowne seemed to have the best chances of preventing him from winning again. Carr had survived a difficult sixth round match against Melville Bucher from Elie, as strong and as brave a golfer as he was a soldier. Bucher, one up playing to the eighteenth green, knocked his second shot close, but Carr played a good one too and holed first from four yards. Bucher just missed and after a hooked drive at the nineteenth failed to match Carr's 4. The latter was still not quite at his best and it took him all his time and another 3 at the eighteenth to shake off Jock Lambie in the quarter-final, before facing a fellow Irishman, Cecil Beamish, who had beaten Bill Campbell and Ian Caldwell in earlier rounds.

The game was full of errors and excitement. At the very first hole Carr drove out of bounds into the gardens beyond the putting green, but he won the hole in 6 to 7 as his opponent spurned safety and put his second into the practice ground. Beamish was out of bounds again, in "the Orchard" at the sixth, but Carr, putting tentatively, allowed him to take control. Two up with three to go, Beamish again drove out of bounds and, with Carr winning the next, the match went to the nineteenth. Carr pushed his second and was saved from the dreaded fate by bouncing from the cop back into the long bunker, short and to the right of the green, from where he would struggle to make his 4. Beamish went for it, as he had done three hours earlier, and unbelievably sliced again, his third visit to the practice ground in the match and his fourth shot out of bounds. This time there was no escape.

Meanwhile Arthur Perowne in the other semi-final against Harvie Ward had been playing well enough to defeat either Carr or Beamish. As it was he was four down at the turn to some brilliant golf by Ward, who won at the thirteenth. Later that evening Henry Longhurst watched him on the putting green in front of the clubhouse and asked him how he felt about his prospects for the next day. "Gee, I just hope when I wake up tomorrow, I've still got it."

He didn't have it next morning, though whether this was caused by the cold blustery wind from the north west or by divine influence, one cannot be certain. As Ward missed a six footer on the sixth green one of those ubiquitous Irish priests was overheard by Peter Ryde, reporting his first Amateur, "Oh, God bless you mun!" Carr was out in 35 and three up, a lead that he held until lunchtime.

Joe Carr driving against Harvie Ward

In the early afternoon Ward started his counter attack and by the Alps (eleventh hole) he was back to all square, but he bunkered his tee shot to lose the next and Carr, with a giant drive and wedge to the long fourteenth, went two ahead again. Even then Ward was not finished as he took the sixteenth with a fine 4 and hit a piercing iron shot second through the wind and onto the seventeenth green. This was the critical test for Carr, who was thirty yards short of the green. He passed it, pitching close and holing for the half. Another half at the final hole was good enough and so Carr had finally achieved the title which had narrowly eluded him in the two preceding years. It also broke a three year sequence of American successes and firmly established Joe Carr as the prominent figure amongst the British amateurs, well deserved both for his free and exciting hitting and his bubbling personality.

1954

The field for the 1954 championship at Muirfield was truly international with entrants from twelve different countries outside the British Isles. Teams from the Commonwealth countries were to join the British in a tournament to celebrate the Bicentenary of the Royal and Ancient at St. Andrews during the week following the championship. Thus there was an abundance of talent from Australia, South Africa, Canada and New Zealand, with Peter Heard, the reigning Australian champion, Peter Toogood, his compatriot, Reg Taylor, a 26 year old who had won the South African Open Championship, and Doe from Canada looking the best of them. Frank Stranahan and Bill Campbell headed the American challenge.

As the championship progressed, the overseas players appeared to be dominating it. There were fourteen left to contest the fifth round on Thursday morning, including most of the stars, although Taylor had succumbed to stiff local opposition in the shape of Reid Jack. By that evening only two were left – Bill Campbell in the top half of the draw and Doug Bachli, one of the less fancied Australian team members, in the lower half. Eric Dalton, the South African test cricketer, had reached the turn in 33 to beat Heard but then lost disappointingly. All square with two to play against Campbell, who had taken two shots in a bunker, Dalton failed to capitalise. He only halved the hole in 6 and lost the eighteenth. Millward had beaten Stranahan in what was described as the battle of the muscle men, and Toogood had lost in controversial fashion to Joe Carr. That match went to extra holes and Carr hooked from the tee at the twentieth. After a lengthy search, the ball was found lying unplayable in muddy ground. A committee man was summoned and, deeming this to be casual water, allowed Carr a free drop. From there he played it onto the green and holed from six yards for the match, leaving an unhappy Australian opponent. Keith Tate, a promising young player from Alnmouth, thrashed the last of the Canadians, Doe, and completed an excellent day's work by beating Gerald Micklem at the nineteenth, for a place in the quarter-final.

Bachli and Tate had a fine match next morning. Tate had come within inches of holing his bunker shot at the eighteenth and Bachli was left with a tricky putt to survive. He holed it and won at the nineteenth to face Tony Slark from Surrey, a surprise semi-finalist, who had worked his way through a less fierce section of the draw. Campbell and Carr meanwhile had taken their appointed places in the other semi-final. This, it was felt, would have made a splendid final and a large crowd followed with the normal sprinkling of Irish priests. Campbell was prepared, having befriended the local minister. He had bicycled to the course each day and as he rode past him that morning he raised his hat. The minister was there to watch the semi-final and slipped over to Campbell. "Don't worry," he said, pointing to the white collared Carr supporters, "We've said a prayer for you." The Scottish ministry outprayed the Irish priests and Campbell, two under 4s, outplayed Carr, winning at the sixteenth. Behind them Bachli and Slark battled it out. Both played steadily to the turn, where the match was square, but then Slark, missing a putt or two, fell behind and also lost at the sixteenth.

Bill Campbell bicycling to work

Although Bachli was a former Australian champion, Campbell appeared to have the stronger game for the final, and the early play confirmed this. He was out in 34 and two up, but his golf became a little untidy thereafter and he was fortunate to lunch one up, as Bachli had failed to take advantage of a Campbell bunker mishap at the eighteenth, which was halved in 6. The American began badly after lunch with a top off the first tee and a hook from the second into the waterlogged area that had saved Carr against Toogood. This time the ball could not be found and no spectator was able to confirm that they had seen it land there.

So Campbell had to make the long walk back to the tee to play another, and Bachli took the lead. Campbell regrouped and, winning the eighth and ninth, was one up again and seemingly in control. He played the next four holes immaculately, but Bachli clung to him and then won the fourteenth. The match then turned swiftly against the American, for, after driving into a bunker at the fifteenth, he attempted too much and took three shots to recover. When he chipped too strongly at the sixteenth and lost that as well, his chance had gone.

The genial Bachli had proved himself throughout the week to be a rock solid striker and a cool and determined competitor in the crisis. Although this championship may be remembered as the one that Campbell lost, Doug Bachli was none the less a worthy and popular winner.

1955

The Walker Cup at St. Andrews, prior to the championship at Lytham, had not only resulted in a resounding American victory, but had caused the ranks of potential British winners to be reduced. White once again could not spare two consecutive weeks away from his solicitor's practice and Blair and Cater also had to put business commitments first. Gerald Micklem had scratched with a rheumatic shoulder, leaving only five of the British team in the draw. It looked likely therefore that the championship cup would again return with the Walker Cup across the Atlantic. In addition to the team members there were a couple of dozen other Americans, including Ken Venturi who had played in the previous cup match and was now a corporal in the U.S. army based in Germany.

There were two American casualties on the first day with Yost and Cherry losing respectively to Jimmy Mahon and Guy Wolstenholme and another, Bill Campbell, the U.S. Captain, on the second day. The committee were called into action in a first round match on the second day when John Maddern, who had travelled from Australia to play, having mistaken his starting time, arrived twenty minutes late, which should have meant disqualification. However the committee, listening to a plea on the Australian's behalf by his local opponent Colin Randall, allowed him to play. Justice was done with Randall winning by five and three. The committee were saved another difficult moment by Bill Sharp, who, finding a fifteenth club in his bag when playing the second hole against Arthur Walker from South Africa, disqualified himself.

At the end of the third day six of the American team still remained and were joined in the last thirty-two by four more of their compatriots. Venturi had however lost a splendid match to Billy Joe Patton. Two of the British team, Carr and Scrutton, carried the British flag into the quarter-finals, by which time only Patton and Joe Conrad of the Americans were left. Alan Slater, a Yorkshireman with nothing more serious than a Leeds championship victory behind him, had done the damage with a splendid day's golf, beating Morey and McHale, two of the American team, in the fourth and fifth rounds. Next day he carried on the good work. He found Carr in one of his wilder moods and was too steady for Arthur Perowne, beating him by three and two in the semi-final. Scrutton had gained sweet revenge on Patton for his Walker Cup defeat by annihilating him in the quarter-finals. His golf was as brilliant as it had been the previous day. In those three rounds he was nine under 4s for the forty holes that he was required to play. The bubble burst against Conrad, who, apart from one difficult match against a fellow team member, had come through a relatively easy part of the draw without trouble.

So an unlikely final emerged – Alan Slater against Joe Conrad, a 25 year old, short but sturdy American about whom there was nothing flamboyant either in dress or behaviour. He came from the same club as Byron Nelson and his approach to the game had been much influenced by him. The first round of the final was played in torrential rain with a small gallery and Conrad took an early lead. A crucial hole was the twelfth, where his ball was stopped by spectators from bounding over the back into the bushes. From a reasonable spot behind the green he saved his 3 to win a hole he might otherwise have lost. That put Slater three down and he lunched four down. In better weather and with a larger gallery, many from Yorkshire, the American won the first hole after lunch to go five up, but Slater, encouraged by the support, came back at him. When he holed for a 2 at the ninth, it looked as though Conrad's lead might be cut to a single hole, but the American followed him in from six yards. That was another turning point and, when Slater took two in a bunker at the eleventh, the initiative was firmly back with Conrad and he held on to it until the match ended at the sixteenth.

There was one American who was especially proud, Chick Evans, who, at the age of 64, had won through two rounds, forty-four years after he had first competed. Conrad was a product of the Evans Scholarship Scheme, having been picked out as a young caddie to go to the North Texas "Tec", which was where he learnt his golf. Conrad turned professional at the end of the following year, but never made the same impact as he had done on the amateur scene.

1956

A controversial change was made for the 1956 Championship at Troon. The field was limited to 200, so that the quarter-final and semi-final matches could be played over thirty-six holes, as well as the final. This, it was felt, would eliminate the element of luck often evident in an eighteen hole sprint and ensure two worthy finalists. The final it achieved was worthy enough, but certainly not one that would have been predicted at the start of the week.

There were some early casualties, with Slater, the runner up at Lytham, losing in the first round and Joe Carr in the second, his first match. Pat Ward Thomas, so it is reported, had been watching the demise of Carr and returned to the press tent with a grim face muttering, "It's a damn shame Joe losing to a hacker like that. What chance has he got of doing any good?" One of his press colleagues was quick to respond. "You must admit, Pat, he's got a better chance than Joe!" The "hacker" was M. Alexander, a Prestwick St. Nicholas man, who carried on to the fifth round.

When it came to the thirty-six hole matches, the top half looked the stronger. Reid Jack, the Scottish champion, was to play Conrad, the holder, with Dr. Frank Deighton to play 18 year old John Beharrell from Little Aston. The previous day Beharrell had beaten Ian Caldwell and Gene Andrews, one of the strongest Americans. Four Scots contested the lower half of the draw and that meant six out of eight, a factor that ensured that the thirty-six hole matches would not be played in isolation. Jack versus Conrad took the largest crowd. Had the match been played over eighteen holes Jack would have lost, as he was three down at lunch, but by winning six of the first eleven holes in the afternoon, he seemingly had the match won. It swung again and, but for three putts on the sixteenth green, Conrad would have been one up with two to play. Jack won the seventeenth and despite a brave pitch by Conrad hung on for a half and the

match at the final hole. Next day Beharrell beat Jack in another tense match that went to the thirty-fifth, and Leslie Taylor from Ranfurly won more comfortably against G. Henderson. So Beharrell and Taylor were the unexpected finalists.

A round of 76 in strong cross-winds and intermittent rain put Beharrell four ahead at lunch, which had increased to six by the fifth hole in the afternoon. He lost the next, but restored his lead with a ninety yard pitch in to the hole for a 2 at the seventh. Four holes later, the match was wide open again as Taylor had won the lot. This was the moment, so it is recorded, that Beharrell went up to the committee chairman who was refereeing and asked, "Please Sir, can you tell me the score?" Taylor reprieved him by bunkering his second shot at the twelfth, where Beharrell holed for a 4. This was three up again and the crisis had passed.

Champion at 18

143

For an eighteen year old British boy to win the Championship was both astounding and exciting. Here was a great prospect for the future, and Leonard Crawley in "The Field" wrote of him in glowing terms.

"John Beharrell, whose charming modesty and general deportment was the envy of every parent among the many thousands who watched him at Troon, is just 18 years of age, and one falls to wondering what it must feel like at that age to have become a famous person in the course of one brief week. His father and mother, who were present to witness his triumph, were completely successful in mingling unnoticed with the crowd all week, and on the rare occasions when a friend spotted one or the other, he or she was almost invariably to be found watching some other match. They deserve our warmest congratulations on their share in John's victory, for, in my judgement it made that victory possible.

The new champion is beautifully built. Five feet ten tall, with broad shoulders, a big bottom and strong legs, he must, I feel sure, be good at all games, but owing to a serious illness in his early teens he was compelled to leave school and take to the fresh air and the game of golf alone. He has been admirably taught by J. H. Cawsey, ... and he has picked up a wrinkle or two from Charles Ward, the greatest exponent of the short game in professional golf since the war, who is now Beharrell's home club professor at Little Aston. ..... His balance, like that of all the world's greatest golfers of both yesterday and today, is superlatively good. He stands still when he hits the ball, and he is still standing still and like a marble statue when the effort of striking is over. This is marked in every stroke from the drive to the putt."

Beharrell apart, the great talking point after the championship was whether the thirty-six hole matches had been a success. There was one Scottish International who, believing that the change had been made purely for the benefit of the selectors, suggested that the finalists should simply appear before the selectors, who would ask each to grip a club and then would point to one, nominating him as the champion!

There is a further story of the selectors, told with relish by Alan Turner. He was walking with the chairman, Raymond Oppenheimer, on the Sunday evening before the championship began and saw a large crowd on the practice ground. In the centre of the gallery was an unknown figure firing shots away to a distant caddie, who scarcely had to move to collect the balls. "He can hit the ball," said Alan admiringly. "He won't do any good with a swing like that," replied Raymond. The player concerned duly lost in the first round and Raymond said to Alan, "I told you so." A fortnight later the same player had won the Canadian Open as an amateur. His name was Doug Sanders.

1957

The 1957 Championship was scheduled for Royal St. George's, but the threat of petrol shortage led to a switch to Formby, a central venue and one that was more accessible by rail. The field was again limited to 200 with the quarter- finals and subsequent matches played over thirty six holes.

John Beharrell the holder fell in the third round to Sandy Sinclair from West Kilbride. Gerald Micklem, the recently appointed Walker Cup captain, caused some early havoc by beating two of his probable team, Joe Carr and Guy Wolstenholme, in successive rounds. The major sensation of the championship was however when Dale Morey, the American Walker Cup player, knocked out Leslie McClue, a young Scottish International, but was eliminated himself. It was a literal knock out as McClue, walking into an unexpected Morey practice swing, collapsed on the eleventh tee with blood pouring from a gash behind his right ear. The game was delayed whilst he received help from a doctor in the gallery, who after twenty minutes or so passed him fit to continue. Morey, who prior to the accident had recovered from four down to be only one down, was as shaken by what had happened and, with his recovery losing its impetus, he was beaten three and two. After the game McClue was taken straight to a local hospital and returned to his hotel with nine stitches in the wound.

The line up for the quarter-finals included three Englishmen, Jack Taylor, Jack Girardet and Tony Slark, three Scots – Reid Jack, Alan Bussell and McClue together with an American Harold Ridgley and Arthur Walker from South Africa, who was qualified to play in the English championship and had won it at Hoylake a few weeks earlier. Reid Jack and Bussell won through to contest the first semi-final and Ridgley, who eliminated McClue, clearly not fully recovered, was to play Walker in the second. Whilst Bussell hounded Jack to the thirty-fourth hole, poor Walker found himself at the wrong end of the Amateur Championship's second largest margin – thirteen and twelve, as his "draw had turned into a hook... and his usually wonderful short game was unable to take the strain." Ridgley, with his faded blue straw hat and weatherbeaten face, was a master sergeant in the United States Air Force, stationed in Britain. As long ago as 1935 he had been in the quarter-final of the U.S. Amateur, and now, at the age of 43, he had added the experience of links golf to his talent for hitting precise golf shots. He was by no means a surprise finalist.

The match that followed was without doubt the best of the championship. Ridgley with some fine putting took an early lead, but Jack, winning four out of five holes from the twelfth, went to three up. He lost the seventeenth to a 4 and, round in 69, was still two up at the halfway stage. He tells the story of how, at lunchtime, he was honoured and delighted to be joined by the great George Duncan, who had been watching some of the morning play. This did not turn out to be the mental preparation he needed, as Duncan told him that he would send him a note, after the final, pointing out his faults!

After three holes of the second round his lead was cut to one and he scrambled untidy halves at the fourth and fifth holes, but his blind second shot to the sixth finished inches from the pin and he had the comfort of a two hole lead again. Ridgley fought hard but could make no further impression. Jack had one piece of good fortune. He pushed his tee shot in to the rough at the fifteenth, where the ball was accidentally trodden into the ground by a spectator. Fortunately a steward had been standing there and told the referee what had happened. A free drop enabled him to obtain his half and another at the next left him two up with two to play. Neither player was on the seventeenth green with their second shot. Ridgley from fifty yards pitched ten yards short of the flag. Jack was just off the front right of the green and he could have run it up the bank or even putted it, but he chose to play one of his "fancy shots" with a wedge. With the hands no doubt tightening on the club, he hit it thin and it ran off the other side of the raised green. It was just Ridgley to play first and he putted dead. Jack, with a shallower bank to negotiate, putted this time but left it four feet short, with more than a little borrow. He calmly studied the line from behind the ball and behind the hole, "Pulled his cap over his eyes, smoothed the blue glove on the left hand, two characteristic gestures..... lifted his centre shafted putter in front of the ball, then behind, and the ball was on its way – straight into the middle of the hole."

Despite the fault identified in George Duncan's subsequent note, a tendency to push, (for which a cure was suggested), Reid Jack's play throughout the championship, with his neat uncomplicated swing, was outstanding. He won all his matches with something to spare. It seemed likely that he would dominate the amateur scene for many years to come. That he did not, was simply a reflection of the fact that, as a true amateur, with a business to run, he could no longer devote the time to it.

The final at the 11th, Reid Jack watches Ridgley putting

1958

More changes to the championship format had been agreed by the committee. In order to contain the field to the required size, there had been fourteen regional qualifying tournaments. Thus the original entry of nearly 500 was reduced to 200, all of whom could claim a right to be at St. Andrews. It had also been decided that seeding should be introduced to achieve a more balanced draw, and sixteen top players were selected. The experiment of thirty-six hole quarter-final matches was discontinued. Only the semi-finals and final would be played over two rounds.

Exemptions from qualifying were limited to holders of national titles together with nominations from the USGA and European Golf Association. One effect was to reduce the overseas entry. There were only a dozen or so from America and one notable player from the Commonwealth, Bob Charles, the left-hander who had startled the golfing scene in Australasia by winning the New Zealand Open Championship as an 18 year old. He had been seeded along with three Americans, Jim McHale, Gene Andrews and Tim Holland.

The first day had the normal quota of excitement and brilliant play. Andrews did the first five holes of the Loop (from the seventh) in thirteen shots and his unfortunate opponent was shaking hands on the eleventh green. Tom Crow of Australia was playing John Thornhill, a useful county player from Surrey, and they came to the eighteenth all square. Both were left with putts of not much over a yard. Thornhill, going first, failed with his. Crow missed and knocked the ball away in momentary anguish. Realising what he had done, he turned to Thornhill and said, "That's your hole and match." The latter responded, "I don't play golf that way," and strode off to the nineteenth tee. It took four more holes to decide the match in the Australian's favour.

Those responsible for the seeding would have been well pleased with their work, as nine of their selections reached the last sixteen and six were left to contest the quarter-finals. The three that had disappeared in the fifth round were Scrutton, at the expense of Carr, Blair and Wolstenholme, who lost to Bonallack. This was one of the outstanding matches of the championship. Wolstenholme was two up going to the thirteenth and played the last six holes in strict par, but Bonallack squared the match and won it with a 3 at the first extra hole. Both had been round in 71.

The quarter-finals went according to form leaving Bonallack and Carr to meet in the first semi-final and Alan Thirlwell, who had narrowly beaten Charles, to play Tim Holland in the second. The latter had beaten Douglas Alexander, a young Scot better known for his footballing prowess, in the quarter-final – but not without an unhappy incident. Holland heard some whispering from a partisan gallery as he lined up his putt for a four on the home green. He walked away, settled again, and holed it. Having retreived it from the hole, he turned to the gallery before the Scot could putt for the half and shouted at them, "If you want to say miss it, say it quietly." Despite the interruption Alexander holed out but lost at the nineteenth.

Both semi-finals saw the wheel of fortune turn. Bonallack was out in 33 against Carr but only two up. As they came to the twelfth tee with the wind blowing from the north west, Carr said to his caddie in a loud enough voice for Bonallack to overhear, "We'll be all right now, he won't be able to handle the left to right wind." He didn't and by lunchtime Carr was two up and, with long and accurate driving up to fifty yards past Bonallack's, he moved serenely ahead to four up with nine to play, a lead which he maintained until the match was over. Thirlwell started against Holland with some putting lapses and was quickly three down, but by the end of the round, which he completed in 73, he had redressed the balance. He continued with some fine play after lunch and Holland, having lost two of the first six holes, drove into the gorse at the seventh. He walked on after only a peremptory search, sensing defeat which in due time came at the fifteenth.

The final was a splendid climax to the championship. Joe Carr, the most exciting British golfer of the decade, who had now harnessed his somewhat unruly swing with a new, slower, smoother rhythm was driving the ball enormous distances. In practice the previous winter he had hit thousands of drives and spent hours putting, knowing that these are the two most telling ingredients of success on the Old Course. Against him the large and amiable Thirlwell, with his solid simple swing, made the game look easy. The story of the match was of Thirlwell taking an early lead which Carr gradually reduced on the way home, until they were back to all square on the eighteenth tee. Here Carr holed for a 3

Carr drives watched by a pensive Thirlwell

to take the lead for the first time. Thirlwell started poorly after lunch, but winning the sixth and seventh, he brought the match alive again. He lost the eleventh and then Carr struck two mortal blows. The Irishman drove the ball onto the putting surface at the twelfth and, with Thirlwell almost certain of his 3, he holed the putt up and across the slope for a 2. At the next Thirlwell's hopes rose again, as Carr drove into "the Coffins", but they quickly faded when Joe, finding a good lie, "coaxed a little five iron onto the green." Three perfectly played halves followed and Carr had won his second championship.

1959

Royal St. George's was host to the 1959 Amateur, having missed their opportunity two years earlier due to petrol rationing. Any thoughts that the American ascendancy in post-war amateur golf might have ended with the hat-trick of British victories, were well and truly undermined by the events of the Walker Cup match at Muirfield, when a seemingly strong British team were whitewashed in the foursomes and lost the singles as well.

One of those to do the damage was a young heavily built college boy with crew cut fair hair who impressed everyone with his powerful shot making. Jack Nicklaus was making his first appearance in Britain. Tom Harvey, then chairman of the championship committee, remembers giving Jack a lift from Edinburgh to Sandwich. As they drove through Kent, nearing the end of the journey, Tom said to Jack, "We are going to make a diversion. There's more to life than just golf," and took him to look round Canterbury Cathedral. Twenty years later, as Jack received the U.S. Open trophy for the fifth time, he used those same words in his speech.

Nicklaus won the thirty-six hole appetiser, the St. George's Grand Challenge Cup, and was amongst the favourites for the championship. As always, in the early rounds of a championship preceded by the Walker Cup, the elimination of Americans was the obsession of the press. Two had returned home, Tommy Aaron had injured his hand in practice and Bill Hyndman was reputed to have a bad back. It can't have been that bad, as he eased to a nine and eight victory in the first round. By Wednesday lunchtime Aaron, Billy Joe Patton and Charlie Coe had all been narrowly beaten with Randall, Hill and Lawrence, all part-time golfers from the south-east, bravely grasping their moment of glory.

With Carr and Blair, who were to play each other in the fifth round, Sewell and Wolstenholme all still in, the British team members outnumbered their American opponents in the last sixteen. Three of them, Nicklaus, Hyndman and Deane Beman, were however joined by two U.S. servicemen, Harold Ridgley of Formby fame and Lieutenant Joe Magee. A crowd of 200, large by Sandwich standards, saw Blair dispose of Carr. Blair, one of three competitors to hole in one within twenty-four hours (the others being Charles Lawrie and Tony Duncan) was three under par for eight holes and four up, but Carr, putting with his three iron as he had done in the Walker Cup clawed his way back into the game and was just one down playing the seventeenth. Here Blair hit another iron shot ruled on the pin, which finished three feet away, near enough for a two and one victory. He then faced Beman for a place in the semi-final, but was unable to find the inspiration of the morning and lost by four and three. That too was the score by which Hyndman beat Nicklaus.

The semi-final matches, over thirty-six holes, were Hyndman against Magee and Beman against Wolstenholme, which looked likely to be the closer of the two. It was all square after eighteen holes, but Beman with his efficient method, a fine short game and deep concentration was out in 32 in the afternoon and gave no chances thereafter. Later he expressed the view that he was hitting the ball at his very best and felt confident for the final. Any thoughts that Hyndman, now in his mid-forties, would have an easy game were quickly scotched by the pleasantly extrovert Magee, who holed nearly as many long putts as he smoked cigars during the course of the match. That and the endless patter made it all the more wearisome for Hyndman, who, at two up with three to play, must have hoped for the game to end quickly and quietly. It didn't. Magee holed another one from twelve yards for his 2 at the sixteenth, putted dead from below the bank at the seventeenth and then holed once more from fifteen yards for a 3 to take the match to extra holes. Thankfully for Hyndman, Magee hit behind his pitch shot at the second, the dry turf powdered and the ball flopped forward only a few yards. The match ended there.

In the final Hyndman's smooth and classical swing contrasted with the mechanical one of Beman, but what the younger player lacked in elegance he made up for with superb control on the fast running fairways and splendid putting. All the golf Hyndman had played in the last fortnight, particularly the thirty-eight holes the previous evening, was beginning to take its toll on his mental reserves and Beman, 33 to the turn in the morning, took the lead. He remained two up at lunch and then won the first three holes in the afternoon. Hyndman, still four down with only six to play, made one final effort with two perfectly played holes to win the thirteenth and fourteenth. Had he found the raised green at the two shot fifteenth, the young American would have been under intense pressure, but Hyndman's ball slid off the bank on the right and finished in thick grass, leaving him no chance of saving his 4. That was all the encouragement Beman needed and the match ended at the next hole.

So, for the eighth consecutive time in home Walker Cup years, an American had taken the championship cup and in the fourteen years since the war their domination was such that they had claimed the title seven times and had won ten of the runner-up medals.

Deane Beman.

CHAPTER FIVE

The Bonallack Era

1960

Less than 200 had entered for the 1960 championship at Portrush, so regional qualifying was not necessary. Furthermore, the committee decided that the extra cost and organisation of these qualifying events could not be justified and therefore for 1961 they would revert to the pre-1956 arrangements with 18 holes quarter-finals and semi-finals and a maximum entry of 256. The handicap limit was set at 3 with a ballot of higher handicaps if that number was exceeded.

Despite a large Irish contingent, only 171 played with just a handful of Americans. Those who took the trouble to travel to Portrush were rewarded with outstanding links golf in a memorable setting. It is difficult to imagine three consecutive holes with greater appeal both for scenic and playing qualities than "Fred Daly's", "White Rocks" and "Harry Colt's" (fourth, fifth and sixth holes). Later in the round "Calamity" and "Purgatory" are two more great holes suggestive of the drama likely to unfold.

There was little to brighten the dull and wet opening day. The main interest centred on the reappearance of Jimmy Bruen, who, despite his wrist trouble, was only a couple over 4s against Billy Steel from Denham for the thirteen holes that took him to four up. On the fourteenth he walked over to Steel and offered him his hand, explaining that, if he won, his wrist would not be able to stand another round. Thus ended the competitive career of one of Ireland's outstanding golfers.

It was not surprising that another Irishman, Joe Carr, was a firm favourite and his play on the second day justified it. He was out in 35, winning easily. Two of the other seeds did better. Blair was out in 34 and Jimmy Walker in 32, both on their way to seven and six victories. By the time the field was reduced to sixteen, the four seeds in the top half, Carr and Walker included, had come through unscathed, but the lower half of the draw was seedless.

Carr needed to be at his best on the Thursday, for Brian Chapman, a recent

Cambridge Blue, having beaten one of the stronger Americans, Tim Holland, in the third round, showed no respect for the favourite's reputation and harried Carr to the last hole. In the afternoon the Irishman played Michael Bonallack in a match which again looked likely to go all the way. They were level with three to play, but Bonallack hooked from the sixteenth tee, took the wrong club for his approach to the seventeenth and lost both holes. In truth Bonallack had failed to take a number of chances, missing time and again from five to six feet, and had now lost twice to Joe in the later stages of the championship. "The greater rewards continue to elude him," wrote Pat Ward Thomas.

Carr's opponent in the thirty six hole semi-final was Walker from Irvine. In the bottom half Bob Cochran, a 47 year old American, had been playing some excellent golf, none better than his start of 4, 3, 2, 4, 3, 3, which put him five up against John Duncan, the Irish Open Amateur champion. He reached the semi-final, as did Gordon Huddy, another Cambridge man, who had twice won the President's Putter as an undergraduate and who in his genial yet determined way produced golf that was the essence of steadiness. Whilst the two semi-finals might not have provided the best golf of the championship, they certainly lacked nothing in excitement. Huddy started strongly against Cochran, but the latter pulled back the lead to two by lunchtime. The match was square again at the tenth and they halved the next in 2. Then Huddy took a two hole lead again, only to see it disappear as a result of a superb second by the American at the sixteenth and some trouble of his own at the next. A long putt stone dead by Huddy at the last ensured extra time, but it was the American who prevailed at the par 5 second with a perfect chip for his 4.

Carr's play against Walker in the morning was his poorest of the championship. Round in 79, he was lucky to be only two down. The quality of golf improved in the afternoon, but Walker was still one up playing the par 5 ninth. Carr hooked his tee shot, pushed his second and, from the rough sixty yards short, missed the green with his third. Walker, just short in 2, chipped neatly to within six feet, a length of putt which he had been holing with regularity, and looked certain to win the hole. This however was a moment for the unexpected and, with Carr holing his chip, a startled Walker missed the putt. The match was still all square with three to play, when another hooked drive committed Carr to a 5. Walker was left with a five foot putt to take the lead again, but missed. Thus reprieved, Carr hit two enormous blows into the wind and onto the green at the 520 yard seventeenth and Walker was never in sight of his 4 there or of matching Carr's 4 at the final hole.

For the second year in succession an American in his forties had to search for mental resilience to overcome the fatigue of a thirty-eight hole semi- final. It was never likely that he would find enough of it, or the skill to overcome Carr, for, although Cochran from Missouri had qualified a dozen times for the U.S. Amateur, he had never made sufficient impact to earn Walker Cup recognition.

The improbable looked possible when Carr three putted the short third to give first blood to America, but from there the Irishman was at his relentless best, long, straight and accurate, and with a round of 69 was six holes ahead at the halfway stage. He added another four in the first seven holes of the afternoon, and although Cochran won a couple back, the match ended at the short eleventh with a rapturous crowd cheering their hero's third Amateur title. Only Ball and Hilton had won more.

A story appeared in the Irish Times that victory had cost Carr some money. Joe, it was said, had been summoned for jury service in Dublin during the week of the championship, but his name was called in vain. The judge, who was a useful member of Portmarnock and to whom the name of J. B. Carr was not unknown, without a flicker of emotion imposed a fine of three pounds. It was suggested by a Dublin press man that a challenge match might soon be arranged between the judge and a well known member of Sutton – for a stake of three pounds a side.

1961

Another exciting new venue had been chosen for the 1961 championship. Turnberry had staged the previous year's Home Internationals and, now fully recovered from the ravages of wartime use, was in excellent condition.

For the second successive year there were no overseas players amongst the seeds. Carr, Walker and Bonallack, all of whom had justified their seeding at Portrush, seemed to have the best chances, along with Blair and a young Englishman of outstanding promise, Martin Christmas, who had finished runner up in the 1960 Brabazon and English Championship. Guy Wolstenholme, who had been England's most successful player over the preceding five years, had turned professional, taking advantage of a new P.G.A. ruling, which enabled him to play for money after only six months.

The champion, an early starter on the first day, began as he had left off at Portrush and was back in the clubhouse in ninety-nine minutes, having disposed of his opponent on the eleventh green. The first seed to go was the Scot Sandy Saddler, who lost to Brian Chapman. That evening Brian was celebrating with a few of his young English friends, including Gordon Huddy. Joe Carr sitting nearby, saw that money was being thrown into the centre of the table and, always game for a wager, came over and addressed the company. "What's up lads? Can I join in?" Huddy nodded and Joe threw a ten shilling note into the kitty. "What's the game?" to which Huddy responded, "Thanks Joe. You've just contributed to our wine bill." Perhaps there was justice in the fact that both Huddy and Chapman lost next day.

Carr and Walker at the top and Bonallack and Christmas in the lower half all reached the last eight. One surprise was the presence there of Laurence Foster from Prestwick. It was still more surprising that he had played a fifth round match in which the aggregate age of the two competitors was 109 years. Alex Kyle, his victim, was the junior by a year. Another survivor was the American serviceman Ralph Morrow, a reinstated professional now based at Prestwick, who looked a real threat to the home players.

Carr versus Walker was the outstanding match of the quarter-finals, perhaps of the championship. These two had played their exciting semi-final at Portrush and had faced each other more than once in the Home Internationals, but Walker had never beaten Carr. On this occasion the Scot took the lead again and again, but each time Carr responded by winning a hole back, until they came to the seventeenth all square. This hole, measuring 515 yards was into a strong wind and Carr was on the front of the green in three. Walker's hooked third was caught by the wind and finished fifty yards to the left. He played the odd to the middle of the green, about ten yards away and from there he holed. Carr having putted past missed the return, but once again he squared the match winning the eighteenth with a 4. Both were on the nineteenth green in two with the Scot nearer the hole and, when Carr three putted, Walker had at last got his man. The Scot avoided reaction in the afternoon's semi-final but, despite playing from the third to the eleventh in six under 4s, he couldn't shake off the American, Morrow, until the eighteenth. Walker's long approach putt there finished stone dead to clinch his place in the final.

Bonallack and Christmas met in the other semi-final. Both had been playing excellent golf in the previous rounds, but Bonallack raced to the turn in 33 and was six up after ten holes. Christmas then found the rhythm of his smooth and graceful swing and with a series of perfect golf shots won the next three holes. He might have won the fourteenth too, if he had holed from eight feet, and Bonallack needed a five footer to halve the fifteenth. That made him three up with three to play and the match ended at the sixteenth, which was as far as anyone had taken him.

Neither finalist could claim to have the most elegant of golf swings, but in terms of ability to control and flight the ball and in their skill at manufacturing the short shots and then holing the putts, they could not be faulted. Bonallack that year had found a new confidence to go with his quiet determination. Since his win in the 1952 Boys Championship, which had marked him as an outstanding prospect, he had been runner up in the Youths Championship, in the English Championship and the Brabazon, but had not yet netted his first major prize. The winter coaching with Ernest Holdwright, a boost from his early season form in winning the Berkshire trophy and finishing fifth in the Martini Professional Tournament and a recently acquired golden goose putter combined to give him this self belief. His play in the final remained as rock solid in straightness, accuracy and judgement as it had been throughout the week. Walker did not play badly. Indeed his score of four over 4s for the holes played in blustery conditions would have been good enough to win most finals. As it was, he was four down after nine, five down at lunch, with Bonallack round in 69, and that was how it remained, apart from a couple of holes exchanged, until the end. Bonallack had won the championship in the most commanding manner and the Scot accepted defeat gracefully. His reward was a Walker Cup place, which two years ago had been denied him as a result of injury.

1962

With the championship back at Hoylake there were more than the 256 entries that had been set as the maximum. So a ballot amongst those with a handicap of 3 became necessary. Many of those that failed to find a place in the draw will have been frustrated when they saw the large number of scratchings amongst the first round results. The last two champions, Bonallack and Carr, were the favourites. In the absence of Jimmy Walker, who had followed his fine performance at Turnberry by winning the Scottish Championship, the pick of the Scottish entry was Ronnie Shade. He had won the Brabazon at Hoylake the previous year and in doing so had set a new amateur course record with his 67 in the third round.

The seeds fell fast and furious, with Martin Christmas, the only point winner for Great Britain in the previous year's Walker Cup match, the first to go. The champion's defence ended in the second round, at the hands of Jackson Taggart junior from Portrush. Bonallack seemed to have weathered the storm when he started for home 4, 3, 3, 2 to convert a one hole deficit into a lead of two, but Taggart won the fourteenth, squared the match with a 3 at the fifteenth and Bonallack followed these setbacks with uncharacteristic 6s at the next two holes. By Thursday morning the only seeds to remain were Joe Carr, John Hayes, the South African champion, and Alec Shepperson, the talented Walker Cup player from Nottingham, who was making one of his rare appearances in the championship. By the end of the day they too had gone. Harry Kinloch had beaten Shepperson and Rodney Foster, a fresh faced 21 year old from Bradford, had eliminated the South African.

The fourth round match between Carr and Brian Chapman, both members of the 1961 Walker Cup team, was the highlight of the championship, outshining everything that went before and after. Carr had been a little lucky to beat 19 year old Bruce Critchley in the previous round, for, having taken the lead for the first time at the sixteenth, he pushed his second at the next and was saved from the road by hitting a small boy who was standing near the fence. Against

Chapman, in a stiff westerly breeze, Carr started positively, winning two of the first three holes. From the fourth Chapman took charge with a series of pin splitting iron shots, leaving him time and again with putts of just a few feet. He played the next eleven holes, to the fourteenth green, in just 35 shots – seven below par. Carr amazingly was only two down, but Chapman was not one to become frightened at the enormity of what he was doing and he retained his composure and his lead to close out Carr on the seventeenth green. At that point the Irishman needed a 4 for a 68, and he said afterwards, "In all the matches I have ever lost, it has always been possible to look back and see where I could have won. In this game I can't. However I had played, I don't see how I could have beaten him."

None of the quarter-finals went beyond the fifteenth green and that left Chapman and Welsh International John Povall to play in the first semi-final and an American, Richard Davies, with Foster in the second. Chapman had continued his fine form for the next two matches, but as the ultimate prize began to glitter his golf became a little ragged. One up after eleven holes he bunkered his drive at the twelfth to surrender the initiative. With a 6 at the fourteenth and a second shot out of bounds into the field at the sixteenth, he became two down with two to play. Povall obliged with one onto the road at the seventeenth, but a half in 4 at the last secured the Welshman a place in the final and left Chapman with just a bronze medal and memories of his finest golfing hour. Meanwhile Foster was unable to repeat the golf that he had displayed in the quarter-final, in which he had been three under 4s for fourteen holes, and the 31 one year old ex U.S. Marine, Richard Davies from California, became a second somewhat unlikely finalist.

The two finalists could not have been more contrasting characters. Doubtless the extrovert Welshman prepared himself for the final, just as he would have prepared for the monthly medal at Whitchurch, drinking a pint or two with his friends. Davies, on the other hand, was an intense and emotional person. He saluted the portrait of Bobby Jones each day as he climbed the stairs to the clubroom. He had arrived a week in advance and was leaving nothing to chance in his effort to find solutions to the penetrating questions posed by the Hoylake links. This had been rewarded with a series of relatively untroubled victories and Povall was the first opponent of international stature that he had to face.

The final began with a sparse crowd in sparkling sunshine and a light breeze. It was soon evident that Povall would not have won the monthly medal at Whitchurch. He was near to level 6s for the first five holes and four down. Davies too was hitting some wayward shots, but a morning round of 81 was good enough to retain half of that early lead. The quality of golf improved in the afternoon as the crowd swelled with supporters from across the border and Povall, duly encouraged, went ahead. After eleven of the afternoon holes he was two up, but with a bunkered tee shot at the next and a 4 by Davies at the fourteenth, the match was square again. The American took the lead at the next and Povall had to hole bravely on the "Royal" green to save the match. A fine second gave him a five yard chance of a 3 at the final hole, but the putt slipped past and Davies holed from a yard for his 4. After the unpromising start it had after all been a thrilling final and Davies had taken his opportunity by playing Hoylake's demanding last five holes in level 4s. Afterwards, with pleasant modesty, he expressed his surprise and pleasure at winning and added, "There are a hundred guys back home who could give me a start and a beating." Maybe, but not many would have matched him over those last five holes.

1963

1963 was another home Walker Cup year. The British team at Turnberry had flattered to deceive in the match with its new format of eighteen hole foursomes and singles on each of the two days. They had established a three point lead at the half way stage, but could only manage two wins and a half out of the twelve matches next day. The contestants moved east to St. Andrews for the Amateur, with the American squad depleted by the absence of Charlie Coe and Deane Beman. Despite this, they were expected to maintain their record of an American win following a home Walker Cup match, which had held good since 1923. The Scots however were hopeful that either Stuart Murray, the reigning Scottish champion, or Ronnie Shade, both of whom had scored two points at Turnberry, might prevent it.

When the championship had reached the quarter-final stage American hopes were still high, but it had been a black Thursday for the Scots. The day had started with thirteen of them in the last thirty-two, including both Murray and Shade, but by the end of the day not one remained. Dr. Ed Updegraff had beaten Shade and Murray had fallen to John Blackwell, a 48 year old greying schoolmaster from Kent. Blackwell had a fine golfing pedigree. He was captain of the Royal St. George's Club, a medal winner at the R & A, holder of the Oxford & Cambridge Golfing Society's President's Putter and a successful Harrovian Halford Hewitt player, but to find him in the last sixteen of the Amateur was something of a surprise and he was not expected to test Murray. As it turned out the Scot was not at his best and Blackwell, starting fast, was three up after five holes. Murray closed the gap, but three putts on the ninth and eleventh greens and a 3 by Blackwell at the twelfth meant that the latter's lead was restored, and despite another Murray counter attack he held on to win by two and one. Two other seeds in the lower half of the draw, Carr and Christmas, were also beaten, which left a top heavy situation as four Walker Cup players, three of the American team and Michael Lunt, were contesting the first two quarter-final matches.

Lunt played Richard Davies, the holder, and came to the fourteenth with a lead of one hole. He was lucky to bounce back into play from the wall and the hole was halved, as were the next two. At the Road hole Davies was on the green and Lunt short and a little to the left with his second, facing one of golf's most difficult shots. "With his putter from below the bank he ran his ball up to within inches of the top of the dreaded bunker. It slowed ominously as it lost its speed, and then turned towards the hole and slipped down the hill six feet past the cup," which was as near as he could have hoped, and he holed the next. At the eighteenth Davies having played his second to the top of the Valley of Sin, hurried forward to mark it before it ran back. It was to no avail, as his putt for a 3 shaved the hole, and Lunt holed for the match.

If there was tension in the morning, there was more for Lunt in the late afternoon in his match against Dr. Ed Updegraff. He was ahead most of the way and, at three up with three to play, he looked to have secured his place in the final. A Scottish "haar" was now enveloping the links, but this did not deter Updegraff, who holed for a 3 at the sixteenth and won the Road hole with a 4. In the murky light both found the green at the Home hole but neither of them were near the hole. The green was now damp and slow and Lunt, putting first, left his ball two yards short. Updegraff followed to within a couple of feet. The words of Pat Ward-Thomas capture the scene:

"There is no place in all the world like the Tom Morris green for these deathless moments of hope and longing and fear. The crowds lean tensely over the green palings and from the windows that seem so close .... over all there is that awful silence. A car hooted in the distance, and heads turned angrily; then all was still again, and there was Lunt slowly, carefully as always, reading his putt. It broke from left to right, some inches had the green been dry, but he struck it on the left lip. For a moment of pure agony we thought he had missed on the right, but it caught the rim and fell; the deed was done, the Americans were vanquished."

In the other semi-final Blackwell had been caressing his way round with steady patient play and a well-disguised determination, allowing his opponent, the other American doctor Ron Luceti, to make the mistakes. Blackwell was two up with five to play. Here he drove over the wall and at that moment must have feared that the lead was insufficient. Unbelievably Luceti followed him out of bounds and ended up losing the hole. With halves at the next two holes, Blackwell finished the job.

The morning round of the final was played in pleasant sunshine with scarcely a breath of wind and ended all square, although the scoring failed to match the conditions. Blackwell took the lead with a fine 3 at the first in the afternoon, which prompted the comment from him, "I always thought it should have been an eighteen hole final!" Lunt squared at the second, reached the turn in 35 and, with Blackwell missing his tee shot at the seventh and taking three putts at the ninth, was two ahead. The twelfth was critical. Blackwell ran up his approach to five feet and Lunt, after a huge drive left his next five yards short, from where he holed. With hopes dashed, Blackwell missed. He hung on to take the game to the seventeenth and, after a miraculous pitch over the Road bunker, it looked as though it might go to the last, but it was not to be and Michael Lunt became a worthy and popular champion.

Lunt recovers at the 13th in the final

His great talent had not before been fully rewarded, although he had been runner-up in the English Championship and the Brabazon Trophy. His slow rhythm belied enormous power. His driving was sometimes erratic, but his fine iron play, a smooth putting stroke and an equable temperament more than made up for that. His triumph meant much to two people, one of whom was there and the other was not. Michael's fiancée, Vicky, had graced the final as his caddie. His father, Stanley, was persuaded to stay at home, leaving god-father Leonard Crawley, whom he had beaten in the final of the English championship the year of Michael's birth, to phone through the scores.

"No-one remembers who came second," so Walter Hagen said. In this case however, the runner-up gained almost as much of the glory. Despite coming from south of the border, John Blackwell captivated the two thousand or so spectators that followed the game. He was everything that one does not expect in the final of an Amateur. He wore a tie and a happy smile. His clubs were a collection of favourites with kinked shafts and wry necks. He putted with his left hand below his right, as an anti-twitch device. He rested on a stool whilst waiting for his turn to play and from time to time he would revive his spirits with some mixture from his flask. "The Field" summed it all up – "Here was a match that was more than a Championship final. It was a game – and a game to celebrate."

1964

The venue for 1964 was a somewhat controversial choice. For the first time it was not a seaside links. No-one could deny that the site at Ganton, with its sandy sub-soil, was eminently suitable for a testing championship course amidst trees, heather and gorse, the latter ensuring that it was not wanting in scenic quality, especially in May. But Ganton is twenty miles from the coast and there is not even a whiff of salt air. Strangely, this seemed to discourage the Scots more than the Americans. They could only muster an entry of about twenty whilst many more than that came flocking across the Atlantic, but without the Walker Cup stars. George Blocker and Dale Morey seemed to be the strongest of them, the former having come close to beating Lunt in the fourth round at St. Andrews, but neither were seeded.

John Blackwell was an early starter on the first morning, perhaps too early, for he found himself five down with five to play to Malcolm Peel. Pride then took over and he won them all back, but as so often happens the man who loses a long lead comes again and so Peel won after all at the twentieth. Another match went the same distance late next afternoon, between David Marsh and David Kelley, both under the scrutiny of the England selectors. The match started brightly, but Marsh playing some errant shots fell behind and, at four down with seven to play, Frank Pennink, who was selecting and writing for one of the national daily papers, decided that he had seen enough and that Marsh was a beaten man. He filed his copy accordingly and was duly penitent next day when he arrived to discover that Marsh had after all won at the second extra hole.

The lower half of the draw was prised open by the defeat of first Shade and then Bonallack, both at the hands of Americans – Brady and Morey. This left only Martin Christmas of the seeds. At the top Lunt, Carr and Thirlwell had all progressed to their appointed place in the quarter-finals. Two former champions had also made unexpected progress. The 52 year old Sweeny, 1937 winner and Kyle (1939) aged 57 reached the fifth round to be confronted there by a couple of Irishmen. Kyle was no match for Joe Carr, but Sweeny, holing a pitch and a bunker shot, beat young Peter Flaherty to set up a quarter-final match with Martin Christmas. The smooth and elegant swing of yesterday was however no match for the graceful one of today.

The first pair off on Friday morning, Lunt versus Carr, were the ones to attract the greatest interest. They had met at a party the previous evening and, talking jocularly about the forthcoming clash, Carr had told Lunt, "Don't let me get three up. You'll never get them back." Starting well and then knocking his tee shot stone dead at the fifth, Carr duly went three up, but Lunt did get them back and was one up playing the sixteenth. Here he took three putts to lose it and it looked as though he would lose the seventeenth, when he hooked into the hollow to the left of the green, but he pitched up and holed the putt. A good half followed and at the nineteenth Carr, missing from close range, was beaten.

Lunt and Christmas both had opponents from the north-east in the semi-finals, though possibly not the one that had been expected in the case of Lunt, as Hall from Durham had beaten Alan Thirlwell by a hole. Christmas's opponent was Gordon Clark, a 31 year old from Whitley Bay, who, having lost in the final of the English championship in 1961, had played for England that season but since then had been overlooked by the selectors. The two seeds appeared to have control of the semi-finals at the halfway stage, but whilst Lunt moved safely on to his second successive final, Christmas lost his way over the inward half and saw Clark seal his fate with a fine second to the back of the eighteenth green.

Lunt could not have been a stronger favourite to win the final, though Clark had shown in earlier rounds, particularly in his fifth and sixth round victories against the American, Morey, and Harrison, the last remaining Scot, that in a crisis he had the coolest temperament to support his sound method. Lunt, despite that slow backswing, was much the longer from the tee, long enough to be able to use an iron and eliminate the risk at the tight driving holes. Normally he had a lovely putting touch, but three putts at the first hole in the final set him off on the wrong foot. It occurred to him that the greens had not had their morning shave and were not as quick as they had been earlier in the week, and this may have undermined his confidence. Clark took the lead and went three up at the thirteenth, where, after a missed second shot, he holed from the front of the green for an unlikely 4. Lunt had however recovered two of the holes by lunchtime and gradually took control in the afternoon, moving to two up after a superb drive to the 280 yard fourteenth hole. The next was halved, but Clark took advantage of Lunt's pulled second to the sixteenth and then holed bravely from six feet to save his 3 and the match at the next. The last at Ganton, round the pines and over the road, is a splendid finishing hole requiring two long and accurate shots and both did well to find the green with their seconds, though Lunt was at the front with the pin well back. He finished the afternoon round as he had started in the morning, with three putts, and Clark won it with a 4. He was reprieved again at the thirty-eighth where both were over the green with their second shots. Clark chipped weakly and failed with his putt, then Lunt, from a couple of yards, missed as well. History had already been made as this was the first final to go as far. It ended at the next, a short par 4, where Clark holed his putt for a 3, thus depriving Lunt of the chance of emulating Hutchinson, Hilton and Lawson Little by winning successive championships.

1965

There was plenty of optimism about the chances of another home bred winner at Porthcawl in 1965, despite an American entry in excess of thirty, which included their new champion, Bill Campbell, who had delighted everyone by winning the prize that his fine golf so richly deserved. It included also Bob Gardner, Bill Hyndman and several others trying for the back-door route into the American Walker Cup team. Dick Chapman, now a rugged looking 54 year old, was also making a sentimental journey, having won at Porthcawl fourteen years earlier. The optimism arose largely from two youngsters, the 18 year old Peter Townsend from Porters Park, who had played in the England Boys team as a 14 year old and had won the Boys Championship twice, and Clive Clark, two years his senior, who had blossomed during the early part of the season. He and Bonallack had won everything. They had tied in the Lytham Trophy; Clark had won the Golf Illustrated Gold Vase, and Bonallack the Berkshire Trophy, but Clark, by finishing four strokes ahead of Bonallack in a tie for the Brabazon had won the prestigious Scrutton Jug.

A lovely hot day, with the sun sparkling on the channel, was just what the overseas visitors wanted, but it didn't prevent one sensation. Bill Campbell was unlucky to be drawn against Richard Langridge, a former England Boys' captain, who had moved to South Africa and won the 1964 South African Amateur Championship. Even so victory looked to be a formality for Campbell as he walked down the hill at the eighteenth having played a fine second shot to the middle of the green. Langridge, one down, was just inside him, but failed with the putt to save himself, or so it appeared. Unbelievably, Campbell whose approach putt had finished within a yard of the hole, missed. At the nineteenth Langridge, with the honour, unleashed an enormous drive to the edge of the green and made a 3, which Campbell could not match.

Another American to make the news was Hunter McDonald, formerly an assistant professional in his native Scotland. He had moved to America, where a job in the oil industry took all his time for several years, after which he resumed his golfing career as an amateur. The quality of his shot making was outstanding in beating Michael Lunt at the seventeenth in the second round. He then played Dick Chapman who had rolled around in 72 to beat Findlay Black in his first match. The Chapman fighting spirit was still in evidence against McDonald, as he splashed out of a greenside bunker at the eighteenth stone dead to square his match, but the younger man returned the compliment with his second shot at the nineteenth.

Of the seven Americans to reach the fourth round, only Bill Hyndman remained by the Thursday evening. Alistair Low from Duddingston beat Gardner and John Povall brought McDonald's run to a peremptory end. Young

163

Townsend, who had distinguished himself by beating two Americans, lost to Foster and the holder, Gordon Clark, who had won his way through to the fifth round without trouble, lost to his namesake Clive. The four Englishmen, Foster, Bonallack, Clark and Christmas neatly spaced in the draw won their way to the semi-finals at the expense of Low, Hales, Hyndman and Povall.

Both semi-finals were excellent games. Bonallack, who had previously had a series of crushing wins, looked as though he would secure another when he became four up against Foster after twelve holes, but he shanked his second at the thirteenth and three putted the next. Thus encouraged, Foster won the fifteenth with a neat chip and putt and so Bonallack, for the first time during the week, found himself under real pressure. Two solid halves followed and then, at the eighteenth, Bonallack with a 7 iron put the ball inches from the pin, as good a shot as he could remember and Foster had shaken him by the hand before they reached the green.

Christmas playing in his third semi-final in five years and swinging as sweetly as ever, missed a couple of short putts which should have given him an early lead. He could not shake off Clark and the match was still all square as they played the eighteenth. Here Clark holed from nine feet for a 3, though a 4 would have done the job, as Christmas had badly bunkered his second.

So the season continued as it had started, with Clive Clark, the young pretender, in fierce competition with "The Duke", as Michael Bonallack was known to his golfing friends. If Bonallack's passage to the final had been easy, Clark had only survived in the second and third rounds by beating Frayssineau from France and David Kelley at the nineteenth. He had faced good opponents all the way, including Gordon Clark and Bill Hyndman. Success breeds confidence and confidence combined with a sound technique and a lovely tempo, not just to his swing but in his approach to every shot, bred more success. Clark showed no nerves as the final began and raced to the turn in 35 to be four up. By the thirteenth he was six up and Bonallack was wondering how he could avoid a double figure drubbing, but he won the fourteenth. By lunchtime Clark's lead was down to three and Bonallack was having positive thoughts again, all the more so after he had put some loose change into the club fruit machine and taken out the jackpot. By the turn in the afternoon the match was level. Clark had not collapsed. Bonallack, out in 34, simply gave him no chances. At the tenth he took the lead and, though Clark continued steadily, Bonallack completed the twenty-two holes from the fourteenth tee to the thirty fifth green in three under par, never losing the honour.

The two of them met again, later that summer, in the final of the English Championship, and again Bonallack, coming from behind, asserted himself. Clark's moment of glory came in the Walker Cup when he holed the putt that gave the British team its first tie on American soil.

The finalists. Bonallack and Clark with Angela Bonallack

1966

After a gap of nearly twenty years the Amateur was back at Carnoustie. On a grey day, with the wind from the east, it can be a forbidding place, but as a championship test there is nothing finer, particularly those last five holes, with the Barry Burn exerting its watery influence at the end of a tight match.

Clive Clark had turned professional. It was now easier and more respectable for an amateur to turn professional and in Clark's case he had the opportunity of touring the world at the expense of the equipment company that was sponsoring him. Two other young players had made the news in the early part of the amateur season. Peter Townsend, described by Walker Cup captain Joe Carr as "the best thing thrown up in these islands since the war," had won the Brabazon Trophy at Hunstanton, seven shots clear of Bonallack, Shade and an 18 year old South African, Bobby Cole. The latter had impressed everyone there and at Sunningdale, where he won the Golf Illustrated Gold Vase.

There were only four seeds in action on the first day and little happened to set the pulses racing. The first match of interest to the press came next morning when Ronnie Shade was playing against an illustrious opponent, Mark McCormack, almost as well known as his three famous clients, though not quite as competent on the links. Tip Anderson was there to caddie for him, but it was to no avail and he lost by three and two. Another famous figure playing late in the day was Bob Falkenburg, who had won the Mens' Singles title at Wimbledon back in 1948. He was no mean golfer, but lost his second round match to Sandy Pirie, a good young Scot. Immediately behind, Joe Carr was battling with Donald Marr, a former Oxford Blue and Sunningdale member. Carr, not quite at his best and unhappy at the lack of pace in the greens, was one down with two to play. Despite a visit to the Barry Burn by Marr at the seventeenth, Carr failed to win the hole. At the eighteenth Marr looked to be in the burn again with his second shot, but it finished just clear of the water at the bottom of the muddy bank. He took off his shoes and socks and knocked the ball to within six feet of the hole. "I would certainly have missed it," he said afterwards in his disarming manner, but Carr had failed with his putt from a little further away and conceded the match.

There were more water sports next day. Shade had been three down to Jimmy Hayes, one of that useful band of Northumbrian players, but he won them all back and took the lead at the fifteenth with a fine 3. Hayes squared again at the seventeenth and at the final hole, which, into the wind, required two good shots to carry the burn, he failed narrowly and the ball lodged on the bank. Shade hit his second thin. It looked doomed, but bouncing just in front of the burn it skipped into the bank up and over. Hayes found a playable lie but his head came up on the pitch and the ball hit the stone facing of the bank and fell back into the water. After one damp and unavailing attempt he conceded the match.

Next morning the dampness came from the sea, in the form of a thick Scottish haar. Visibility was down to a few yards and the start of play was delayed for two and a half hours. By then there was little chance of completing a second round and the championship committee, now under the chairmanship of Gerald Micklem, decided that the fifth and sixth rounds should be played next day and the semi-finals and final, over eighteen holes, on the Saturday.

Only two seeds, Gordon Cosh and Shade, remained for the fifth round as the three English hopes, Bonallack, Foster and Townsend, had all lost on the last green the previous afternoon. Hyndman and Campbell, the American favourites, had also been eliminated. Cosh and Shade won through against fellow Scots to meet in the first semi-final. Local hopes that there would be a third Scot in the last four were dashed when Charlie Green, who had out-putted Sandy Pirie in the morning, took as many putts on the first four greens in the afternoon as he had taken for nine holes against Pirie. That put him three down to young Cole. Green found his form on the way home, but Cole gave nothing away and, halving the last six holes, he won at the eighteenth. His surprise opponent in the semi-final was a 48 year old Frenchman, Henri de Lamaze, who had played several times in the championship without making progress. His economic swing with minimal leg action was perhaps more suited to the shorter tree lined courses around Paris than the windswept British links. In France for twenty years he had been almost unbeatable and had won so many French Amateur Championships that the cup seemed to be his personal property.

Next morning, Shade soon took charge of the first semi-final and, reaching the turn in 33, was four up. Although Cosh fought gallantly and had reduced the deficit to a single hole by the fifteenth, that was as near as he could get and the match finished at the seventeenth. The second semi-final began with an

Gerald Micklem watches the champion in full flow

incident. At the first hole Lamaze played his second shot to six feet from the pin, whilst Cole was still looking for his tee shot. When it was found, it was clear that Cole should have been the first to play. The referee pointed this out to Cole and Lamaze's shot was recalled. Although the hole was halved, the incident seemed to unsettle the young South African more than Lamaze and he was soon three down. He was still two down after ten holes, but from there his long hitting into the wind gave him the advantage, no more so than at the 240 yard sixteenth where he played a magnificent tee shot. That put him ahead, and he took his place in the final at the next.

Pat Ward-Thomas described Cole's swing as "a movement of compelling beauty in the width, outline and constancy of its arc, generating quite abnormal clubhead speed." His great length belied the fact that he was a mere nine and a half stone and five foot nine inches high. By comparison Shade was the honest shire-horse against a thoroughbred racehorse. The Scots cheered their own man in the final and kept him going. He won the short thirteenth to square the match, but the Cole power was too much for him at the next three holes and the South African won them all, hitting the sixteenth green yet again to clinch his victory, and share with John Beharrell the distinction of winning the championship at the age of 18.

1967

The first day of the 1967 Walker Cup at Sandwich, in which the British players could only manage two and a half out of the twelve points, provided an ominous warning for the championship at Formby. The entire American team stayed on to play and all of them were seeded. There were four absentees from the British side, as Craddock and the two Scots, Saddler and Pirie, had returned home after the match. Now that Townsend had joined Clive Clark in the professional ranks, the new home star was Peter Oosterhuis, a 19 year old, but he too had to give the championship a miss because he was on 'A' Level duties. All looked set for a resumption of the time honoured practice, broken only in 1963 by Michael Lunt, whereby a member of the visiting American Walker Cup team took home the championship cup.

The first round saw the demise of two of the American team, Lewis and Allen, and Rodney Foster from the home team. It had also seen Bill Campbell playing at his best. He needed 4 for a 67 in his first match and was much impressed by the young Scot who took him to the penultimate hole. His name was Bernard Gallacher.

Ten seeds remained in the last sixteen for the fifth round matches and, of these, seven were Americans. Two memorable contests between British and

168

American team members took place that afternoon. Michael Bonallack played Downing Gray in a repeat of the first day Walker Cup singles, which had been halved, and Michael Attenborough was matched against Marty Fleckman.

Bonallack had hurt his back the previous day and his swing was somewhat restricted, but his short game was as sharp as ever and the match as close as their previous encounter. The mounting tension was momentarily eased by an amusing incident on the thirteenth green. Gray was at the front and Bonallack on the steep bank to the left. It was not clear who was to play and the referee, Dr. John Lawrie, was called into action. He paced from Gray's ball to the pin and from pin to Bonallack's ball with stride shortening as he mounted the bank. He then turned to the players and a little breathlessly, with his pronounced stammer, gave his decision. "E-e-e-xactly e-e-e-qual." The two protagonists waited for the hilarity to subside, tossed a coin and the match proceeded. Bonallack squared at the fifteenth and went ahead with a delicate pitch at the seventeenth, where Gray failed to get down in two from the bunker at the front right of the green, but at the eighteenth, after a huge drive down the breeze, he put his second a few feet away and holed for his 3. The nineteenth was halved, but Gray missed the green at the next and failed narrowly with his putt to save the match.

It looked as though Attenborough would join Bonallack in the quarter-finals and reduce the American challenge still further. He was one up playing the eighteenth and played a similar second to the one that Downing Gray had played a few minutes earlier. It nestled five feet from the hole. "Follow that," he might have said. Fleckman did, from 130 yards, and holed it for a 2. It was no surprise that a shell-shocked Attenborough failed to make his 4 at the nineteenth and lost the match. He recently recounted that the two of them had sat together at the Walker Cup dinner. Fleckman was not a great conversationalist and all that Michael had discovered from him was that he preferred stroke play to match play. As they returned to their hotel in Southport, Michael asked, "Does that alter your opinion of match play?" The response was, "I told you, I only rate stroke play." A couple of weeks later Fleckman was leading the U.S. Open after two rounds, but collapsed with a poor third round. Michael resisted the temptation of sending a cable to discover if he had now changed his view on stroke play.

Meanwhile Bob Murphy, another of the Americans, had lost to the Scot Bill Murray, which left four of the U.S. team, each playing against a British opponent, to contest the quarter-finals. When Bonallack's back went again in his match against Ron Cerrudo, it looked possible that all four Americans might reach the semi-finals, but Gordon Clark, playing as steadily as ever, hung on to beat Jim Grant and earn a tilt at Bob Dickson. He had won all his Walker Cup matches and had only been extended at Formby by Shade who had taken him to the seventeenth in the fourth round. That afternoon Clark's driving became uncharacteristically ragged and he missed more fairways than he hit. He could not afford that against the tall Dickson whose wide, upright and rhythmic swing was propelling the ball far and straight. Maybe the pressure of following such shots caused Clark's errors and he duly lost at the fifteenth. The two young Americans, Cerrudo and Fleckman, contested the other semi-final and it could not have been more exciting. All square at the eighteenth, Fleckman holed for a 3. Cerrudo lined up his putt for a half from six feet, stood back waiting for a train to pass, and then rattled it into the hole. At the nineteenth both were on the green in two, but Fleckman unexpectedly took three more and Cerrudo was through.

The final between two outstanding young members of the United States team was memorable for more than one reason. They played the first round in less than three hours, halved all but two of the holes and both were round in 71. Despite this, Cerrudo, who had lost his lead at the seventeenth, called to his caddie who was walking from the last green towards the clubhouse, "Fetch me my shag bag," and turned towards the practice area. Play in the afternoon maintained the same pace and the quality of golf was even higher, with Dickson's putter coming alive around the turn where he took a three hole lead. Cerrudo came back, winning the thirteenth and fourteenth in 3 apiece, but Dickson holed one more putt, from twelve feet, for a 2 at the sixteenth and that was two up with two to play. A half in 4 at the seventeenth finished a splendid match.

Formby is not the longest of championship courses and, with its pine trees protecting golfers from the winds off the Irish sea, it was at its most benign that week, but, even so, Dickson's score of twenty-three under par for eight rounds of golf was quite outstanding. Cerrudo too was below par for his week's work. Great things were expected of these two in the future. Both turned professional, Cerrudo later that year and Dickson the following year, having first completed the double by adding the U.S. Amateur title to his victory at Formby. Neither was to make the impact that had been anticipated.

1968

The two likeliest contenders from overseas, Bill Hyndman and Dale Morey, had both scratched and none of the others looked likely to mount a strong challenge at Troon. If effort alone had been the requirement, then Don Givens a 27 year old American must surely have gone all the way for he arrived there on the Wednesday prior to the championship, played three rounds a day to learn the intricacies of the course, and then retired to the practice ground and was firing shots long after darkness had driven away the other enthusiasts. Sadly his reward was a six and five defeat in the first round.

Four of the eight seeds, all British, had been eliminated by the end of the third round. Attenborough and Gordon Clark had fallen at the first hurdle and Oosterhuis and Foster two rounds later. This left the two Scots, Ronnie Shade and Gordon Cosh, as the main threat to a final between the two supreme British amateur golfers of the post-war years, Joe Carr and Michael Bonallack, the likelihood of which turned from possible to inevitable as the championship progressed. Carr had reached the quarter-final without meeting any player of international standing. There he had beaten Scott Cochran and it looked as though his semi-final opponent would be Shade, but a 42 year old Surrey player, Reg Glading had other ideas. Shade gave him all the encouragement he needed on the easier front nine and Glading was three up. He was still three ahead with five to play, but a bunkered tee shot at the fourteenth allowed Shade, who had also missed the green, to win it. At the fifteenth Glading was in trouble all the way and conceded the hole. He played the sixteenth untidily, but was relieved to hole from five feet for a half. Shade got his three at the seventeenth to square the match and the Scottish supporters were breathing more easily. They cheered again as Shade hit a wonderful second to the home green. Glading was just wide of the green, but able to use a putter, which he did to the best possible effect, knocking the ball into the hole. Shade missed from four yards to save the match and the handshakes were greeted with muted applause. In the afternoon Glading fought bravely to take Carr to the seventeenth green, but he lacked the necessary fire power and the result of the match was never really in doubt.

Bonallack had played splendid golf throughout. In the first round his opponent, Leslie McClue, had played fourteen holes in level par, but still lost by five and four. On the penultimate day Bonallack was five under 4s in beating Charlie Green by four and three, and three under in his semi-final victory against Geoff Marks, the conqueror of Gordon Cosh.

Carr versus Bonallack conjured up memories of Ball and Tait down the coast at Prestwick in 1899, although, in truth, Carr at age 46 was coming to the end of his outstanding career. The six Irish National titles to add to his three Amateur gold medals, a host of West and South and East of Ireland championships, twenty-one years heading the Irish team and ten Walker Cup appearances were all behind him. Bonallack too could boast a string of victories and International appearances, but at the age of 33 he was at his peak.

A plane load of Joe Carr's friends and supporters flew in from Dublin and, so it is said, the first order on the flight, before breakfast was served, was for sixty-two gin and tonics. They arrived too late for the preliminaries. "What ball are you using?" Joe had asked on the first tee. "Dunlop 6," replied Michael with a smile, knowing that this was the make and number that Joe always used. After a little more good natured banter Joe finished the conversation with, "Well I hope you lose the bloody thing."

Troon begins with three friendly two-shotters, before the full examination starts, and Carr got his 3s at the first and third, interposed by a Bonallack 3 at the second. The latter took charge with a 2 at Troon's famous Postage Stamp and a 3 at the ninth. As they came to the tenth tee, turning for home into a fresh north-westerly wind, left to right, Bonallack put his finger up to test its direction in full view of Carr. "Remember 1958," he said. Carr was unable to cope with it, as Bonallack had failed in that semi-final at St. Andrews. So at lunch Bonallack was six up. Carr holed for a 3 again at the first in the afternoon, but this time Bonallack followed him in and it became a question of what the margin of victory would be. It was seven and six.

Bonallack had been at his imperious best throughout the early part of the season. During the previous winter he had gone to the Leslie King Golf Clinic in London for weekly sessions, and whilst his swing may have looked the same, there were some minor changes which enabled him to hit more from the inside, draw the ball and gain thirty yards or so in length. With this adjustment and his magnificent short game he was almost unbeatable. The Amateur Championship victory had been preceded by successes in the Brabazon, Berkshire Trophy and Golf Illustrated Gold Vase. More followed – the English Championship, Essex County Championship and the St. George's Grand Challenge Cup. In the Open Championship he was leading amateur, having been in contention up to the ninth hole of the final round at Carnoustie. Later that year, in the World Amateur Team Championship, he had the lowest individual score. It is impossible to imagine such a record ever being matched in one season.

1969

Royal Liverpool were celebrating their centenary and, as the founding father of the championship, it was only appropriate that they should host it. The Almighty showed his approval with some uncharacteristically benign weather, unheard of at Hoylake for a full championship week. For those prepared to lift their heads on the tees beside the Dee estuary, the vista of golden sand and blue haze of the Welsh hills was magnificent.

A number of home players were looking to improve their chances of filling the vacancies in the Walker Cup team, left open by Shade and Oosterhuis turning to the professional ranks, but many of the fancied contenders fell in the early rounds. Perhaps the beautiful greens at Hoylake, smooth and fast, give an opportunity for lesser men with a putting streak to beat the better strikers. Gordon Cosh and Geoff Marks fell in consecutive second round matches and late on the third day the crowd mourned the departure of the ever popular Joe Carr. He lost on the last green to another champion, the American Peter Bostwick, who was champion of the world at real tennis. One wonders how he might have faired against Bob Falkenburg, playing a few matches earlier.

Although Michael Bonallack was the only seed in the last eight, there was a truly international look to it, with Dale Morey and Bill Hyndman from America, the young South African Dale Hayes, a Belgian, Philippe Toussaint, a Scot and two other Englishmen. One of these was a Hoylake member, Michael Pearson, who had played for England fifteen years earlier, but was now very much a part-time golfer, though his swing was as slow and smooth as ever. He had raised home hopes with victories against O'Brien, the Irish champion, and Scottish International Bill Murray, but against Billy Davidson, his opponent in the last eight, those hopes were dashed. The Scot won a couple of early holes against the odds with a chip in and a long putt and held on to gain a semi-final place against Bonallack, who had been at his best against Dale Morey.

The other semi-final was between Hyndman, and the 16 year old Hayes, a sturdily built young man, who was in receipt of thirty-seven years. Hyndman had been conserving his energy in earlier rounds, as none of his previous four games had gone beyond the thirteenth green. Hayes on the other hand had one close call, against Roland West of Altrincham, a Cheshire County player. When they came to the nineteenth tee it was apparent that there would be a delay whilst the players in the match ahead waited for the green to clear. Hayes' caddie threw the driver over and steamed off with the bag to find some cooling liquid refreshment. It was only when the time came for Hayes to play that he realised that the driver was not the required club that day for the tee shot at Hoylake's renowned first hole, a sharp dog leg around the practice ground. There was a stiff breeze from the north and had he aimed the ball down the fairway it would have pitched in thick rough close to the refreshment tent to which his caddie had repaired. There was only one thing for it, so he lined himself up only a little to the left of the green and unleashed an enormous drive that carried a generous chunk of the out of bounds and ran across the fairway to within about sixty yards of the pin. It was not surprising that West was unable to follow that.

The semi-final between Hayes and Hyndman looked as though it would be as exciting. They were all square as they played to the short thirteenth, where both bunkered their tee shots. Hayes played an excellent shot to within a couple of feet of the hole and with hopes high stood back to watch Hyndman play from under the face of the same deep bunker. He splashed the ball up and out. It landed softly and trickled on into the hole. That was the turning point and Hayes lost the match at the sixteenth. Meanwhile Bonallack, with golf improving as the championship progressed, disposed of Davidson.

The final was an appropriate climax to Hoylake's celebrations, with the top British amateur facing one of the best of the Americans, who had three Walker Cup appearances behind him and a championship runner-up medal, won ten years earlier. Bonallack was quick to show his intentions with a twenty foot putt to win the first and Hyndman was struggling to stay with him for the rest of the morning round, which ended with a lead of three holes for the Englishman. In the afternoon a huge putt for a 2 at the Dowie by Hyndman raised a momentary smile. For the rest it was all Bonallack and he moved serenely on to five up with five to play. Hyndman holed from seven yards to save the match at the fourteenth and won the fifteenth as well, but Bonallack's sixty yard pitch and single putt for a 4 clinched it at the next. The Dun green at Hoylake is an ideal place to finish a match and the large crowd, including those invited from clubs that had staged the Amateur, ambled back across the first fairway in the warm sunshine to watch the presentation in front of the clubhouse. The guests then left to prepare themselves for the club centenary dinner at which the speakers were to be Selwyn Lloyd, the club captain, Gerald Micklem as captain of the Royal and Ancient, Willie Whitelaw and Joe Carr. Guest of honour was Michael Bonallack, now with his fourth championship medal, a feat matched by Hilton and beaten only by the great John Ball.

Hoylake champions at the Dinner. From the left: Micklem (R & A Captain), Bonallack, Carr, Selwyn Lloyd (Club Captain), Davies, Tweddell and Kyle

174

1970

For scenic qualities there is no championship links to compare with County Down, with its massive dunes, banks of colourful gorse and heather and the backdrop of "the Mountains of Mourne coming down to the sea." A dry spell had bleached the fairways and greens, so that it was not only a test of straight driving, always important at Newcastle, but of nerve and finesse on the short shots. Despite the problems of Ulster, the entry far exceeded the 256 maximum, and only a few of the three handicappers were successful in the ballot.

The Americans came in greater numbers than ever, led again by Bill Hyndman, runner-up at Hoylake. Amongst them, playing on the second day, was Mark McCormack, once again unlucky with his draw. He had faced Shade at Carnoustie in 1966, and this time it was Charlie Green. McCormack finished strongly to convert a three hole deficit into all square with one to play, and after a free drop from a car park area to the right of the eighteenth, he pitched to within five yards leaving himself that putt for the match and the first major surprise of the championship. It didn't drop and, after a half at the nineteenth, he hooked his tee shot at the twentieth, enabling Green to survive his nervy finish. A few matches behind Joe Carr was bringing disappointment to his supporters by falling to a young South African, Kevin Sullivan, and son Roddy, who had come from four down to beat Mike Kelley of Ganton at the nineteenth in the first round, added to the Irish gloom by losing later that afternoon.

Four seeds survived to the quarter-final. Michael Bonallack and Bruce Critchley were in the top half, whilst Hyndman and Green met on the Friday morning, with the winner certain to have an Ulsterman as a semi-final opponent, either John Glover or Brian Hoey.

For the third time in five years Green reached the quarter-final only to lose, and it was some relief to Hyndman that the game finished at the sixteenth, for three of his previous four games had gone to extra holes. In the second round he had to contend with a 3, 3, 4 finish by Matt Lygate, which won all three holes. Another 4 at the nineteenth (par five) was matched by Hyndman and the twentieth was halved in 4 as well. There was a long wait for the match ahead to clear the next hole, giving time for Lygate's hot spell to cool, and he missed the green, leaving the American to win with a 4. In the fourth round Hyndman needed to chip into the hole at the nineteenth to win against McCrea from Walton Heath and in the next game Rae of Irvine was two up with three to play. This time Hyndman finished strongly with 3, 4, 4. Rae missed his chance of winning at the nineteenth from five feet and bunkered his second at the twentieth to lose.

Bonallack and Critchley duly met in the first semi-final. For once Bonallack's play was somewhat ragged and, with three putts at the short tenth, he went two

175

down, but Critchley was unable to take his chance. He lost the eleventh, could only halve the twelfth after Bonallack had deposited his second into a bunker fifty yards short of the green and then at the tight thirteenth, instead of hitting an iron from the tee, took his driver and was in the gorse. Bonallack now took control and he stroked in a twelve yard putt for a 3 and the match at the seventeenth.

Hyndman was playing Hoey in the other match and, despite the former's superior striking, the match was close with Hyndman one up playing the eighteenth. Hoey played his second shot first and Hyndman did not see it finish, but assuming that it had not reached the green, played short with an iron which left him a chip over a greenside bunker. As they approached the green he realised that Hoey was on with his second and suddenly his pitch became crucial. He played it well, although not dead, and extra holes loomed, but Hoey stubbed his first putt and missed the next. Hyndman could breathe easily.

So Hyndman and Bonallack were to meet again. The former with aching joints and blistered feet needed a doctor that night, but came out next morning fresh enough and was round in 69. Against Bonallack that was sufficient for only a slender single hole lead. As he always seemed able to do, Bonallack started fast after lunch and won the first three holes. The American's resistance was broken and hole after hole slipped sadly away until, mentally and physically drained, he surrendered the match on the eleventh green. The afternoon was still young as Bonallack collected the championship cup. "I hope you don't bring it back again Dad," his daughter Glenna had said as he left home for County Down. It was Glenna's responsibility to keep it clean, so she was in for a disappointment.

The feat of winning three successive Amateur Championships and five out of ten put Bonallack's record beyond comparison and, when one adds to that the five English Championships, also won within those ten years, and his numerous other victories, it was a decade of golfing supremacy almost beyond belief. It could not be said that the competition was weak for this was a period of solid development in the British amateur game, with Carr, Lunt, Foster, Christmas, Shade and Green all outstanding players, not to mention the strong American opposition and the transient youngsters like Clark, Townsend and Oosterhuis.

How could all this be achieved by one who was a genuine amateur? The fact that he worked in a family business environment will have helped, but the role of sales director of a coach and container building company was no part time one. Much of his practice was done at Thorndon Park, near to the factory, during his lunch hours. On the way home in the evening there was more practice, mostly putting sessions with his friends at Thorpe Hall. Weekends were entirely devoted to competitive play during the season and his wife Angela, from her own experience, understood the demands of golf at international level and accepted that there would be no normal family holidays.

Michael had been a good all round sportsman at school. This gave him strength, balance and that instinctive feel with the hands, but he was never a fluent, free and natural swinger of a golf club. His method, and the knowledge of how it worked, were acquired during his winter coaching first with Ernest Holdwright and then Leslie King, though he remembers three hours with Bobby Halsall at Birkdale at the age of 17, as he was transferring his thoughts from Lords and the Haileybury versus Cheltenham cricket match to Formby and the Boys Championship. Those three hours may have done more to shape his golfing future than any others, as without them it is unlikely that he would have won at Formby and channelled all his sporting talent to golf.

Throughout his golfing career his long game was based on ever changing swing thoughts and, as he said, "If they lasted a week, I won." Even so it was not his driving and iron play that opponents feared. It was his touch around the greens and the inevitability with which he holed the putts of awkward length. A strong competitive instinct and fierce determination were masked by modesty, a genial temperament and an ever present sense of sportsmanship. No one was more liked and respected in the golfing scene.

CHAPTER SIX

Double Champions

1971

The home team had won the Walker Cup at St. Andrews during the previous week and the euphoria carried over to the championship at Carnoustie. History however suggested that a home-bred winner was unlikely, the more so because there was plenty of grass on the fairways and the fast, smooth greens suited the American team, who, having failed to unravel the mysteries of the Old Course, were now happy to be reunited with their wedges. For the British team it was not surprising that there was reaction. This showed itself on the first day with George McGregor duck-hooking from the first tee and Hugh Stuart perpetrating five three putts. They survived, but Rodney Foster and Scott McDonald did not, and Michael Bonallack, seeded to meet Lanny Wadkins in the final, only did so by the skin of his teeth. Phil Cobley of Langland Bay had a ten foot putt for a 3 on the eighteenth to beat him. He didn't hole it and Bonallack got his 3 at the nineteenth.

Jim Simons, the youngest of the American team, looked likely to be the first American seed to be eliminated, as he came to the sixteenth three down to Ian Hutcheon. Most would settle for a 3, 4, 4 finish at Carnoustie and that is what Simons achieved, but it shouldn't have been good enough to win all three holes. It was and he finished the job at the twentieth. A press man, having witnessed his recovery, asked him as he returned to the clubhouse, "What do you think of being joint favourite with Wadkins and Melnyk to win the title." His answer was succinct, "Not much of the bookie."

The third day saw carnage amongst the American team. Lanny Wadkins, who had a severe cold lost to Hopkinson, a good player from the Midlands, but the American made no excuses. "I simply played bad," he said, paused and then added, "in fact horrible." Jimmy Gabrielsen lost to Trevor Homer and Miller and Giles were also losers, the latter to an 18 year old Lancastrian, Andrew Chandler, at the twenty-first hole.

By Thursday evening there were four seeds left in the top half. The Americans, Simons and Tom Kite, were to play against two of the successful

British team, Hugh Stuart and Roddy Carr. In the bottom half only Steve Melnyk of the seeds remained. He had some early scares, needing a bunker shot and single putt against his opponent's three putts to win by a single hole in the first round and taking a hole more to win his second match.

Neither Stuart nor Carr could manage their morning assignments and so Peter Moody, a recent Cambridge captain, who had beaten Hugh Campbell in the quarter-final, remained the solitary British player in the semi-final. By losing the first five holes to Melnyk he gave himself no realistic chance and did well to contain the margin to four and three. Kite and Simons had a splendid match with the former taking a two hole lead at the turn. For the bespectacled Kite, with his scholastic appearance and neat game, it was "the spectacles" that cost him the match, not the pair he was wearing, but the awesome bunkers guarding the fourteenth green which he failed to carry. That levelled it and he lost the seventeenth, where, having driven into a fairway bunker, he played a great recovery shot only to find another bunker beside the green, from which he thinned the ball over the back. Two superb second shots into the wind at the home hole ended the match. Kite found the green with a four wood and Simons followed him on with a one iron to earn the half that he needed.

Steve Melnyk, aged 24, was favourite to win the final. A heavily built young man, he was a long hitter but, as so often happens with big men, combined it with a delicate touch around the greens. He had won the 1969 U.S. Amateur Championship and had followed it by winning the Amateur medals in the Open at St. Andrews and the Masters. His presence in the Walker Cup team and the Championship had however been in doubt, as he had received a three month suspension of his Amateur status from the USGA for accepting a gift of a few dozen golf balls from a manufacturer. Most of Jim Simons' experience had come from college golf. He had failed to win a match in his two Walker Cup outings and, in addition to his first round escape, had looked certain to lose in the fifth round, where a fellow American, Mike Sanger, missed a putt of about a yard to beat him at the nineteenth. The two finalists had played golf every day for two weeks. Melnyk had even gone to Rosemount on the one free day. With heavy legs and weary minds the scoring in the final was not good. Melnyk had taken a three hole lead, but it looked as though Simons would square the match at the eighteenth. Melnyk however saved his half from the bank of the Barry Burn and regained his three hole lead soon after lunch. Simons came again and, but for a misjudged second into the burn at the tenth, where he had intended to play short, he might have taken the lead. A 3 at the twelfth set Melnyk going again and he won, like Carnoustie's previous winners, Turnesa and Cole, at the sixteenth, one of golf's most testing short holes.

This was the last time spectators were charged for admission. Gate money had only marginally exceeded the cost of collecting it and there was little chance of an improvement next year at Sandwich where crowds were traditionally smaller.

1972

There has always been a contrast in the quality of the field in a home Walker Cup year and the intervening years. Steve Melnyk had turned professional, as had Warren Humphreys and Roddy Carr, respectively champions of England and Ireland. The entry for Sandwich was further weakened by lack of support from the Scots, of whom there were only sixteen. The cost of competing, particularly with so far to travel and at a venue where accommodation expenses were high, was a clear deterrent to those that were not in contention for international team selection. Money and miles did not however deter the Americans. There were forty four of them in the list of entries, though Hyndman had scratched. Only Dick Siderowf and Ed Tutwiler had Walker Cup experience, but a couple of others seemed to have a genuine chance.

It was one of the Scots who made the news in the first round, the 14 year old David Robertson. He was only a little over five feet and had the chunky appearance of a rugby forward, which he was for his school second fifteen. His golf was however mature beyond his years and he had seven 3s in nine holes from the fifth in winning his match against an unfortunate American, Peter van Ingen. Robertson lost next day.

One American who created a stir was the glamorous wife of Kemp Richardson. She was caddying for her husband in his third round match against Doug Smith of Duddingston. Richardson had hooked at the thirteenth and after a few minutes' search there was a gleeful shout from his wife, "Here it is darling," and he turned round to see her proudly holding the ball aloft. Richardson conceded the hole, but won on the final green. "I would probably have lost the hole anyway," he said, but the matrimonial relationship might have been severely strained had the result gone the other way. Richardson played some of the finest golf of the week in the next round beating Michael King, one of the seeds. Charlie Green also lost that morning, leaving only Bonallack and Foster of the seeds, both in the top quarter of the draw. Foster had one of those special days, beating two good Americans on the last green. Three down on the fourteenth tee against Marty West, Foster drove out of bounds. His next was close to the boundary fence, but he played a long raking shot not far short of the green and chipped in for a 5 and a half. That, and the vicious rain storm that was in progress, undermined West and Foster won the last four holes. In the afternoon against Siderowf, he went all the way again, winning with a magnificent three wood to the home green. Bonallack was waiting for him next morning.

Kemp Richardson was to play Thirlwell in the other quarter-final in the top half of the draw, which looked stronger than the lower half where Findlay Black, a former Scottish international, Trevor Homer, a Staffordshire county player, Peter Berry, a 19 year old English youth international, and Roger Revell, aged 21 from Surrey, were contesting the other place in the final.

The two to win through on the penultimate day were Thirlwell and Homer. In the morning Thirlwell won at the twentieth, but not before a dramatic nineteenth where he chipped in for a 3 from off the back of the green and Richardson followed him in from eight yards. Against Bonallack, whose putting was not up to standard, Thirlwell was two up with three to play. He missed the green at the short sixteenth and Bonallack took that chance, but didn't take advantage of it, as he drove into a bunker at the next. Thirlwell, still needing his 4 to clinch the match, hit a superb three wood from one of those nasty cross slope lies that one finds at Sandwich. Meanwhile Homer had been in difficulties against Black. Three up after eight, Black chose a 4 iron instead of a putter from the edge of the ninth green. He chipped it over the back and thereafter the holes came with a rush for Homer. In the semi-final he beat his close friend Roger Revell with the same powerful and accurate golf that he had been playing all week. He was, as he had been in all his matches, close to par when winning at the fifteenth.

So to a final between two amiable giants, neither of whom had come to Sandwich with high expectations. Thirlwell, now 43, was an England selector and was staying with his wife and daughter in their caravan, to combine his selectorial duties with a family holiday. Homer, who had recently been dropped from his county side and had finished only third in his club championship, had never before achieved the results that his elegant and lazy swing merited. He didn't sleep much before the final, nor did he change his socks. He had washed his lucky red pair, worn in each match, and wore them again though they were still damp. He said afterwards that playing against someone who struck the ball with such authority made it easier. He knew what to expect and what was needed. He was round in 69, but only one up, Thirlwell having holed another chip to salvage the eighteenth. The first hole in the afternoon was crucial. Homer, after a

Trevor Homer

couple of untidy shots, holed a huge putt for a 4 and Thirlwell three putted. That set the pattern. Thirlwell took three more putts at the fifth and Homer covered the seventh, eighth and ninth in just eight shots to build an unassailable lead. Soon an incredulous and unassuming champion was crowned on the fifteenth green. There was however much sympathy for the ever popular Thirlwell, who had lost a second final with honour and dignity.

1973

The composition of a team to retain the Walker Cup at the Country Club in Boston was uppermost in the mind of the press and players who assembled at Porthcawl. There were plenty of vacancies with two of the winning team now in the professional ranks, one, David Marsh, appointed as non-playing captain and a number of others who had not retained their form. The task of the selectors was made more difficult by the early defeat of some of the contenders. Hugh Stuart, with a back problem, was beaten by Richard Eyles, whose back might well have been worse than Stuart's, as he had been in a serious car crash only five weeks earlier. Michael King and John Davies, of the probables, also lost.

When, during the next two days, Bonallack, Green and Homer were all beaten, six of those already pencilled onto the team sheet had been eliminated. Bonallack was another back victim. Two up playing the fifth, he felt a severe twinge as he hit his four wood second shot up the hill and onto the green. When he got there and bent over his putt his back locked and, unable to straighten, he had no alternative but to concede the match to Peter Holt of Coventry. Homer had begun his defence with a bye and an easy second round victory, but his next opponent was the man he had beaten in the final at Sandwich and Alan Thirlwell gained revenge, winning at the twentieth.

Next day the 18 year old Howard Clark from Moortown, the 1971 Boys Champion, did his cause no harm by beating two Americans, Culligan and Morey, winning both matches on the seventeenth. Morey was a particularly good scalp, for although the wrong side of 50, he had won his three previous matches out in the country and was eleven under par for the holes he had played. Next morning Howard Clark continued the good work with a round of 69 to beat his namesake Gordon. This set up a semi-final against Peter Moody, the one remaining seed, for in the other half of the draw Rodney Foster had failed to take his chances against Harry Ashby, the reigning English Champion. Ashby's semi-final opponent was Dick Siderowf, a 34 year old New York stockbroker, who had come through to this stage without spectacular play. He had won his fifth round match against Matt Lygate after dropping four shots at the first five holes and against Allan Brodie in the quarter-final he was not much better, three over to the turn. With the Scot still one up with two to play, he looked the more likely semi-finalist, but he dropped his pitch into the bunker at the front of the seventeenth green and lost the hole. Thus reprieved, Siderowf went on to win the match with a 3 at the nineteenth. The semi-finals were disappointing. Siderowf, with improved golf, won comfortably against Ashby, while Howard Clark, with shots out of bounds at a couple of early holes, gave Moody the lead and he was too steady to give it back.

Peter Moody, aged 25, had reached the semi-final of the championship at Carnoustie two years earlier and had won the previous year's Brabazon at Hoylake. His game was ideally suited to links golf with a low flight to the ball and a dependable short game. That and his calm temperament and dogged determination gave the home supporters hope, particularly when the day dawned with a stiff wind. Siderowf was as impassive and determined, but the better striker and longer hitter. It was however Siderowf's putting that decided the final. In the first ten holes he had just thirteen putts, which gave him a lead that Moody never looked likely to retrieve. Just when the possibility of recovery seemed there, Siderowf would play a telling stroke, such as his three wood to the third green and his one iron to the thirteenth in the second round. By then the match was all but won.

Victory for Siderowf, as true an amateur as they come, opened the door for his second Walker Cup appearance. Defeat for Moody, surprisingly in view of his record over the two preceding years, denied him the place that he felt he had earned and, disillusioned, he withdrew from the golfing scene. It is sad that he did not stick around to purge his disappointment and answer his detractors.

1974

One unsatisfactory trend in the last five years had been in the finances. With the loss of gate money, the Amateur Championship accounts had gone into deficit and it was accepted by the committee that a subsidy would be required from Open Championship profits. Expenses were curtailed without compromising standards and the entry fee was raised to £10. This did nothing to discourage the size of the entry at Muirfield which was 350, resulting in the need for a ballot and only four out of seventy-six with a handicap of 2 found their way into the draw. With fifty-seven entries from U.S.A., some with dubious handicaps, it was decided that in future all American entries should be vetted by the USGA. It was also agreed that for 1975 alternates should be allowed for those that scratched.

Joe Carr, now off 2 handicap, was one of those to suffer the indignity of being balloted out, whilst Michael Bonallack had to face a different indignity. In his case after sixteen years as a seed, every year since seeding began, he had to take his chance in the draw. He played Phil Smith from Dalmahoy, on the fringe of the Scottish team, but, despite recovering from four down at the turn to all square with four to play, he lost at the seventeenth. For Smith this set up a long awaited shoot out with his brother-in-law, Scott McDonald, and the one hole victory he achieved in that match was even sweeter than his victory against Bonallack.

Two of the fancied seeds fell at the first. Ian Hutcheon, the Scottish champion, was lucky to be playing, as the previous week he had been hospitalised as a result of an electrical short circuit at work, so it was no surprise that he lost to the promising young Northumbrian, Peter Deeble. The defeat of Neville Sundelson, the 1972 South African champion, who had just won the Brabazon Trophy, was however unexpected, and the manner of it even more so. He lost by six and five to Alan Liddle of Alloa, who had never played Muirfield before, not even a practice round.

Next morning the holder played another young Scot, Mike Miller. Dick Siderowf had won easily on the Monday morning and decided to head off to St. Andrews in the afternoon for a first look at the Old Course. He arranged with the starter to join three others who finished their rounds without knowing that they had played with the reigning Amateur champion. Twenty-four hours later his reign had come to an end. Miller, having missed a putt of two feet on the seventeenth, hit a fine long iron shot ten yards past the flag at the eighteenth and holed for the match.

The last eight included Trevor Homer, Hugh Stuart and two good Americans, Jimmy Gabrielsen and John Owens. Gabrielsen had been a member of the 1971 Walker Cup team and Owens, aged 47, had a string of Kentucky titles behind him. Homer beat the latter by a single hole and in the semi-final was matched against Hugh Stuart who looked as though he might be the man to end Scotland's long wait for another champion. Homer however thought otherwise and reaching the turn in 35 was three holes ahead. The lead began to vanish and with a shank at the fifteenth the match was square again and Scottish hopes very much alive. Not for long, for a couple of clumsy chips by Stuart handed the initiative back to Homer, who clinched his place in the final with a solid 4 at the home hole. Gabrielsen, who had entered primarily to fulfil an ambition to play at Muirfield, won both quarter-final and semi-final with plenty to spare against Peter Davidson and Martin Poxon.

The final between Gabrielsen and Homer was a repeat of a third round match at Carnoustie in 1971 when Homer had beaten the then seeded American by two and one. The wind, which had blown from the west all week, had dropped and Gabrielsen's decision, after taking 83 in a practice round, to use the 1.62 ball should perhaps have been reversed. The standard of golf was excellent and after twenty-five holes only four had been exchanged, Homer winning three of them. With eight left to play Homer went three up, but, as in his match with Stuart, the holes slipped away and the match was square with three to play. Homer took the lead again at the sixteenth and the seventeenth was halved, opening the way for what was perhaps the most fateful final hole of any championship. Homer with the honour drove into a bunker, left it in with his first recovery attempt and had hit his fourth shot onto the green before Gabrielsen, after a splendid drive, played his second. It was a solid one with a 6 iron, but a little long and left, and it bounded from the slope at the edge of the green to the back of the greenside bunker. From there, with a difficult stance on the bank, he thinned it into the "Island Bunker". He was strong again with his next and didn't lose his turn. His putt was by no means dead and, after Homer had played, he missed it. This left a bewildered and relieved opponent, despite the fact that he had played five shots, with two putts from a couple of feet for the match.

Gabrielson's fateful bunker shot

The memory of that hole will doubtless haunt Gabrielsen, a delightful personality, for the rest of his life. The consequence however for Homer was perhaps more damaging. He was, at heart, an amateur golfer and had successfully combined championships and international appearances with the management of an engineering business. Now as double champion the temptation to try his luck as a professional was too great to resist. It was, he subsequently admitted, a decision that he bitterly regretted. He was neither successful nor did he enjoy the life. In 1979 he was reinstated as an amateur, but the appetite for competitive golf had gone.

1975

This time there was no euphoria following the Walker Cup match at St. Andrews. A strong American team with a new crop of college boys, including Jerry Pate, their young Amateur champion, Craig Stadler the previous winner, Curtis Strange, Jay Haas and George Burns, had won with something to spare. For the championship at Hoylake there were only eight seeds and not sixteen as in previous Walker Cup years. Five of the Americans were picked and as it turned out, apart from Siderowf, they were the wrong ones.

The first day was horrific. Icy gale force winds brought frequent squalls of rain from the Irish Sea which turned intermittently to hail. One Canadian competitor remarked that it was the first time he had seen white horses on casual water. The wind was so strong that, during the course of the morning play, the committee moved forward the dreaded sixth tee and the carry was transformed from impossible to almost impossible. If readers will excuse one personal memory, this is the time to record one unimportant match. It was won by Willie Ferguson, a former Irish International from Malone, on the last green. The loser, cold, wet and dispirited, returned to the clubhouse where he was greeted by a member of the local press, who asked how he had fared. Never at his most communicative after defeat, he referred the enquirer to his victorious opponent. That was a mistake, as in the local press next day, under the sub-heading "Behrend beaten" appeared the following quotation from Willie Ferguson. "It was nip and tuck for fourteen holes, then I threw some 6s and 7s at him and that was good enough," – which was not far from the truth.

Other than Bill Campbell, who had made his eighth Walker Cup appearance in twenty-four years, all the American team who played that day survived. The second round however saw the demise of three of them. Jerry Pate lost to Neville Chesses, which meant that his first visit to the U.K. had ended without a single victory, as he had failed to win any of his four matches at St. Andrews. Curtis Strange and Robert Burns were both beaten on the last green, the former by Mike Kelley and the latter by a promising young South African, Gavin Levenson.

There were however a couple of unhappy incidents that day. One involved Mike Hughesdon from Sunningdale who came to the nineteenth against Long from Australia. Hughesdon, from a good position short of the corner, was to play his second shot first and walked forward to remove a small white post in the little trench on top of the cop that surrounds the practice ground. He returned and played a fine shot, only to see the Australian walking over to enquire ominously whether he was entitled to move a post defining an out of bounds. He was not and the match had to be conceded. The irony was that no posts are there for members and they had been positioned at the request of the R & A Committee. The other incident happened at the third hole, involving a volatile young member of the American Walker Cup team, who, not for the first time, threw a club angrily back at his caddie after an unsatisfactory stroke. The caddie had had enough and, grounding the bag, headed back to the clubhouse. The young American stood there astonished, not knowing what to do. A few minutes elapsed before an official told him to play on and, sadly perhaps, a spectator came to his rescue and lumped the bag for the rest of the match.

After the first day the weather improved and remained fine and sunny, though with a testing breeze, for the rest of the week. The quality of golf improved as well and there was some fine play, none better than by the 18 year

186

old Nick Faldo who disposed of John Davies, one of the three British seeds. Faldo was not the only youngster to catch the eye, as 17 year old Sandy Lyle, who had beaten Charlie Green, and Nick Price from Rhodesia, a year his senior, moved forward to meet in the fifth round. The latter won to take a place in the quarter-final. The others to reach this stage included three of the American team – Vinny Giles, Dick Siderowf and John Grace, whilst Mark James, the most successful of the home team at St. Andrews, had come through the bottom quarter with a series of comfortable victories. There was also some local interest in the quarter-final as Robin Biggs of Royal Liverpool, with the same outstanding chipping and putting that had earned him victory in the Oxford and Cambridge Golfing Society's President's Putter, had collected some fine scalps, not least that of the Irish Walker Cup man Pat Mulcare. Geoff Marks was however too good for him and deprived him of a place in the semi-final against James, who had beaten Price.

Giles versus Siderowf and James against Marks ensured an Anglo-American final. The battle of the Englishmen ended at the sixteenth, where James holed from sand, but Marks had lost with honour, as James needed a couple of 4s for a 69. The sixteenth was where the excitement started in the other semi-final. Giles played a superb second to win the hole and take the lead. He should have won it at the next, where he pitched close, but missed the putt for the match. The fates ultimately forgave him, but only after a delay of nearly an hour, at the twenty-first.

Vinny Giles may not have been the most consistent striker on the American team, but he had the capacity for the unexpected and nothing is more unnerving in matchplay than to lose a hole one expects to win. James played well to be only two down at the halfway stage. It looked as though he might win the first hole after lunch, but Giles played one of those shots, a long chip and run into the hole for a 3. From there a combination of Giles' play and the effect of hay fever conspired against James and the American, a past U.S. title winner, won the match out in the country, to become one of a dozen players to have won both championships.

One cannot conclude an account of the 1975 championship without a comment from twenty years later, on the strength of the field. Six of the competitors, Pate, Strange, Stadler, Faldo, Lyle and Price went on to win one or more of "the Majors" and a number of the others forged highly successful professional careers, James, Levenson, Koch, Haas and Gordon Brand. Was this the strongest field of all?

1976

The attraction of St. Andrews meant another large American entry. Amongst them were two of the last three winners, Giles and Siderowf, and the young Curtis Strange, who had preferred to renew his relationship with the Old Course rather than accept an invitation to play in the Memorial tournament at Muirfield Village.

By one of those twists of fate two other youngsters, Brian Marchbank and Sandy Lyle, were drawn to play in the first round. These two had competed twice in the Boys Championship with Lyle winning in the semi-final in 1974 and Marchbank avenging that defeat in the following year's final. Now, to add a bit of spice to the contest, Lyle was seeded. It began with all the tension that might be expected and, when Marchbank's tee shot found a divot hole, he mishit his second and fluffed short of the burn for 3. Meanwhile Lyle was in the burn with his second but chipped and putted for his 5 to win the hole. The golf improved, until Lyle, two up after thirteen, surrendered one of the holes by driving over the wall and onto the Eden at the next. He was still one up at the seventeenth where he struck a splendid four iron onto the green, a shot which he must have felt would clinch it, but Marchbank put it inside him with a club less and holed the putt. At the eighteenth neither was close to the pin with their approach shots and Marchbank was still four feet away in 3, with Lyle inside him, but not dead. Marchbank holed and Lyle missed and slumped forward, dropping his putter in anguish. Lyle's friend from Shropshire, Ian Woosnam, was Marchbank's opponent in the second round, but he suffered the same fate.

The third day saw the defeat of four more seeds, including Curtis Strange and Geoff Marks. John Davies was the solitary Englishman to reach the quarter-final, with four Scots and three Americans, all of whom had in recent years proved their championship credentials, Giles, Siderowf and Gabrielsen. Davies had played with great authority and, but for a close game with Michael Hughesdon, had won all his games out in the country. In the quarter-final he played Giles, who had been under par for his week's work and started in the same vein to be two up at the turn. Davies counter-attacked on the way home and Giles helped with a couple of errors, three putts at the fourteenth and a drive over the fence at the sixteenth. That was two down and the Englishman finished him off at the Road hole. In the afternoon Davies, resisting reaction, continued to play solidly but Ian Carslaw was equally impressive, until, fighting his natural draw, he fired one the other way off the seventeenth tee, into the hotel, to lose the hole. That was the margin of his defeat. In the bottom half of the draw Siderowf had several close encounters, not least in his victory at the twentieth against the Canadian Graham McIntyre, who twice had short putts to beat him near the end. In the semi-final against Allan Brodie he was two down with six to play and the Scot, as at Porthcawl, looked like winning, but the stretch home was playing at its most testing with an unhelpful cross wind. A combination of some weak shots by Brodie and a few telling putts by the American swung it in his favour.

As John Davies was waiting for the match to finish, he expressed a preference for playing the American, not just because he had beaten Siderowf in the 1973 Walker Cup, but he hoped for crowd support which would not have been forthcoming if his opponent had been a Scot. The final was always close. In the morning both played well and Siderowf, round in 72, was one up. Three putts at the first in the afternoon cost him that hole and set the pattern for an error-strewn afternoon, particularly in the closing stages. Davies fell behind with a shanked second at the thirteenth, but won the next and the sixteenth. At the seventeenth, he took the left route which cost him a five, whilst Siderowf, whose drive had threatened the hotel, came from the right edge of the fairway and made his 4. The latter, with the honour on the eighteenth, watched his tee shot anxiously as it headed towards the white rails guarding the Bruce embankment. All was well and from there he played a lovely pitch, but he failed with his putt for a 3 and the match went to the extra hole. Perhaps it would have been better if he had holed it, for Davies would then have been spared the memory of three putts on the nineteenth, which enabled Siderowf to join Lawson Little and Frank Stranahan as the third American to win a second championship.

Dick Siderowf pitches from near the Bruce Embankment

The 1976 championship may be remembered as the one that Davies lost, for "the Badger", as he was known to his friends, had played through the week with the confidence, almost arrogance, of one who seemed destined to win. Near the end however, with the prospect of victory and appearances in the Open and Masters, he seemed to lose his aggressive flair. Later Davies joined the celebration party in the secretary's office overlooking the first tee and the first person he saw was Gerald Micklem, who had so much wanted the Sunningdale member to win. "That's the last time I'm watching you, Badger," he said, shaking his head in despair.

1977

Three Americans were seeded for the 1977 championship at Ganton. One was the holder and the other two were the current U.S. Amateur champion, Bill Sander and his predecessor, Fred Ridley. Gordon Murray, the Scottish champion, and John Davies were also seeded, but Jim Nelford, who had won successive Canadian Championships, and Sandy Lyle, recent winner of the Brabazon, were not.

The young Scot, Brian Marchbank, one of the early starters, was in the news again. At the short fifth, having played a perfect tee shot, which caught the edge of the hole and lipped out, he watched his French opponent Patrick Lemaire go one better. That knocked Marchbank off-course and the Frenchman went on to win at the fifteenth.

On the second day much of the excitement took place at the seventeenth hole, a great one-shotter of nearly 250 yards, with gorse to carry and an elevated green with trouble on either side, more so to the right where cavernous bunkers and more banks of gorse awaited the errant shot. First Siderowf arrived on the tee one down to Bernard Meldrum, a Yorkshire player of earlier vintage. Siderowf's hopes rose when Meldrum topped. Somehow he avoided the gorse and found a decent lie close to the ladies' tee, still a shot of 160 yards. From there he hit the green and holed for a 3, which, with Siderowf taking 4, won him the match. A little later Bill Sander arrived on the tee two down to George Ellis from Hilton Park and he too lost the hole. A few matches behind John Davies appeared with Ian Carslaw in a repeat of their St. Andrews semi- final. Both missed the green, but there was a long delay after Carslaw, having been permitted relief by the official on duty, dropped the ball in a spot which Davies felt was nearer the hole. The committee chairman was summoned and confirmed that the rule had been correctly applied. It was however Davies who pitched close to the hole and finished the match. Later that afternoon the third American seed, Fred Ridley, failed to reach the seventeenth against Martin Bentley, losing a hole earlier. "My mother could have beaten me," was his post-defeat comment.

Gordon Murray's third round match with Steven Bennett of Grimsby ended in disarray. They shook hands on the eleventh green, reporting the match result to the scoreboard official as a win for Murray by seven and six, and strolled off for refreshment at the nearby halfway house. A few moments later clarification was sought from the main scoreboard. How was it that the match score was seven and six when there were still seven holes to play? The competitors were summoned back to resume the match, Bennett by then without his caddie. Murray won, but not before he had shed a couple of holes from his lead. He survived to the fifth round, the only seed to reach that stage.

Amongst the quarter-finalists Sandy Lyle looked the likeliest winner, having beaten Nelford in the previous round, though Bonallack, taking advantage of the defeats of first Sander and then Davies in his section of the draw, was also beginning to look as though he might move closer to John Ball's record. In the event Lyle lost to the tall Scottish international, Paul McKellar, who had beaten Mark McNulty, the best of the South African squad, in the previous round. In the semi-final he was to play Peter McEvoy, a 24 year old law student, who had graduated from the England youth team to full international status the previous year.

That Peter McEvoy had reached the semi-final was amazing. He had headed for Ganton expecting a difficult game against Walker Cup man Geoff Marks, but when he arrived he found that Marks had scratched. His first three matches were against Americans and in the second round he had to be at his best to beat Robert Morman by a hole. In the next two rounds he hit the ball superbly, but in the fifth round against Les Walker, a tough Yorkshireman with a reputation of never losing once ahead, he found himself three down with three to play. His fine rhythm had disappeared and he could do little right. If Walker had found the green with his second shot at the fifteenth, he would probably have won the match there. As it was McEvoy got his 4 at the sixteenth and a winning 3 at the next. Both were bunkered with their second shots at the eighteenth, Walker to the left and McEvoy at the back right of the green. It was Walker to play first and he played without knowing that McEvoy's ball was plugged at the back of the bunker with only a few yards of green to the pin, a near impossible shot. Walker splashed it out to within ten feet and the match looked over. Not only did McEvoy achieve the impossible by extricating the ball, but it finished within twelve feet of the pin, from where he holed. It was not surprising that the gritty Yorkshireman had no answer and after two more holes McEvoy completed his great escape. Now in the semi-final he was back to his best and, although McKellar, four down with eight to play, was four under par for the next seven holes, he held his game together to win by two and one.

Meanwhile the first semi-final between Michael Bonallack and Hugh Campbell, who had played several times for Scotland in the 1960s, was in extra time. The former had missed a five foot putt to win at the home hole. It looked all over at the twenty-second, but Campbell holed an awkward one from about twelve feet. That Bonallack could bring himself at this critical moment to say, "Good putt, well holed," and sound as though he meant it, was typical. Two holes later Campbell hooked wildly into the bushes and the match seemed likely to end there. It did, but not as expected. Campbell's ball was found on a grass track and from there he hit it with a five iron to the edge of the green. He putted dead and Bonallack, with a holeable putt to win the match, went for it and missed the return.

After so much excitement the final was bound to be an anticlimax. McEvoy was again at his most solid and with Campbell slipping a few putts past the hole, the Midlander was five up after eighteen holes a lead he maintained to the fourteenth in the afternoon. If ever one shot was to reshape a career, it was that bunker shot against Les Walker in the fifth round.

Peter McEvoy

1978

An ever present American, Frank Strafaci, created a stir on the first morning at Troon. Strafaci, from Garden City, who had played in championships throughout the 1950s, reaching the sixth round on one occasion, continued to attend, though latterly he had met with less success. He rose early on Monday morning after a golfing weekend at Nairn, took the 7 o'clock flight from Inverness to Glasgow and a taxi to Troon to meet his morning starting time against a compatriot, W. A. Bergman. He survived that first day, but only because on arrival he discovered that he was indeed drawn to play at 10.18, but on the Tuesday. He duly lost next day to complete a run of ten consecutive first match defeats.

On the second day a Canadian and two young South Africans made the news. The thoughts of Doug Roxburgh, a former Canadian Champion, had doubtless turned to flight timings for his journey home as he went to four down with five to play against Ian Carslaw, a semi-finalist in 1976. The latter let him in at the fourteenth. The Canadian won the fifteenth and then finished with three consecutive birdies, to leave Carslaw with a shorter but more painful journey back to Glasgow. Wayne Player, son of Gary, and Philip Jonas, two highly talented young South Africans of whom much was expected, both lost to senior opponents, the former to an American reinstated as an amateur, F. W. Campbell, and the latter to 55 year old Leslie Taylor, the losing finalist in 1956, making a nostalgic championship reappearance. Beharrell, the winner then, was also playing and won his first match, but that was as near as the two of them got to a repeat final.

For once the seeds vindicated their selection. All of them were still intact on the Thursday morning and it is probable that all of them would have reached the last sixteen, but for an unhappy rules decision. Gordon Murray was all square playing the eighteenth hole against Tim Planchin from France, who had sliced his ball wildly into bushes adjacent to the committee caravan and scoreboard. A red rosetted official was quickly on hand and Murray watched incredulously whilst he supervised "line of sight" relief, allowing Planchin to pick the ball out of the bush and drop it without penalty leaving a clear shot to the green. He played it well, holed the putt for a 3 and Murray was out of the championship. The press were quick to realise that the rule under which the Frenchman had been given relief was a temporary rule that applied in the Open Championship, where scoreboards, tents and stands abound, but was not amongst the local rules for this championship. Later in the day Colin Maclaine, chairman of the championship committee, admitted that a mistake had been made by one of his most experienced referees. This was no comfort to Murray, who felt that his chance of a place in the Great Britain team had been jeopardised, and it was little solace to him or the Scottish press that his defeat was avenged that afternoon by Alan Sym, a local member.

Six seeds remained to contest the quarter-finals. Three in the bottom half were Scots, Ian Hutcheon, Paul McKellar and Allan Brodie. Brodie had won the previous year's Scottish Championship at Troon, beating McKellar in the final, and now with a series of massive wins, eight and seven, seven and six, five and four and seven and six, looked as though he was the man to beat. Nothing inspires John Davies, the odd man out at the bottom, more than an American or a Scotsman with a high reputation and, in cool and blustery conditions, he was level par for seventeen holes in beating Brodie. His opponent in the afternoon semi-final was McKellar, but Davies did not have a restful lunchtime, spending it on the telephone with his solicitor dealing with some unhappy matrimonial problems. When he emerged to the first tee it was not surprising that his mind was not fully on the task of winning a place in the final and he lost four of the first five holes. That was too big a start to give to a player of McKellar's quality.

In the top half of the draw Peter McEvoy had been working his way steadily and comfortably through, other than an early scare in the second round against John Glover. In this match he was two down with six to play. Such was his early season form and his confidence that it never occurred to him that he might lose and he duly won at the nineteenth. In the quarter-final and semi- final he met South African opponents, the seeded Gavin Levenson and David Suddards, the South African Strokeplay champion. McEvoy was close to par in beating both of them by four and three.

The two finalists had met in the semi-final at Ganton. McEvoy had won on that occasion and his superior technique made him favourite to win again, but Paul McKellar, Scottish Strokeplay champion, was assured of local support. Conditions that morning were the most difficult of the week with a strong north westerly wind making the second nine as testing as any championship stretch. McEvoy's morning round of 79 represented sound golf and he was three up. The match restarted in the afternoon with the large crowd soon having cause to cheer. McKellar drove the first green and won that hole. He did the same again at the third. At the short fourth both were bunkered at the back of the green. McEvoy playing first was some way short and then, to another huge cheer, McKellar hit the pin, rebounding four feet away. McEvoy holed and McKellar missed and the crowd were silenced. He was on his way again and, reaching the turn in 34, was four up. Once they turned for home McEvoy, with rhythm and balance holding in the wind, never looked like surrendering the lead. So he became the fifth player to win consecutive championships.

From a young hopeful a year ago, he had become the much needed figure-head in the amateur game. He had never relied on coaching. His fine natural swing had been tuned in the period between school and university, during which he hit five hundred balls a day. At the beginning of this year he had discovered a new secret, "kicking the right knee into the shot on the downswing". That was the swing thought with which he won at Troon. For the rest of us golf is not that simple.

1979

The last afternoon of the Walker Cup at Muirfield converted a close and tense match into another defeat for the home team. Only Allan Brodie could provide a point for Britain, and he, with a couple of the other British team members, had withdrawn from the championship. All the American team with the exception of Hal Sutton, who had returned home, were seeded, as were two of six recent champions from the Commonwealth.

The recognition of Hillside as a championship venue was one which gave general pleasure. Many thought that it provided as stern a test as nearby Birkdale, with the Liverpool to Southport railway line providing an extra element of fear at the start. For the Americans, with definition provided by trees and towering dunes and softer fairways and greens than one normally associates with links golf, it was a splendid stage. It was therefore surprising to see two of their number lose in the first round. Another seed to fail on the first day was Gordon Brand. He had fought valiantly from four down with five to play to keep the match alive at the eighteenth, accompanied then by a large crowd, though it was not clear whether this was in deference to Brand, to his opponent Francis Speight, son of the famous scriptwriter, or to Speight's caddie, the local footballing idol, Ian St. John. In the event Brand chipped dead for his 4, but Speight holed from six feet, denying the crowd extra holes.

More distinguished scalps were taken on the second day. Two South African champions, Suddards and Norval, were beaten and the Australian champion, Clayton, also lost, but this was less surprising as the victor in this match was Dick Siderowf, captain of the victorious Walker Cup team. John Davies, his victim in the 1976 final, was another first round loser. He had come south from Muirfield with his game in disarray and his confidence gone. On the practice ground his swing looked as good as ever, but he could not take it to the course, where all sense of rhythm had vanished. He provided Duncan Evans, a young Welshman, with an easy win.

Early next day Peter McEvoy's run of seventeen championship matches without defeat came to an end. All square after thirteen holes of excellent golf the match turned suddenly and fatally against him. His opponent Ian Bradshaw played the fourteenth with a drive, wedge and putt for a 3, a great long iron second into the breeze at the fifteenth and a chip stone dead at the long par 3 sixteenth, to win all three holes. Bradshaw thus confirmed his right to a place in the England team, which he had earned by finishing runner-up in both Lytham Trophy and Brabazon.

It looked likely that the American flagship, 34 year old Jay Sigel, would also sink that afternoon, but with guns firing at the end, he converted three down with four to play into a victory against John Graham of Alnmouth. His finish of 3, 3, 4, 4 was two better than par and good enough to win all four holes. Later in the day Dick Siderowf lost heavily to Wayne Player, still only 17. Well though the South African played, Siderowf's defeat stemmed from a disastrous first nine holes, in which one ball found the railway line and two others were lost.

The quarter-finals set up four intriguing international matches with American Scott Hoch, a recent college product playing Bradshaw, Brian Marchbank against the Australian Tony Gresham and Sigel paired with Stuart Robson, an experienced Surrey County player. The three overseas players won. The fourth match involved the Canadian Doug Roxburgh against Lashman Singh, the Indian champion, whose short game had beguiled some good opponents in earlier rounds. This was the match that provided the day's excitement. The Indian came to the eighteenth one down and drove into the large bunker that bites into the fairway at drive length. From there he played a miraculous five iron to the green and, with his charmed putter, holed for a 3 to take the game to extra holes. Here the charm turned to a curse and three sad putts ended his splendid championship, but provided another afternoon's "lumping" for Doug Roxburgh's recent bride, who had come to England, so she thought, to enjoy their honeymoon.

For the first time in eighty-six championships not a single home player had reached the semi-final, yet the pedigree of the four that remained could not be questioned. Three were seeds and the fourth, Tony Gresham, though nearing 40, had a string of Eisenhower Trophy appearances behind him and was thought, by no less a judge than Gerald Micklem, to be amongst the world's best amateurs. In his match against Marchbank he had justified that assessment, reaching the turn in 32. Against Hoch however he was unable to repeat that form and the American led all the way, to win by three and two. As for Sigel, he never lost a hole against Roxburgh and their match ended at the thirteenth.

So yet again in a Walker Cup year there was an all American final. Sigel and Hoch had been the two most successful players at Muirfield, dropping only half a point between them. There is no doubt that the crowd sided with the older man. They were attracted by his slow rhythmic swing and his placid demeanour, whilst Hoch's excitability had caused disquiet in an earlier match. His South African opponent, Van Niekirk, had paused for only a moment before picking up Hoch's putt for the match from the lip of the hole on the eighteenth green. The American immediately claimed that his ball was still moving and that he was entitled to ten seconds. That, as it happened, was the U.S. Tour interpretation at the time, but not relevant in this championship. Hoch showed his unhappiness as he walked to the nineteenth tee, but all was well for him as he won two holes later.

In the first round of the final Sigel, with a fine score of 70, established a three hole lead. In the afternoon the play became tentative. Sigel had lost his lead after five holes, but Hoch threw the initiative back at the next by finding an unplayable lie from where he dropped and then chipped into a bunker. More holes were exchanged, leaving Hoch one down after the long eleventh. From there Sigel took control again and finished the match with a fine long iron shot to the sixteenth green. Poor Hoch had lost a third consecutive championship final, having previously been beaten in the final of the U.S. Amateur and the North and South. He admitted cheerfully that he intended to turn professional later in the year and added, "At least you're paid for coming second."

It was by accident that Sigel, at the age of 34, was still playing as an amateur. At college his ambition was a place on the Tour, but a domestic mishap undermined that. He had put out a hand to prevent a door slamming, missed the frame, and the glass had shattered on it, resulting in 76 stitches, ten days in hospital and prognostications that he would never play golf again. It was nearly twelve months before he did restart and by then thoughts of the tour had vanished. He used his degree to build up an insurance business, which he was able to combine successfully with the pursuit of amateur honours. Few have held together the quality of striking and competitive intensity for so long and very few have achieved so much. Now, however, sixteen years later, he has fulfilled his college ambition by joining the U.S. P.G.A. Seniors' Tour. Good luck to him.

The 1970's produced seven great champions. Bonallack, of course, won in 1970. Thereafter there were three double winners – Homer, McEvoy and Siderowf – and three other outstanding Americans, Melnyk, Giles and Sigel, each of whom had won or subsequently won the U.S. Amateur Championship.

Jay Sigel at the 10th in the final

CHAPTER SEVEN

The Transient Years

1980

A new condition agreed with the U.S.G.A., that American entrants should have a tournament pedigree as well as the required handicap, meant that far fewer came over to Porthcawl. In 1978 at Troon more than seventy Americans had played, of whom nearly two-thirds had lost in the first round. On this occasion there were just eighteen. Jay Sigel was not amongst them, but he had written a graceful letter to the R & A explaining that he had an exemption to play in the U.S. Open. A shortage of Americans was counterbalanced by a strong Australian and South African presence.

The seventeenth hole at Porthcawl is a par 5 of 508 yards. The drive is blind onto an angled fairway with the ground to the right sloping down to some gorse. This was the hole that provided much of the strife and drama in the first round. Ian Bradshaw, the man who had brought McEvoy's run to an end at Hillside, was all square with an American, Steve Cisco. The latter, with the honour, pushed his drive well to the right and, after Bradshaw had driven, he played a provisional. This started left but, fading back, appeared to finish on a line similar to Bradshaw's. When they had climbed the hill no ball was visible on the fairway and after some searching one was found on the left, another on the right and a third much further to the right, close to the bushes. There was one problem. All three balls were the same make and number. After discussion it was established that Bradshaw was using an American size ball, whilst Cisco was using the 1.62. Bradshaw's ball was clearly the one on the left, but the question then arose as to whether Cisco could positively identify the ball near to the bushes as his first one. There was further debate before the arrival of a committee man, who, having heard the evidence, ruled that it could reasonably be assumed from the line of flight that the ball near the bushes was Cisco's original tee shot. The decision was accepted without demur and the hole was halved, as was the eighteenth, but Bradshaw lost at the nineteenth to continue an unhappy run of form which was to put his place in the England team in jeopardy.

The same hole was soon to be the scene of another rule altercation. The official on duty at the sixteenth green, and the writer should have a clear memory of it all, had noted that two Americans were taking their time, but, as the match was a close one and the game behind had finished, he decided to say nothing. They halved the sixteenth hole in silence, drove from the seventeenth tee and disappeared over the hill, leaving the official a pleasant period of quiet contemplation basking in the sunshine beside a shimmering sea. Another game passed through and then, some twenty minutes after they had driven off, the tranquillity was disrupted by the two Americans reappearing. One claimed that the other had spent more than five minutes looking for his ball and the other disagreed. The white armband and red rosette of office had become a burden and the rule book was no help. It was a question of fact. The official wandered forward over the hill, where there were a few spectators. Yes, they had seen it all, but couldn't possibly comment as to how long the search had taken. After more questioning it was established that the player, who claimed the ball was lost, had a watch with him, which he said he had consulted. His opponent had no watch. The decision was thus made that the ball should be deemed lost. It did however require the intervention and support of the committee chairman before the owner of the "lost" ball would accept the decision. Four hours and twenty five minutes after setting out the match ended at the eighteenth. The loser was reported to have said, "One of the great things about playing in the Amateur is the friends you make"!

The best of the Australians and the South Africans, Gresham and Groenwald, both seeded, had lost in the second round. Despite that five of the eight seeds had won their way through to the fourth round. By the end of that day all of them had lost. Most of the damage was done by two other South Africans and two Irishmen. Duncan Lindsay Smith and David Suddards had accounted for Geoff Godwin and Allan Brodie, whilst in the bottom half of the draw the English and Scottish Champions, Roger Chapman and Keith McIntosh, lost respectively to Arthur Pierse and Ronan Rafferty. These four reached the quarter-final with two Welsh Evans, Duncan and Hugh, an American, Charles Harrison, and Paul Downes from England.

The form of 16 year old Rafferty had been sensational. His first match was against Peter Davidson, one of the selectors, and from the tenth to the fourteenth the Irish boy holed consecutive putts of twenty, forty, twelve, twenty and thirty-five feet. As Davidson said afterwards it was all unnecessary as he had already been picked for the British team! In the fourth round Rafferty showed great composure at the end of a tight match against Michael Bonallack. He followed two long shots close to the seventeenth green with a masterly chip to secure his 4 and then, after a poor first putt at the eighteenth, he holed the second one for the match.

It was however the other Irishman who won a place in the semi-final. Arthur

Pierse from Tipperary was a late-comer to competitive golf. He was in his 20s before he acquired a single figure handicap and, as an antique dealer, golf was a secondary interest. He beat Hugh Evans by two and one, whilst Duncan Evans, two under for seventeen holes, was doing the same to Rafferty. The semi-final between Evans and Pierse began dramatically, with Evans playing his second from the beach and then chipping close to the hole. Pierse, putting for a 3 from seven yards, cannoned into Evans' ball and knocked it in to lose the hole. The game continued with a liberal supply of birdies until Pierse, one up after twelve holes, looked like adding to his lead at the thirteenth. Evans, however, holed from sand, which may have won him two holes, as with the honour at the short fourteenth he hit the green and Pierse missed it. Now with the initiative Evans held on and, taking advantage of a poorly played seventeenth hole by the Irishman, clinched his place in the final. His opponent was David Suddards, who had won an all South African semi-final by a similar margin.

The two finalists could scarcely have been more different. Suddards, from a golfing family, had experience at international level and of winning national championships. He was small of stature, just ten stone, and his golf was neat and effective. The tall and well built Evans had a more powerful and elegant swing. Aged 21, he had won the 1979 Staffordshire Championship and, although he had played for Wales in the previous year's Home Internationals, he had been omitted from their side to play in the European Team Championship. This was just the spur he needed.

When the day of the final dawned, the lovely weather had vanished and the vilest of wet and windy days had taken its place. Whether the match could continue was in question as the greens flooded, but committee chairman, John Salvesen, and the head greenkeeper, armed with squeegees, went ahead and swept the greens clear as the two finalists prepared to play their second shots. Conditions undoubtedly favoured Evans, who had plenty of experience of the fickle British weather. He maintained the rhythm of his swing and with many fine iron shots completed the round in the near miraculous score of 73. Suddards did well to be only four down. After lunch, in marginally less unpleasant weather and with the scent of a first Welsh victory, a few more spectators gathered to cheer their man home. He didn't let them down and the match ended at the fifteenth.

1981

Nothing attracts those from across the Atlantic as much as a visit to the home of golf. Despite the new conditions, the overseas entry was close to half the entire field, with not only Americans but South Africans, Australians, Canadians, Indians and a Continental challenge headed by the French.

One American who was well prepared and in good golfing form was the winner of the last St. Andrews championship, Dick Siderowf, but after a poor first nine against John Huggan, a drive into "the Beardies" at the fourteenth cost him any chance of mounting a recovery. Duncan Evans, the holder, all square with two to play survived narrowly against another champion, Mohta of India.

The second day was a bad one for youth. Jesus Lopez, a talented young Spaniard who had been in the semi-final of the Boys Championship, lost to Michael Hughesdon and Paul Way and Wayne Player were unexpectedly beaten. The major surprise was however the defeat of the seeded Ronan Rafferty by Colin Maclachlan, a west of Scotland player and R & A member. Heavy rain caused a two hour delay after they had played the first four holes, at which stage Rafferty was one up. When the cannon boomed for the restart it was Maclachlan who left the blocks faster and took a lead of three holes with five to play. Four up looked a probability at the fourteenth, but Rafferty holed bravely from twelve feet and Maclachlan missed from well inside him. With a 3 by the Irishman at the fifteenth he was back to one down, but that was as near as he came to saving the game, as the last three holes were halved in excellent 4s.

With the previous day's matches unfinished because of the rain delays, the third day began at 7 a.m. and finished nearly fifteen hours later. It was a bad day for the favourites, with the exception of Shergar in the Derby. Duncan Evans and Peter McEvoy lost. So did the Canadian Doug Roxburgh. At the end of the day, of those remaining in the last thirty two, half were from overseas, with eight from U.S.A. four from Australia and two each from South Africa and France.

There were more surprises next day, with only Tony Gresham of the seeds surviving. The main upsets were the defeat of two Englishmen, both Walker Cup probables. Geoff Godwin was two up with five to play against John Carr, Joe's youngest son. Father had not expected him to reach the closing stages as he had not yet attained international standing, but he had the Carr temperament and the benefit of Tip Anderson as caddie, arranged by dad. Carr should have won at the home hole, where a splendid run up through the Valley of Sin left him close to the hole. He missed and was punished by needing three extra holes, before a five yard putt won him the match. Peter Deeble's defeat by the 26 year old Frenchman Philippe Ploujoux was the second surprise. Deeble had been four under par in his morning match against John Davies and he was close to level par in the afternoon, but could make no impression against Ploujoux, whose putting carried him through to the last eight.

In the third quarter of the draw Gresham reached the semi-final, in which he was to play the winner of a section dominated by the Americans. Five had reached the fourth round in the bottom quarter and of these Joel Hirsch from Chicago won through. He was no great stylist, but he had passed his first major test by beating McEvoy in the third round. Now, opposed to the experienced Gresham, he won once more against the odds. The day's honours, however, belonged to the Frenchman, Ploujoux, whose dazzling display of putting continued. On the first six greens of his morning match against Colin Dalgleish he had five single putts to go two up and he was still two under par in winning at the sixteenth. Against John Carr in the semi-final he holed four more huge putts, the most crucial of which came at the sixteenth from forty feet to retain his two hole advantage. A half at the seventeenth set up a final that no-one would have predicted.

Ploujoux had started golf young and, as a 15 year old, had entered the Boys Championship at Dunbar. He arrived late on the tee and was disqualified, but as a consolation he was taken for a round at St. Andrews, which was his only previous experience of the Old Course. He had been in the Continental youth team against Great Britain and had won the French Championship at the age of 22.

A plane load of supporters from Paris came to swell a surprisingly good local crowd, but they missed the Frenchman's tentative start, which left Hirsch two up after four holes. They arrived as the match reached the thirteenth, by which time Ploujoux was in the lead, and they saw him hole another giant putt at the fifteenth, one of three from more than twenty yards during that morning round. This may have undermined Hirsch who compounded his problems with self-inflicted mistakes. He finished the morning round with a 3 to win one back and reduce the margin to four down. Ploujoux went further ahead in the early part of the afternoon and weathered a minor crisis around the loop, which could have been a major one had he not holed from nine feet at the twelfth after leaving his approach putt from below the bank woefully short. From there he proceeded steadily and was one under par when he won on the sixteenth green. It was a first for France and the supporters doubtless celebrated his sparkling display of putting with their own sparkling brand on the return flight.

1982

The Royal Cinque Ports club at Deal is best known for hosting the Halford Hewitt. Each year in early April more than 600 golfers come to this south-east corner of Kent to battle for the honour of their school, often in driving rain or squally showers. The greens then are firm and fast but a little thin. June 1982, for Deal's second Amateur Championship, was a pleasant contrast. A hazy sun shone all week with the gentle breeze scarcely stirring the Channel. The fairways were fast running, the rough light and the greens smooth and receptive to a well struck shot. The holes from the twelfth back to the clubhouse, so fearsome into the prevailing wind in the Spring, were not baring their teeth that week.

It was a Halford Hewitt player who created the first shock. Charles Giddins, an old Harrovian, was six under par for seventeen holes against Philippe Ploujoux, who, although scoring well himself, could not extend the defence of his title beyond the first round.

The U.S. Collegiate Championship had been held that weekend and Stephen Keppler, one of a growing number of young British golfers who had been accepted into the American scholarship system, flew back on the Sunday night, which meant that he was able to snatch only a couple of hours sleep before his mid-morning starting time. It didn't seem to affect his play and he won by five and four. Another college man, Nathaniel Crosby, holder of the U.S. Amateur title and now therefore a famous son of a famous father, had come on the same flight. He was not playing until the second day and had time to prepare himself, though no opportunity for a practice round. Unlike his father, who had started with a brace of 3s at St. Andrews in 1950, he started 6, 5, 5 and was three down to the 16 year old David Gilford, recent winner of the Carris Trophy and mature beyond his years. There was no recovery and Crosby was soon on his way back to California. McEvoy lost as well, as did the two most recent silver-medalists, Hirsch and Suddards.

By Thursday afternoon only one seed, Peter Deeble, had reached the fifth round. A member of the previous year's American Walker Cup team, Frank Fuhrer, looked threatening; so did two of the British players now past their prime, Bonallack and Christmas. The former was President of the English Golf Union and had come to Deal primarily to watch and support the young Englishmen. Luck had extended beyond the golf course, for he had drawn the Derby winner, Golden Fleece, in the R & A committee draw, but his good fortune ran out next day in the fifth round when he met Philip Parkin of Wales, a young man whose golf proved much too good. He was 31 to the turn and five up, on the way to inflicting the past champion with his heaviest defeat. Deeble, Fuhrer and Christmas lost as well that afternoon, the latter to the American Kristan Moe, who was four under par. Even so Christmas took him to the nineteenth.

The international challenge ended next morning in the quarter-finals with defeats for Moe by Andy Stubbs, for the South African Winsnes by Parkin and Kinell from Sweden by Martin Thompson. This left a Welshman and three Englishmen to contest the semi-finals and ensured an all British final. Stubbs played Parkin in the first match and in the other Thompson played the third Englishman, Peter Hedges, youth versus experience. The latter had recorded most of his golfing achievements in the 1970s. He had played twice in the Walker Cup (1973 and 1975) and was an ever present member of the English team between 1973 and 1978. He had one other advantage in that he was a long standing member of Deal. This had carried him through three difficult matches, for he had beaten Dalgleish, Fuhrer and young Richard Boxall in successive rounds. So Hedges and Parkin, who had followed his resounding victory over Bonallack with a good win over the South African, looked the likely finalists. As so often happens it was the other two who won.

Andy Stubbs, at 22, had already showed his matchplay ability by reaching the final of the previous years' English Championship. He was however a lightweight hitter and had benefited from the fast running fairways, without which he might have been left far behind from the tee. The 18 year old Martin Thompson, son of a Middlesbrough doctor, was a product of the E.G.U. training scheme, having been coached for several years by Roger Jennings, who rated him as one of the best he had ever seen. Thompson had led the previous year's England Boys team against Scotland. This week he proved his temperament in tight matches as, up to the final, he had been to the seventeenth hole or beyond each time, twice winning in extra holes.

It is difficult to say how much the outcome of the final was affected by a mishap to Stubbs. As he came down from the elevated fifth tee he slipped over on his ankle and was clearly in pain. Any such injury provides some physical restriction and now Thompson was fifty yards or so beyond him from every tee. It did not however break Stubbs' mental determination or the quality of his short game and, playing with great courage, he eased the pain by winning three of the last four holes before lunch. Both had been round in 69. During the interval he was taken to the local hospital, where torn ligaments were diagnosed and a painkilling injection administered. Restarting with an injury is difficult and Thompson soon took the lead again. But for a little anxiety in the closing stages, when thoughts of taking his place in the Open Championship, the U.S. Masters and the Walker Cup team began to play on his concentration, he kept control and won at the fifteenth.

1983

The Walker Cup teams headed north to Turnberry after their encounter at Hoylake. It had been a splendid contest with the Americans fighting off a strong British challenge during the early part of the last afternoon.

There was a new format for the championship. There would be thirty-six holes of strokeplay qualifying during the first two days, with eighteen holes over the championship (Ailsa) course and eighteen over the Arran. The leading sixty-four players would qualify for matchplay. Such a system had been discussed several times before by the Championship Committee, not least under the powerful advocacy of Cyril Tolley in 1946, but by 5 votes to 4 his proposal had been defeated. The revised arrangement enabled more to participate, an increase from 256 to 288, and assured all entrants of two competitive rounds, even if only one of them was over the primary venue. There were some casualties amongst the Walker Cup men. Rick Fehr of the Americans and David Carrick and Lindsay Mann from the home side all failed to make the qualifying score. Philip Parkin, one of three from the British team at an American university, led the field, adding a 73 on the Ailsa to his 66 on the Arran. It was posted as 74 and he had an anxious few minutes with the officials sorting out his score at the short fourth hole, which he had holed in 3, but signed for a 4. It was just as well that it wasn't the other way round. Martin Thompson, the holder, recovered from a first round 76 on the easier course with a fine 72 on the Ailsa. Two who had not played at Hoylake, the Northumbrian Deeble and a Californian policeman Foreman were joint second and Billy Tuten, 143, and Jay Sigel, 144, were the best of the American team.

There were fifty scores of 149 and better, with another twenty-two tied for the remaining fourteen places, for which a sudden death play-off had been prescribed. This can produce drama, but for the players who have to wait on the brink after completing their round, for the press, anxious to finalise their copy, and for the officials bursting for a gin and tonic, the prospect of starting at 8 p.m. to find fourteen qualifiers from twenty-two hopefuls can be a nightmare. Play-offs such as these can last an age, with four players playing the first hole and then waiting behind the green whilst two more four balls and two groups of five complete the hole. Some would qualify, some would be eliminated and then in deteriorating light the process would start again with the balance. The fates however were kind and one hole sorted it all out, with a chip in and a three putt amongst the very last group, fourteen players had scored a 4 or better and the remainder trudged sadly home.

Perhaps they were the lucky ones, for next day was one of continuous rain, which the greens and fairways were unable to absorb. A round in the mid 70s was a good score and delays for casual water rulings frayed tempers, not least for one American, who, in his match against a Scot, felt that three decisions had gone against him. There had been arguments as to where the ball should be dropped in the rough, where it should be placed on the green and whether his opponent could sweep away casual water on the line of a putt. After losing the match he walked unhappily away without the formality of a handshake. Two of the American Walker Cup team, Hoffer and Tuten, lost, missing presumed drowned. That night the Royal and Ancient set their moto-mops to work and from 2 a.m. to 11 a.m. they removed seven thousand gallons of water from the course, which was sufficient to enable the day's programme, sixteen matches in the morning and eight in the afternoon to be completed. Thompson, the holder, went out to Foreman and Oldcorn, undefeated in the Walker Cup, also lost, but a combination of reaction to his Hoylake high and a severe cold were perhaps more responsible for that than the skill of his opponent.

Five of the team members remained for the quarter-finals, which saw two

Anglo-American battles, Keppler against Tentis and Deeble versus Sigel. Parkin played Thomson, a solitary Scot, in one of the other two matches, whilst two Americans battled it out for the other semi-final spot, Holtgrieve versus Foreman. Wales beat Scotland and the two Englishmen surprisingly beat the Americans. The all American battle was the closest morning match. Holtgrieve had established a comfortable lead, but with seven dropped shots in the last nine holes, it vanished and he was lucky to survive at the nineteenth. His driving, so solid at Hoylake, had become erratic but, thankfully for him, Deeble was also spraying his shots in the semi-final and that gave Holtgrieve the necessary encouragement to win his place in the final. In the other semi- final Parkin went one down to Keppler after ten holes, the only time he had been behind in the second nine throughout the championship. It was a situation he quickly rectified and came through to win at the seventeenth.

Parkin with his bubbling personality and stylish golf had been marked a couple of years back as a player for the future and had confirmed it in 1982, following his semi-final medal at Deal, with a seven shot victory in the Youths' Championship. His opponent in the final, Jim Holtgrieve, from St.Louis, was in his mid 30s and had successful appearances in two Walker Cups and two World Amateur team championships behind him. His driving problems continued in the final and were largely responsible for four bogeys and two double bogeys in the first round. He did however pitch in for a 3 at the eighteenth to reduce the

Philip Parkin driving at the 17th hole in the final

deficit to two holes and raise his hopes. Parkin took control again over the first six holes in the afternoon, winning four of them. The American won a couple back, but another wild drive at the thirteenth put the Welshman five up and he finished it at the next.

1984

The championship was back at Formby in 1984, the club's centenary year. The links had been altered recently, as wind and tide had taken their toll of the old eighth and ninth holes. This had necessitated four new holes, scenic and testing, but somehow not as satisfying as the ones they had replaced.

The championship followed the St. Andrews Trophy match at Saunton, so most of the European team had entered, which, with the normal sprinkling of Americans, gave the field a strong international flavour. The qualifying arrangements had been altered to avoid the trauma of sudden death. This was just as well, as this time twenty-three with scores of 150 would have been playing for fourteen places. Instead a card play-off decided ties for the final places. Philip Parkin was again the top qualifier. With rounds of 70 and 71 he finished a stroke ahead of Peter McEvoy, whilst the young Spaniard Olazabal, who had won the previous year's Boys Championship at Glenbervie, demonstrated his taste for Formby with a new course record of 69.

Next day in the first round of matchplay Olazabal found himself two down with three to play against Neil Roderick, the Welsh Strokeplay champion, but he answered the crisis with a 2,4,3 finish to win all three holes. Paul Mayo aged 21, holder of the Youths' Championship, who was sharing a room with fellow Welshman Parkin, provided the best golf of the day. He chipped in for a 3 at the first, but despite a couple more birdies found himself one down to Peter Deeble with five to play. He completed the next four holes in twelve shots, hitting the ball to within ten feet or less at each hole. That made it seven birdies in seventeen holes and a two and one victory. The following afternoon his room-mate made the news. Parkin lost by four and two to the Scot, Colin Brooks and, whilst the latter was asking his landlady for a room for another night, Parkin was explaining to Michael Bonallack, the new R & A Secretary, that he had decided to turn professional. He had enjoyed his life at Texas University and his experiences in amateur golf, but this had only been possible with the financial support of his parents and he felt that he should not impose further on them.

The closest match of the day was between Colin Montgomerie and the last remaining American, Kristan Moe. A fine match was soured however by an unhappy incident in which the Scot won a hole through the American, having marked his ball, failing to replace it in the correct position on the green. The game went to extra holes and Montgomerie was saved from a similar fate at the nineteenth by a voice in the crowd reminding him that his marker had been moved a putter's head to one side. He replaced the ball correctly, holed for the half and won at the twentieth.

The aggregate age of the four semi-finalists added up to about three-quarters of Formby's one hundred years, but their golf on that penultimate day was some of the finest ever played there. In the morning Montgomerie was seven under par for fourteen holes in beating Brooks. Meanwhile David Gilford, all square with Angus Moir after seven holes, played the next five in 3,3,2,3,3 to ensure his place in the semi-final against Olazabal. In the afternoon Montgomerie continued his fine play and comfortably disposed of Curry, who had beaten McEvoy in the morning. The other semi-final was an exciting contest. Gilford came from two down at the turn to all square with two to play, but Olazabal's 4,3 finish was good enough, enabling him to win by a single hole for the fourth time in five matches. More remarkably, he had done it with a 3 at the eighteenth for the third time.

Jose Maria Olazabal lived in the shadow of Seve Ballesteros in northern Spain. As the son of a greenkeeper, he came to golf early and it was soon clear that he was destined for stardom, having played for the European Boys side against the British at the age of 15. Now, aged 18, he was holder of the Spanish Boys, Youths and Amateur championships. Winning came naturally to him. Montgomerie was two years older and had played for the Scottish Boys and Youths teams. Having won a scholarship to the University of Houston, he was intent on winning a senior cap and then perhaps a career in golf.

He started well in the final, winning two of the first four holes, but Olazabal counter-attacked and was two up after fourteen holes. In hindsight the next, a fine two-shotter with a two-tier green, was probably the critical hole. Both of them were short with their seconds, on the green but below the bank. Olazabal putted first from twenty yards and left it ten feet short. Montgomerie, about twelve yards away, failed to get his putt dead and when Olazabal holed the Scot missed – a two hole swing.

The Spaniard completed the first round in 72 and was still three up. For a moment in the second round, after Montgomerie had holed across the seventh green for a 3, it looked as though he might mount a challenge, but Olazabal followed him in. When the Spaniard holed his second with a sand iron from 110 yards at the eleventh the damage was done beyond repair.

Next year Olazabal won the British Youths Championship and the silver medal for the leading amateur at the Open. Is it too much to hope that some day he will complete the nap hand?

1985

Royal Liverpool would naturally have liked to host the centenary championship but requests from Formby and Lytham to host the Amateur during their centenary years (1984 and 1986) had been granted and this meant that a Scottish venue was required. No-one could argue with the choice, new to the list of championship venues, Royal Dornoch with its spectacular scenery.

Hoylake members did however have their day, as jointly with the R & A they held a centenary celebration coinciding, as in 1885, with their spring meeting and annual dinner. Ten champions accepted the invitation to attend including two from the 1930s, John de Bendern and Charlie Yates, and one who travelled from Australia, Doug Bachli. The guests played in the club medal, but Hoylake that afternoon was at its most unforgiving with a north-westerly gale buffeting the stiffening joints and making the downwind chips and putts as speedy as Augusta. The scores were incidental as the main purpose of the weekend was the dinner for guests and members. With closed circuit television relaying proceedings from club room to dining room and vice versa it was a memorable evening.

The weather a month later at Dornoch was not much better, nor was the scoring of the holder. Olazabal started with three 5s to be four over par and followed that with a brace of 7s, reaching the turn in 43. Improved golf over the second nine seemed to have given him a chance of salvaging a score of better than 80, but more problems at the seventeenth, where he lost a ball and had two unplayable lies, meant an 8 and condemned him to a non-competitive round at the other qualifying course, Golspie, next day. For the record, he scored a 68 but that still left him six shots above the limit. Colin Montgomerie with 74 and 75 was also a couple of strokes too many. The Golspie defences were lowered on the first day by Ian Stephenson, a left hander from Moortown, with a 64, but next afternoon his score at Dornoch rose with the north-east wind to 83 and he lost a qualifying place on a count-back. The leading score of 137 came from Dana Banke, one of ten Americans to qualify out of more than fifty who had entered, such was the lure of Dornoch.

The first round of matchplay saw the defeat of several past Walker Cup men. McEvoy lost to young Stephen Richardson from Hampshire, Peter Hedges to Billy Bremner, son of the Leeds and Scottish football star, and Ian Hutcheon to Colin Dalgleish.

Two 17 year-olds, Patrick Hall from Yorkshire and Peter Baker from Shropshire won through the second and third rounds to take their places in the last eight. Baker was particularly impressive. Under the scrutiny of the Walker Cup selectors he was two under fours in beating a reinstated amateur, Cecil Bloice, who had played a major part in Scotland's European team championship victory. The two youngsters were joined in the quarter-finals by another Englishman, Graham Homewood from Middlesex, and three Scots, George Barrie, John Huggan and David James, the first two of whom had played at senior international level. An Irishman and an American completed the eight. These two seemed the strongest, but they were to play each other in the quarter-final. Garth McGimpsey from Ulster had been a regular in the Irish team since 1978 and his opponent, Duffy Waldorf, was a bustling confident young man of sixteen stone, who had beaten Dana Banke in the previous round and was intent on securing a Walker Cup place.

Their match next morning fizzled out like a damp squib on the fifteenth green with McGimpsey, having taken an early lead, never letting Waldorf back into the game. Peter Baker however, from two down with four to play against David James, did make a strong recovery and was all square playing the final hole. He was addressing his second in light rough, when unseen by anybody other than himself, the ball moved. He stood back and called over the referee, explaining what had happened. Graham Simmers, the man in charge, had to confirm that a penalty shot had been incurred and Baker, failing narrowly to get down in two more, lost the match but gained the respect of all around him. The two other Englishmen beat their Scottish international opponents to complete a semi-final quartet, in which Garth McGimpsey beat Hall by three and two and Homewood won by five and four against James.

It was a truly amateur final. McGimpsey, aged 29, had no thoughts of swapping his job, as a sports goods distributor, for the professional circuit and the younger taller and stronger Homewood, who had never previously achieved more than a place in the Middlesex County team, had come north without major ambitions. McGimpsey weathered an early crisis. He lost the third hole and looked like losing the fourth when he drove into gorse, but, after dropping under penalty, managed a half in four and

Garth McGimpsey

holed for a three at the fifth. This set him going on an uninterrupted march to victory. He was round in 70 in the morning, five up, and moved smoothly to an eight and seven victory in the afternoon.

Whilst that evening McGimpsey paraded the cup in front of his hotel to the strains of the bagpipes, others were watching on television the success of another Ulsterman, Barry McGuigan, who was winning his world title fight. It was quite a day for the Irish. Meanwhile a couple of Homewood supporters must have wondered whether it had been worthwhile. Graham's father had been 'phoned the night before, to bring a jacket up for the presentation, and English Golf Union President, John Wild, travelled overnight by train, standing in the corridor, having been unable to book a sleeper. For them the result was a disappointment, but they could be proud of their man, both for his deportment and for his many fine golf shots. His consolation was a place in the England team later in the year.

1986

To coincide with the club's centenary, the championship went back to Royal Lytham and St. Annes for the third time. No American professional had won an Open over these famous links, but it had been a happy hunting ground for American amateurs. Bobby Jones had won the Open in 1926 and Lawson Little and Joe Conrad had won the two previous Amateur Championships. From the qualifying rounds it looked as though the Americans might be successful once more, with Dana Banke heading the field for the second successive year. He added a round of 71 at St. Annes Old Links to his first day 71 at Lytham. The largest crowd on the first day was at St. Annes following another American, Jack Nicklaus junior. He was round in a respectable 73 and then 'phoned home for instructions from father.

Qualifying arrangements had again been altered so that the leading sixty-four players and ties all moved into the matchplay stage. On this occasion it meant seventy-five players with scores of 152 or better. The eight top qualifiers were seeded into the second round. For the remainder it was the luck of the draw, as to whether they were required to play in the first round. David Carrick, who had the ninth qualifying score was unhappy with the arrangement, especially when he discovered that he had a first round match against Peter Baker.

There were two surprises on the first day of matchplay, both at the nineteenth. Lee Vannet, a member of the Scottish team in the 1984 Home Inter-nationals, was dormie one down to Banke, but played a miraculous chip shot from tangled rough, that had his American opponent joining the applause, partly no doubt to warm his hands in the biting wind. Banke bunkered his tee shot at the nineteenth and failed to match Vannet's 3. Later in the afternoon Garth McGimpsey started as though he was in no mood to relinquish his title.

He won the first two holes against Duncan Muscroft, a former boy champion who had, as caddie, his father, that shrewd Yorkshire professional. McGimpsey, from the apparent security of three up with six to play, suddenly hit trouble and, with two bad holes and two good ones by Muscroft, he was one down. He squared it again at the eighteenth, but lost the nineteenth to a chip and a putt against three putts.

The afternoon of the next day saw young Nicklaus, the last of the Americans, playing David Curry, an England International from Northumberland, for a place in the quarter-final. Another large crowd followed eleven holes of tight and even play. Then Curry, in his own words, "stiffed it" from sand at the short twelfth, holed from twelve feet for a winning three at the thirteenth and took advantage of a Nicklaus error at the next. That was three up with four to play and he won the match two holes later.

Curry was one of six Englishmen to reach the last eight with a Scot, Bryan Shields, and Paul Mayo from Wales. McEvoy versus Baker, Walker Cup partners at Pine Valley the previous year, looked like being the outstanding quarter-final match, but it ended early with Baker, not quite at his best, losing. McEvoy and Curry, who had beaten Mayo, met in the second semi-final, which looked likely to decide the championship, for in the first one neither Geoff Birtwell, who had played his best golf for Lancashire and England more than a decade earlier, nor the uncapped Shields, aged 20, seemed to have the same credentials. None the less they had an exciting match and came to the eighteenth all square. Both hit similar seconds towards the left edge of the green, but the Scot found a bunker and Birtwell skipped to the right and finished well. Shields skimmed his recovery into another bunker and conceded the match, leaving Birtwell the winner by a single hole for the fourth time in five matches.

In the other match Curry established an early lead against McEvoy, but the latter fought back from three down and, despite finding trouble off the tee at both seventeenth and eighteenth, saved himself with fine recoveries. He was however badly bunkered at the nineteenth and this time failed to make his three and lost the match, a defeat, he subsequently said, which hurt more than any other, because he felt certain that whoever won would win next day.

David Curry

His assessment proved correct. Geoff Birtwell had been a member of Lytham, but now played at Fairhaven. "Lytham was too difficult for me," he said, as an explanation for the move, and he seemed to find it that way in the final. Curry's first round of 71 established a six hole lead, but he started poorly after lunch. The first was halved in 4 and, bunkered at the second, he lost it. When he drove out of bounds at the third Birtwell's hopes rose. The latter, short for two, played a wedge third shot towards the middle of the green. It landed on Curry's ball, which apparently shot sideways into the rough. Curry's caddie, having checked with the referee that it could be replaced on the green, picked up the ball. It was Birtwell's and after a further conference with the referee, who had sanctioned the caddie's action, it was replaced in the rough. The outcome was a halved hole and, thus reprieved, Curry slipped his game back into gear and won the next six holes to achieve the largest winning margin since Lawson Little in 1934.

1987

After the exciting Walker Cup matches at Hoylake and Pine Valley and the recent successes in the Ryder Cup and Curtis Cup, the disastrous result at Sunningdale was an unexpected setback. It did little to raise hopes of a British victory at Prestwick, now reinstated as a championship venue after a gap of thirty five years. The American team were enchanted by the club's history, bemused by some of the blind shots and disappointed only with the mean weather.

The leading qualifier was young Andrew Hare from Sleaford with a score of 136. Paul Mayo, Bill Loeffler and Billy Andrade were all a stroke behind. Peter McEvoy and Garth McGimpsey, two controversial omissions from the British team at Sunningdale, also made their point to the selectors. The axe fell at 145. Andrew Rogers of Ealing, in the last game out, needed two putts for a 72 and a total of 146, which would have enabled himself and fifteen others to qualify for the matchplay stages. He holed it, eliminating the fifteen and restricting the qualifiers to sixty-four, and for his pains earned an eight and six defeat from Andrade next day. One of those on 146 was the Scottish favourite, Colin Montgomerie, who had recovered from a first round 76 on the easier St.Nicholas course with a 70 at Prestwick. Three of the American team were also left on the sidelines, Billy Mayfair being forced to withdraw with a stomach upset after a first round 69 and Jim Sorenson and Buddy Alexander taking a few shots too many.

The first day saw just two of the British team progress, David Curry and Paul Mayo, whilst Bob Lewis, who beat Hare, Len Mattiace, Andrade and Jay Sigel all advanced. The latter was involved in one of nine games to go to extra holes, a splendid match with Paul Broadhurst of Atherstone in which the American was five under par for the nineteen holes.

The second day created an unlikely hero, John Wilson from Troon. He had come into the championship as an alternate for one of the scratchings and, having exceeded his expectation by qualifying, he then proceeded to remove Garth McGimpsey in the first round. In the second round he played a more prominent Ayrshire player, Jim Milligan, and beat him at the home hole. After a short celebration in the clubhouse he came out to meet his afternoon opponent, Dennis Edlund from Sweden, only to discover that his clubs had disappeared. After some frantic enquiries he established the worst, that they had been put in the boot of a friend's car, who had unwittingly driven away with them. Just in time another competitor, having lost in the morning, came to his rescue with a similar set of irons, but the driver was a metal one and the putter much heavier than his own. Wilson found an extra twenty yards length from the tee and the putter worked like magic, as new putters often do. It was not long before he found himself in the exalted company of the quarter- finalists. The other drama of that afternoon was the match between Paul Mayo and Jay Sigel. The latter now 43, had won at the twenty-fourth hole in his morning match against the young Scot, Gary Orr, who had the disappointment of seeing a two hole lead with two to play disappear against the American's 3s. Sigel must surely have been feeling a little weary as he ventured forth against Mayo and he was behind most of the way, but his competitive spirit brought him to the tee at the eighteenth just one down. Once again he squared the match with a 3, though Mayo had missed from three feet. The Welshman made up for it at the nineteenth with a second shot as close to the pin and this time he made no mistake.

Next morning Mayo played Wilson, reunited with his own clubs, but the rest had done them no good and Wilson must have longed for the metal driver and the heavier putter. He lost by six and five. Mayo didn't have it so easy in the afternoon, for in a desperate game with the last of the Americans, Len Mattiace, a 19 year old from Florida, he went to the twenty-second, where Mattiace obliged by driving over the Pow Burn and out of bounds.

Peter McEvoy had been having less trouble. He went to the sixteenth in the first round and each of his other four games had ended at the fifteenth. David Wood had helped by removing first Brian Montgomery and then David Curry from his section of the draw. Russell Claydon from Gog Magog did the same for him in the quarter-final against Bob Lewis, a veteran of four Walker Cups, by recovering from three down with five to play and taking the game in extra holes.

An all British final in a home Walker Cup year was solace for the Sunningdale misery and a Mayo versus McEvoy confrontation for the second time (the latter had won a third round match at Formby) was a fitting climax. Conditions were miserable, but the quality of the golf and the excitement made up for that. McEvoy's long game was at its best but Mayo, despite finding a few bunkers from the tee, stayed with him by means of some splendid pitching and putting, and took a lead of one hole into lunch. With nine holes to play Mayo still held his lead with the same pattern of play, fine striking by McEvoy and superb work by Mayo with his beryllium pitching wedge, with which he was spinning the ball back on the firm greens. He went three up at the thirteenth, but McEvoy, at last holing a long putt, won the fourteenth and followed that with a 3 at the fifteenth – back to one down again. Mayo's answer was to drive the 296 yards sixteenth and hole for a 2 and then, with yet another pitch and putt, he sealed his victory at the Alps.

1988

The championship at Porthcawl began as the last one in 1980 had ended, with driving rain and gales lashing the links. Within half an hour play had been suspended, but one benefit of a strong wind is that it quickly dries the pools of casual water. It didn't seem to have much effect on Steven Dodd of Bryn Hill who played one of the best rounds ever played at Porthcawl. The standard scratch score for the day was set at 77. Despite dropping two shots in the last three holes he was round in 68. There were only four other scores of 75 and under that day. With a 77 at Pyle and Kenfig, the other qualifying course, Dodd tied with Liam McNamara of Woodbrook as leading qualifier and the qualifying score of 155 was the highest so far recorded. Gordon Clark, who had won the championship twenty-four years earlier, was one of three former champions to qualify. David Curry and Peter McEvoy were the other two. One distinguished non-qualifier was 65 year old Bill Campbell, now captain of the Royal and Ancient Golf Club, who had first played in the championship at St. Andrews in 1950. His scores of 78 and 80 would, under the conditions, have won him a match or two in earlier days.

Sixty-seven qualifiers meant that there were three first round matches and the first of them saw McEvoy lose to Christian Hardin from Sweden, the major surprise of the first day. The most extraordinary finish that day was in the match between an Australian, Roy Vandersluis, and 20 year old Gavin Lawrie from Prestwick St.Nicholas. The latter, one up playing the eighteenth, saw his opponent's hooked second shot carry into the clubhouse area, apparently out of bounds. Guarding against a similar mishap in the strong crosswind he held his ball to the right and it dropped in rough on the far side of the green. It was then discovered that the Australian's ball had ricocheted from wall to wall onto a path from where it somehow trickled through an open gate back into play. From there he was able to make his 5. Lawrie with a downwind pitch out of thick rough, did what most would have done, chipped it over the green and failed to get down in two more. Clearly shaken, he drove wildly into gorse at the nineteenth and the Australian had achieved an unlikely victory.

There was strong overseas representation in the last eight with two Swedes, a Frenchman, a South African and an American. It might have been stronger still but for two unheralded Englishmen, Carl Suneson of Ladbrook Park and Nigel Graves of Brockenhurst, who had beaten the Frenchman Thomas Levet and a highly talented young South African, Ernie Els. In the quarter-finals next morning they did further damage to the foreigners by eliminating another Frenchman, Eric Giraud, and one of the Swedes, Anders Haglund. This left Graves contesting one semi-final with 20 year old Ben Fouchee, the 1987 South African champion, and Suneson playing Christian Hardin, the other Swede. The two English youngsters had their chances. Suneson was three up at the turn, but lost four holes in a row and the match at the seventeenth. Graves, one down playing the eighteenth, put a fine three iron second close to the hole and won it, but failed to take his chance at the twentieth where a yard putt for the match evaded the hole. He surrendered at the next, after pulling his second shot onto the beach. So a Swede was to play a South African in the final, which led to some unfounded speculation that Hardin would not be permitted to play, for South Africans were banned from participating in sport in Sweden.

The best weather of the week was reserved for the final, which was followed by a couple of hundred spectators. Christian Hardin, aged 24 with a fine, powerful swing, was in the lead for most of the first round, but he missed a short putt at the seventeenth and saw Fouchee chip in for a 3 at the eighteenth which meant that the Swede's lead at lunchtime was down to a single hole. With three 4s at the start of the afternoon round, he had soon regained his three hole lead, only to lose it again in the next four holes. After a tense period in which seven consecutive holes were halved, Fouchee took the lead for the first time at the fifteenth. The six-teenth was halved, leaving the South African one up with two to play. Hardin responded with a pitch and putt 4 at the

Christian Hardin is applauded by R & A Captain Bill Campbell

long seventeenth to win it, thus taking a final to the thirty-sixth for the first time for twelve years. Here he followed Fouchee's tidy second shot with a better one, a seven iron to twelve feet. The South African, from more than twice that distance, raced his putt at the hole. Hardin failed narrowly with his, but it didn't matter as Fouchee missed the return. Amidst the applause as they left the green, some compatriots emerged to lift their man from the ground and throw him three times into the air, an unusual Swedish variation of the old practice of chairing the champion.

1989

With the championship at Royal Birkdale to mark their centenary year and nearby Hillside providing the second course, there was no respite in the quest for a position in the top sixty-four, as low scores at Hillside are just as hard to come by as at Birkdale.

The eighteenth at Hillside is a tough par 4 of 440 yards. If, from the tee, a player can avoid the apparently magnetic bunker, he is left with a long downhill shot to a narrow green with trouble to the left and right. This was the hole at which Philip Robinson of Knebworth, one of the late starters in the second round, holed a three wood for an eagle two. At that stage there were sixteen players with scores of 153 anxiously eyeing the scoreboard. A par by Robinson at that hole would have made it seventeen and all of them would have qualified. The freak stroke left Robinson on 151 and the other sixteen packing the bags into their cars.

Jim Milligan, the 25 year old Scot from Barassie and one of the Walker Cup certainties, led the qualifiers by three shots with a 71 at Birkdale and 70 at Hillside. Craig Cassells, an England youth player now playing at Murcar in Aberdeen, must have feared the worst after his first round of 79 at Hillside, but on the second day he managed the lowest score at Birkdale, a 68, and dejection turned to elation. One of the other qualifiers was not so happy. Ernie Els, after finishing with a score of 149, practised at Hillside before driving back to Birkdale to check his starting time for the match play. He parked a few yards away from the championship office, chatted briefly to the Secretary and returned to find the rear window of his estate car shattered and the clubs gone. It was not surprising that, with borrowed clubs, he succumbed next morning.

Close behind him two of the top players went to extra holes. The burly Russell Claydon, with his forceful if unusual style, was not only the reigning English champion but had surprised his supporters with an outstanding performance in Australia, finishing second in a field of world class professionals. He was drawn against Ben Jackson, a friend from another Cambridgeshire club. Claydon seemed to have earned a reprieve, for, having lost his ball at the eighteenth with the match level, he managed a 4 with his second one for an unlikely half in 6. On the nineteenth he found the green with his second and Jackson did not, but optimism quickly faded as the latter chipped up and holed his putt, and Claydon, not quite dead, missed.

Peter McEvoy was now re-established as England's top amateur after his performance in leading the British team to success in the Eisenhower Trophy and achieving for himself the lowest individual score. He had been one up playing the eighteenth against Drew Elliott, a young Scottish international, and he too lost his tee shot after pushing his drive close to the fence. Elliott was not as generous as Jackson had been and they went to the nineteenth, which was halved. McEvoy looked certain to win at the twentieth but Elliott saved himself with a chip and putt from an awkward spot. That primed his survival instinct and he saved himself again with a long putt at the twenty-first and twice more at the twenty-second and twenty-fourth. A chance came for him at the twenty-sixth where McEvoy was bunkered, but with two for the match from about fifteen yards, he failed with the second from five feet. Two holes later he three putted again, from the back of the tenth green and McEvoy had won. If Elliott had holed his three foot putt, a new record would have been set for the longest match in an Amateur Championship. As it was, it equalled the Munn versus Palmer match of 1908, but mercifully for Elliott the walk from the tenth green back to the Birkdale clubhouse is shorter than the one faced by the defeated Munn at Sandwich.

McEvoy made progress next day winning his two matches, but not without a further scare. James Cook from Leamington, noted for his gritty temperament, was three down with five to play and salvaged two of them. It would have been all three if McEvoy had not holed from eight feet on the home green to save himself from more extra time. This meant that he was to meet the other former champion, Garth McGimpsey, in the quarter-final.

The Irishman won next morning at the seventeenth after a stern tussle, but it was by no means the match of the day as all the others bar one went to the eighteenth green or beyond. Craig Cassells beat Jim Payne to face McGimpsey in the first semi-final. With a 3 at the eleventh and a 4 at the long fifteenth the former went one up, but threw it away immediately with a wild shot into Birkdale's willow scrub. The seventeenth was halved in 4 and Cassells' hopes rose again when McGimpsey bunkered his tee shot at the last, but his own drive missed the fairway and he couldn't reach the green. After McGimpsey had played his third shot to nine feet, it was still anybody's game. A couple of minutes later it was all over. Cassells had pitched to six feet and, having watched McGimpsey's putt slip past the hole, knocked it in for a place in the final.

The other semi-final was between 22 year old Steven Dodd from Bryn Hill near Barry and Steven McCraw of Australia. Dodd had been taken to the twentieth by another Australian, David Harding, in the first round and when he became one down with two to play against McCraw it looked as though Australia might gain their revenge. Dodd had other ideas and, with two of the highest quality shots to the middle of the seventeenth green for a 4 and the same again at the eighteenth for a 3, he won both holes.

Dodd, the Welsh strokeplay champion, was built on the lines of a flank forward. Despite a fluent swing and calm temperament, he had lacked the self confidence required to achieve consistent results. None the less he was the more relaxed of the two at the start of the final. It may be that Cassells, with a more intense approach and greater awareness of the potential rewards, felt the pressure more. Whatever the reason, he never found a rhythm to his swing, lost the first three holes and, whenever recovery looked possible, a drive would find another bunker. He came from the course after the first round totally dis-spirited and seven down. His play improved in the afternoon and, at only three down with seven to play, there was still a chance for him. Then, at the thirteenth, a par 5 down the prevailing wind and easily within range, he missed the green and a relieved Dodd put a five iron shot a yard from the pin to go four up again. Two holes later he had become the fourth Welsh champion within the decade, quite an achievement for a country with less than one hundred and fifty clubs.

1990

With the championship at Muirfield, Luffness was the other qualifying course. It extends to the side of Gullane Hill from where there are splendid views of Aberlady in the foreground and the Forth stretching down to the bridges in the distance. It is short by modern standards, just 6100 yards and it yielded over twenty scores of under 70 in the calm of the second day, with 66s by Adam Hart, Brian Shields and Liam White. The former, a 19 year old from West Hill in Surrey, led the qualifiers, having achieved a 72 in the sterner conditions of the first day at Muirfield. He tied with a 34 year old American, Michael Brannan, whose golfing c.v. included a Walker Cup appearance in 1977 followed by a period as a professional which was ended, after little success, by a shoulder injury. His 68 on the first day at Muirfield was exceptional. The two days had been bad for the Scots with not one qualifier from the team that had recently won the European championship. Five of the six had entered and even Jim Milligan, the hero of the Peachtree Walker Cup match, had been six strokes over the qualifying score of 148.

The benefit of being a top seed proved illusory. Following his previous day's success, Adam Hart had described himself to the press as "pretty unknown", and he duly confirmed it by losing three and two to Greg Kennedy of U.S.A. The second seed, Brannan, lost narrowly in the last match of the day to Michael Macara of Maesdu, who had been one of twenty-two qualifiers required to play a first round match.

The results next day gave an unusual look to the last eight which contained not one Scot nor an American. A Dutchman, Rolf Muntz, played Jim Carvill from Ireland in the first quarter-final. Cassells, the losing finalist at Birkdale, played Gary Winter, a young Cumbrian. Gary Evans, who had tied for the Brabazon Trophy played the Welsh Boys champion Richard Johnson, and in the fourth match his Welsh colleague Macara, who had beaten Gary Wolstenholme at the twenty-third hole in the previous round, was matched against Olivier Edmond from France, the joint winner of the Brabazon. The two Welshman surprisingly won their quarter-final matches with Macara again needing extra holes against the Frenchman. Cassells outplayed Winter with some excellent golf, whilst Muntz, having three putted the two previous holes, needed a five foot putt at the eighteenth to save his match against Carvill. He holed it and another longer one at the nineteenth, both with a lightweight putter purchased in Edinburgh for £10 earlier in the week.

Looking at the pedigree of the others, Craig Cassells must have felt optimistic about his chances of going one better than last year. Muntz had already overrun his stay in Scotland. The Netherlands golf officials had booked the return journey for him and a Dutch colleague on the assumption that neither would qualify. His golf was however improving as the week progressed and against Cassells it was rock solid. He had several opportunities to extend an early lead during the first nine holes, but Cassells scrambled his pars with sound chipping and putting. From the turn the pattern was the same and all holes were halved until Cassells, one down playing the seventeenth, ran another delicate pitch close. This time he missed to lose the match.

The other semi-final was even closer. All square with two to play, Macara hit two drivers onto the seventeenth green (550 yards) and followed it with an eighteen foot putt at the home hole to remove his young Welsh compatriot. So it fell to Michael Macara, aged 24, who had a couple of Welsh Strokeplay victories behind him and had been playing for his country since the age of 17, to attempt to extend the run of Welsh successes. That seemed to be a more likely outcome than a champion from Holland, though Rolf Muntz, aged 21, had much in his favour. His mother had been an international player and he was at Leiden University studying psychology, which was developing strength of mind to go with his strength of body. With a well organised swing he was a longer hitter than the more slightly built Macara. What is more Muntz, with a bye to the second round, had played only 118 competitive holes in reaching the final, whilst Macara had amassed 146.

The first round of the final ended with the Dutchman one ahead, largely by courtesy of the short sixteenth, where he had saved his three from over the back of the green, against three putts from Macara. Muntz took his lead to four up by winning three holes early in the afternoon and his long straight driving began to take its toll on a tiring Macara, whose fade was turning to a slice. The sixth hole was crucial. Muntz raced his chip onto the fringe at the back of the green. From there he holed with his lucky new putter, leaving Macara an awkward one for a half, instead of the win that he had anticipated and needed so desperately. He missed it and, when Muntz had also won the eighth hole, taking the Hagen route via the practice ground, that was six up. The match ended four holes later. There is no doubt that Muntz's mental approach was a significant factor throughout the championship. He had eliminated thoughts of what his opponent was doing, playing "card and pencil" matchplay. "You can do anything if you believe you can do it," he said and believed that he could hole the putts when it mattered. "The ball is small and the hole is large."

Muntz was thus the fourth continental winner of the championship in ten years, and this confirmed the growing strength of golf in Europe, not only in the professional game, but amongst the amateurs.

1991

The reasons for moving the Amateur Championship from its traditional early summer date to September seemed compelling. It should be the climax of the golfing season and September weather was likely to be more favourable. The Walker Cup was another consideration. With the championship in September and the match against the Americans a week earlier, it would enable the selectors to pick a team on current season's form. It also ensured a strong American presence in the championship and all but two of their team came to Ganton from Portmarnock. One unforeseen problem had however denuded the entry of six of the British team, for, in order to participate in the P.G.A. tour school, they were required to file entries in early September, which jeopardised their amateur status.

It was Ganton's centenary year. Sadly in September it is not quite the same there as at the end of May, when the gorse in full bloom provides a spectacular setting to many of the holes. Ganton without golden gorse is like a gin and tonic without lemon and ice. The fairways were bronzed and fast running, which meant that it did not play to its full length of 6800 yards. That apart, it was a fine test and with fast firm greens and difficult pin positions low scoring required a high degree of skill.

Much of the interest during the qualifying attached to two non-team Americans. One was Gary Nicklaus, younger son of Jack. The other was 32 year old David Szewczul from Connecticut. He was staying in Scarborough and went over to North Cliff, the other qualifying course, to practice during the morning and then drove sedately across to Ganton. Having prepared himself for his 2.40 starting time, he went over to the tee to discover that he should have been fifteen miles away, back at North Cliff. Disqualification was confirmed despite an impassioned plea by his wife. The fact that it had cost five thousand dollars for them to make the trip brought sympathy from Michael Bonallack, but no reprieve.

David Duval of the American team was the top qualifier with a 73 at Ganton and 68 at North Cliff. He was joined for the matchplay stage by sixty-five others with scores of 148 or better. Three of the American team failed to make it, one of whom was the reigning U.S. Amateur champion, 41 year old Mitch Voges, who was so overcome with fatigue and a sense of anticlimax after all that had gone before, that he admitted he would have taken eight putts on the last green, if that was what was needed to miss the cut. Milligan and Hay of Scotland also failed, which meant that the Irishman Padraig Harrington was the only qualifier from the British team.

On the first day of matchplay, Nicklaus took the crowds, as Nicklauses do. He was playing Klas Eriksson, aged 20, one of three Swedes to qualify, and the latter was two up after eleven holes. Nicklaus squared the match with 3s at the twelfth and fourteenth but lost the fifteenth. A half in 3 at the par 4 sixteenth followed and Nicklaus, having saved himself with yet another 3 from sand at the long par 3 seventeenth, made his fifth 3 in seven holes to win the eighteenth. Eriksson, badly bunkered at the nineteenth, emerged smiling with his hand outstretched in a gesture of surrender against golf that Gary's father might not have matched over those seven holes.

At the end of the first day the prospects of a British victory looked slim, as nearly half of the survivors were overseas players, but by the penultimate morning there were only three Americans left, Duval, Bob May, who had annihilated an exhausted Sigel the previous evening, and George Zahringer, a more than useful player from New York. Young Nicklaus had lost to Mark Pullan. The Americans were joined by three Englishmen, and two Scots.

The two young Americans, Duval and May, predictably won their quarter-finals and contested the first semi-final, and those that watched felt that this was the match that would decide the championship. The second semi-final was between England International Gary Wolstenholme, aged 31, son of Guy, and Wilson Bryson from Drumpelier, a hitherto uncapped Scot, who had beaten Zahringer in the morning. Neither semi-final generated much excitement. Duval lost the first but, despite some wild driving, held his man until the ninth, a par 5 hole of 494 yards, where he unleashed an enormous drive, which with the assistance of the wind and the baked fairway finished more than 350 yards from the tee. It left him with only a sand wedge for his second, but that scuttled over the back of the green and he took three more to lose a hole he should have won. May followed it by winning the short tenth with a 3 and, now three up, the outcome was virtually decided. By the time he had claimed his victory on the sixteenth green, Wolstenholme was finishing his match at the fourteenth.

The final began with May looking the stronger, for Wolstenholme has never been known for long hitting despite his height. The former was out in thirty-six and led by two holes. May did however have an unusual method with a twirling action at the top of his back swing and, if his rhythm disappeared, so did his accuracy. That was what happened, which was just the encouragement Wolstenholme needed. His iron shots suddenly began to find the middle of the greens and the putts started to drop. He was home in 32 and had converted a two hole deficit into a lead of two. He continued after lunch in the same rich vein, reaching the turn in 34 to give him an unassailable lead. May, no doubt exhausted from 21 rounds in fifteen days, had nothing left and, with yet another drop from an unplayable lie at the twelfth, conceded the match there.

How sad that Gary's father, Guy, was not around to see his son with the cup that he, for all his golfing talent, was never able to win.

Gary Wolstenholme

1992

Carnoustie had been overlooked as a championship venue since the 1975 Open and it was twenty one years since they had last staged an Amateur. The links management were determined to win back an Open and nothing had been spared in preparation. Members had taken their plastic turf round with them through the winter to preserve the fairways and as a result the links were in magnificent condition – so good that a member of the championship committee, who had been walking the course prior to the championship to confirm the local rules, looking down from the left of the sixteenth green, asked, "What do you want me to do about this temporary green?" It was explained that he was simply looking at the forward tee for the seventeenth hole.

Carnoustie from the championship tees measures 7235 yards and under normal conditions not many scores under 70 might be expected. There were only two under 80. Gales estimated at fifty to sixty miles an hour lashed the competitors throughout the first day. The first three cards to be returned were 88, 91 and 97, and that set the pattern. There were forty cards of 90 or more and even at Panmure, the other qualifying course measuring nearly a thousand yards shorter, there were a dozen in the 90s. Of the three past champions McEvoy achieved the lowest score with an 84 at Panmure. Muntz and Wolstenholme each took 87. Next day McEvoy failed to qualify but the other two scraped in, with the Dutchman producing a high class second round of 75 at Carnoustie. Winds were still strong, but the previous day's gales had done the damage to swings and morale. The qualifying score was 163 and only 19 year old Michael Welsh from Hill Valley was able to handle conditions sufficiently to break 150.

The story of the third day, the first round of matchplay, was created by Benedict Genese (not Ben as he explained to the press, as it sounded like "Bend your knees!"). He had started early from his home near Stirling to meet a 10.56 starting time against Calvin O'Carroll, the young Welsh International, but road-works between Perth and Dundee delayed him badly and he arrived in the car park as his name was being called. He sprinted to the tee without his shoes and clubs, but by the time he was ready to play, it was past 11 o'clock. The penalty was to lose the first hole and commence the match at the second, one down. Some three and a half hours later he did play the first hole, as the nineteenth. He halved it and was thus one up for the eighteen holes he had played, but he lost the match at the next where O'Carroll chipped dead from a difficult spot.

It was youth to the fore in the third and fourth rounds. The oldest competitor left in the last eight was 24 year old Mike Meehan from U.S.A. Three teenage Scots had survived with a teenage Welshman and three young Englishmen. Steven Gallacher, nephew of Bernard, who was only 17 and Scottish champion, had played Raymond Burns, an Irish International, in the previous round. Burns' pitching and putting had enabled him to hold a lead until the fifteenth, but when another good chip would have put him three up with three to play he fluffed it. That was the lifeline that Gallacher needed, for he caught him at the eighteenth and won it at the first extra hole. The tall bespectacled Steven Dundas, an 18 year old from Haggs Castle, who had been semi-finalist in the Scottish Championship, had an even better day by defeating two Walker Cup men, the American Danny Yates and Irishman Padraig Harrington. Against the latter Dundas was one down with two to play, but Harrington obliged with one into the Barry Burn at the seventeenth and worse, over it and out of bounds, at the last. The third Scottish teenager, Hugh McKibbin from Troon had eliminated Michael Welsh, the leading qualifier, also on the last green.

The three Scots were in the top half of the draw and Gallacher and Dundas made it to the semi-final. Dundas had survived a poor round in the morning against Meehan in which he was two up at the turn despite taking forty shots. Against Gallacher he started strongly and was four up after eight holes, but the Scottish champion rallied by winning the ninth, tenth and eleventh. His confidence returned. He had been coming from behind all week and now he had his man on the run, but a tramliner of a putt by Dundas at the short thirteenth broke the momentum and when Gallacher failed to carry "the Spectacles" with his second shot at the next and then left his third in, Dundas was firmly in charge again.

Meanwhile the Welshman, Bradley Dredge, had beaten off the English challenge by defeating first Lee Westwood on the eighteenth and then Matthew Stanford. Stanford had played the best golf of the day in the morning, covering the first nine holes into the wind in 33 against Ian Garbutt, but he could not reproduce it in the afternoon. Dredge was four up after nine and playing too well to allow the Englishman back into the game. Thus the final was to be between Dundas and Dredge and not Gallacher and Stanford, as might have been predicted by most of those who had set out to watch the semi-finals.

Both Dredge and Dundas had come through their national Boys and Youths teams and were to make a first appearance in the Home Internationals to be played later in the month. Both were playing full time golf, with Dredge working for his parents, whilst Dundas was at college in Dallas mixing psychology and business studies with his golf.

The weather was benign for the final, but after a week battling against the wind, it can often be difficult to retain rhythm in still conditions and that was Dredge's problem. He had lost confidence with his driver and, though he was only one down after fourteen holes, he lost the last four before lunch. Dundas had holed a long putt at the fifteenth, recovered from sand at the sixteenth and played fine shots to the middle of the last two greens. Dredge was unable to mount a serious challenge after lunch and, when he did look like winning a hole, the short eighth, Dundas holed from sand for his 2 to go seven up, a lead he maintained until the end. It was an unhappy day for Wales, but a glorious one for Scotland, who, at last after thirty-five years, could celebrate another victory.

1993

A return to Portrush and the traditional date at the end of May produced a memorable championship. Apart from the quality of the links and its splendid setting, the Irish enjoy their amateur golf and watch it in their thousands, as they had demonstrated two years earlier in the Walker Cup at Portmarnock.

Initially the omens were not good, as the weather for the qualifying was little better than it had been at Carnoustie, especially in the cool nor'-easter of the second day. Two of last September's medalists led the field at the end of the first day. Matthew Stanford, with a 67 on the easier Valley course, outscored Bradley Dredge who was round in 69 on the Dunluce. The latter commented to the press how much it had hurt to watch the Masters on television with Steven Dundas playing in it. Dundas himself had a respectable first round 73 on the Valley course but next day, needing a 4 at the par 5 eighteenth to qualify, cut his second out of bounds and finished with a 7. He was not alone in his misery. Garth McGimpsey was the only former winner to qualify for McEvoy, Muntz and Wolstenholme were all condemned to the sidelines, as was the New Zealander Philip Tataurangi, winner of the individual medal in last October's Eisenhower Trophy. Scottish International Craig Watson headed the field with an excellent second day 73 on the Dunluce to add to his first round 68.

Surprisingly, only Gary Vanier of thirty American entrants had reached the matchplay stage and he was unlucky enough to draw Stuart Cage of Sand Moor, the English champion, in the first round. This meant that no American had reached the last thirty-two, the first time since the war. The crowds on the first day of matchplay followed Garth McGimpsey, a great favourite at Portrush, as he had won the North of Ireland Championship title four times. He was playing Stanford, who had represented Great Britain in the Eisenhower Trophy, but the game didn't live up to its "match of the day" billing. McGimpsey won the third with a 2 and, having watched Stanford top his second only a few yards at the fourth, played two more careful shots onto the green and three putted for a 6. Stanford missed a shorter one and couldn't even halve the hole. From there it was one way traffic and the Irishman won at the twelfth.

There was much fine golf over the next two days, but it all paled to insignificance when compared with what followed in the final. It was not just the match of the championship or of the decade, but possibly the finest thirty-six hole match ever played in an Amateur. Neither Paul Page, aged 21, of Dartford nor Iain Pyman, a year younger, from the Sand Moor school of excellence, had played for the full England team. Both had played at boys' level and Pyman was Yorkshire champion. Page had reached the final without going beyond the sixteenth hole, but to suggest that he had a favourable draw would be quite untrue. Each of his opponents had played at senior International level, Niall

227

Goulding of Ireland, Stuart Cage of England, against whom he was five under par, and Alvaro Prat, the Spanish champion, were the first three. In the quarter-final he beat Padraig Harrington and in the semi- final Raymond Russell, two Walker Cup probables for the match at Interlachen later in the year. Each time he had gone into the game as underdog.

If Pyman's victims did not have quite the same pedigree, he had to work much harder for his place in the final. Only one of his five matches ended before the eighteenth and that was his quarter-final against Mikael Lundberg from Sweden. Twice he had been to the twenty-second hole. Dale Baker from Downpatrick took him there on the first day, as did another Ulsterman, Dr. Neil Anderson, in the semi-final. In that match Pyman recovered from two down with six to play and twice at the extra holes it had looked as though he would lose. At the nineteenth he made his 4 from an unlikely spot at the back of the green and at the twenty-first Anderson had a twelve foot putt for a winning 2. He missed it and his drive at the twenty-second put paid to any further chance.

The first round of the final saw Paul Page take the initiative. He won the first and went two up with a 3 at the eighth. Winning the tenth and twelfth as well, he was four ahead and that would have been the score at lunch but for a fine 4 at the last by Pyman. Page was round in three under, 70, and Pyman had equalled par. Not many people could have believed that Page would beat his morning score in the afternoon, yet only finish level. A half in 3 at the first in the afternoon set the mood for a crowd of about 3000. Pyman holed from twenty-five feet for a 3 at White Rocks (the fifth) to start the fireworks. He holed a longer one at the next, for a 2, and that was back to one down. Page steadied the ship with his second 3 of the day at the eighth, but to cheer and counter-cheer Pyman replied with three more successive birdies, only one of which Page could match. The Yorkshireman made his only mistake of the afternoon at the twelfth but squared the match again at the next. A half in 3 at the fearsome short hole, Calamity, was followed by an enormous drive from Pyman bounding down the hill at the 368 yard fifteenth. He was able to play his second with a putter and made his 3 to take the lead for the first time. At the sixteenth a six iron second shot left him a ten foot putt, which by then was routine. He had covered twelve holes in forty-one shots (six under par) to move from three down to two up. Surely there could be no more excitement. But there was. Page won the seventeenth with a 4 and chipped neatly to the holeside at the last for yet another birdie. He stood back to watch Pyman complete the formalities, but he didn't. He missed from less than a yard and sank to his knees in anguish. Perhaps it was a pity that he didn't hole it, for the thirty-seventh hole was anticlimax with Page failing to make his par. How lucky that the venue was Portrush and that so many were there to watch what had been an enthralling, scintillating match.

As for Iain Pyman he proved his worth as champion with an outstanding performance in the Open Championship at Sandwich a month later, winning the amateur medal with a score of 281. For Paul Page there was the consolation of a Walker Cup place. Pyman turned professional after playing at Augusta and performed creditably in his first season on tour.

Of the fourteen champions since 1980, only Ploujoux, McGimpsey and Wolstenholme have remained as amateurs. Duncan Evans and Martin Thompson have been reinstated but do not play in top amateur competition. The others, Olazabal apart, have so far met with only modest success in their new careers. Why should it be otherwise?

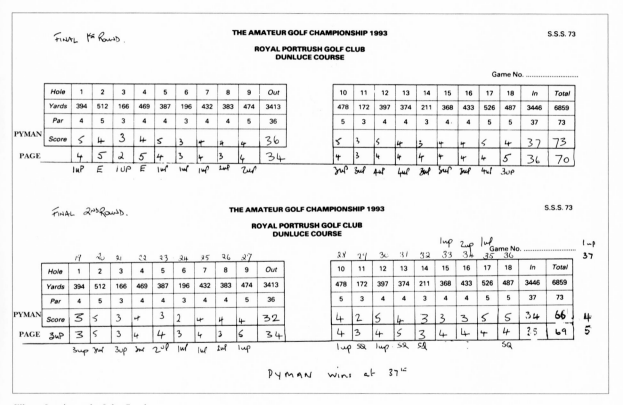

The referee's card of the final

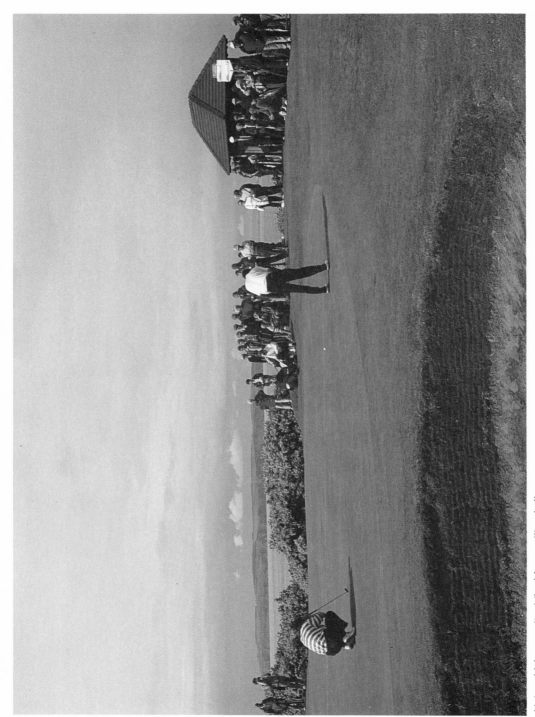

Nairn. 11th green. Semi-final James v Turnbull

CHAPTER EIGHT

Ninety Nine Not Out

The committee's decision to take the championship to the north of Scotland for a second time was an inspired one. Nairn is more accessible than Dornoch and as rewarding. For many of the competitors it was a first visit and they will surely have been entranced by it all, the architectural quality of the links, the perfect greens, the vivid gorse and the spectacular views across the Moray Firth to distant snow-capped mountains. The club gets other things right. The superbly sited new clubhouse combines all the necessary comforts with a functional simplicity. They also had the happy idea of selecting, as their President for the year, Lord Whitelaw, who developed his golfing skills there sixty years ago. His presence added to the occasion and jogged the memory that in the early 1950s he had won several matches in the championship and served on the committee.

The one thing that Nairn could not offer was docile weather. Strengthening winds and lashing rain on the Monday afternoon meant that the later starters were at a disadvantage. One of them, Euan Little from Portpatrick, had a particularly unhappy time beside the shore at the long seventh. He cut his tee shot onto the beach (a water hazard) and playing his second from the sand, lost it. Dropping another ball, he chose a safer line but the ball headed for gorse on the other side of the fairway and, after a further lengthy search, it could not be found. By the time he had again returned to the beach, the tide was coming in and the point from which he had played was under water. He identified what he believed to be the spot and played the ball as it bobbed on the swell of the tide. This time he found the sanctuary of the fairway and it all added up to an 11, the same score that he had taken at the hole on his previous visit to Nairn for the Scottish Boys Championship. In future he would come equipped with a rule book, a tide table and a pocket calculator.

There were other hard luck stories and some surprises, not least the failure of David Fisher, English champion, who, needing a par at the last to qualify, was so prodigal with his putts that he missed by two shots. Steven Gallacher, with a 74 at Nairn to add to his first day 71 at Nairn Dunbar, led the qualifiers by four shots.

One of four players to tie for second place on 149 was the Englishman Warren Bennett, who, as holder of the Australian Amateur title and the Lytham Trophy, was one of the favourites.

It was a pity, people thought, that Gallacher and Bennett were in the same half of the draw. It would have made the perfect final. Such thoughts tempt providence and, sure enough, neither survived their first match. Gallacher looked like saving himself after winning the eighteenth to take Matthew Blackey from Hayling to the nineteenth, but the latter holed there from ten yards for a win. Bennett lost a high class contest at the last, but he had let slip a good chance of squaring the game when he had allowed the diminutive Damion Berridge to escape with a half after driving out of bounds at the short par 4 fifteenth.

The closest match next day was the one between Bradley Dredge and Craig Watson. They had played together in the qualifying competition and had identical scores, 76 in each round. This time it took another twenty three holes to separate them, with Watson recovering from two down with three to play to beat the Welsh Walker Cup man. The outstanding golf of that afternoon came from the Swede, Kalle Brink. He pitched into the hole for a 2 at the first against Graham Homewood and, by the time he had won the match, he had three more of them and another three birdies to be eight under par for the twelve holes. The Swedes were looking ominous as Martin Erlandsson, a Tom Kite look-a-like, had put paid to Scottish International Barclay Howard to join Brink in the quarter-final.

Seventeen year old Carl Duke, a member of the England Boys team, seemed likely to create the surprise of the quarter-final against Brink. His golf for the first nine holes was almost as good as the Swede's had been the previous day, but Brink never let him out of his sight and Duke was only one up with three to play. Heavy rain fell as they drove at the sixteenth and with the deluge intensifying and flashes of lightning, play was suspended. They sheltered for twenty minutes contemplating the second shots from the right rough to the green over the burn. When they restarted, Duke dropped his into the water to lose the lead, but regained it with a 3 at the seventeenth. The eighteenth was out of range for the second shots and both were on in 3. The youngster putted close. Brink conceded it and carefully studied the twenty footer to save himself. He holed it and won the nineteenth, the first time he had been ahead.

The other half of the Swedish threat had been extinguished by Allan Turnbull from Peebles and Brink soon found himself up against it in his semi-final against Gordon Sherry from Barassie, a Stirling University student. The Scot was one over 3s for the first six holes, four below par and four up on the Swede, to whom he never gave the opportunity of counter-attack.

The other semi-final was closer, but it left English International Lee James from Broadstone, who had beaten Watson in the morning, a little disappointed in that he was only level par for the seventeen holes he had needed to defeat Turnbull. In his four previous matches he had not been taken beyond the sixteenth green and was a cumulative sixteen under par.

A Scotland versus England final always attracts interest. Gordon Sherry aged 20, a member of the Scottish team, admitted to having lost a stone from his massive frame following the intensive fitness training introduced by the Scottish Golf Union, but he still had six and a half stone and a foot in height to spare against his opponent. James, a year older, had graduated through the England Boys, Youths and full International team though he had never won a major amateur event.

A strong westerly wind greeted the finalists, and at the start it was James who showed greater accuracy and judgement, especially his putting. This had been so solid all week, following a tip from his coach in Dorset to hold his hands higher. He reached the turn in level par, a great performance with seven of the first nine holes against the wind. He was however only one ahead and that was how the morning ended, with James round in 71 to Sherry's 72. Again in the afternoon James drew first blood, but after ten holes there was still only one in it. James widened the gap by following a winning 4 at the twelfth with a ten foot putt for a 3 at the thirteenth, after the Scot had shaved the hole with a longer one up the slope. Sherry responded immediately with a 2, but that was the end of his challenge and a splendid and sportingly contested final ended in anti-climax with both taking three putts at the seventeenth.

The name of Lee James was thus the ninety-ninth to be engraved on the famous trophy. The other rewards for a newly crowned champion are now so great, with invitations to the Open and the Masters and near automatic selection for the international teams, that for the loser, who may have failed by a mere hair's breadth, there is much sympathy. Gordon Sherry, the large and amiable Scot, was however soon over his disappointment. It had been a memorable week for him too and surely there would be more to come.

*   *   *

For the hundredth championship it is back to Hoylake, the place where Thomas Owen Potter first dreamed of a tournament to decide who should be "champion amateur golfer for the year". The links have never been better. Spring weather dictates how a course looks and plays in early summer, but one can be confident that the greens will be fast and firm. The smooth approaches, the revetted bunkers and a good grass covering on the fairways will all help to confirm that Hoylake is it's old immaculate self. There have been some changes, new bunkers, subtly sculpted pathways from tees to fairway and a redesigned hole. Some lament the passing of the old Dowie (seventh hole) with its shallow cop that gave scant defence to the dreaded "out of bounds" penalty, but most will welcome the alteration. The green is the same, but the flatness of the hole has gone. A raised tee, a watery fate in front of it, grassy hollows, bunkers and dunes to the right and a reshaped bank to the left have combined to produce a scenic and challenging hole. If the wind blows from the west the new hole won't be easy, nor will Hoylake yield to anything but the best.

The qualifying rounds will also take competitors to Wallasey. They will find there some memorable holes amongst the sandhills and an excellent finish to the round. It will be a pleasant surprise for those who have not been before. One wonders however if the change in 1983, when stroke play qualifying was introduced, may have deprived the championship of some of the excitement. The best players may fancy their chance of winning a place in the top sixty-four in stroke play, in preference to winning two rounds of match play, but many in the field would rather leave it to the luck of the draw, with the opportunity for some early giant-killing. The new format has certainly dimmed the interest of the first two days for press and spectators.

What of the field? Twenty or so flags of the nations represented will flutter in front of the clubhouse, though perhaps the Stars and Stripes will hang a little limply as, sadly, the cream of the American amateurs may not be present, even though 1995 is a home Walker Cup year. For the first time the two events have been separated in the golfing calendar. Despite this there will be no shortage of talent from at home and overseas. The names may not trip from the tongue as readily as those of Ball and Tait and Hilton in the early years, of Tolley and Wethered between the wars and of Stranahan, Carr and Bonallack in the fifties and sixties.

There is no purpose in attempting to compare the top golfer of one generation with another. Even the fascinating statistics prepared by John Littlewood don't tell the full story and don't give an answer to the question – who was the best? Ten years ago, at the dinner to celebrate the centenary of the Amateur Championship, a short ode completed the offering of one of the speakers. Here it is again:

> If Ball and Tait were here today,
> What sort of golf would they display?
> Could they, compared to Lunt and Carr,
> Propel balata balls as far?
> And would Bonallack at his peak,
> With gutty and wood-shafted cleek,
> Upon such men inflict defeat?
> Who'd reign supreme of golf's elite?
> I've got this feeling in my bones
> That all would lose to Bobby Jones.

1994

The 99th Champion

235

Bob Jones – an appreciation

by
Charles R. Yates

Bob, who was born in 1902 was moved at age seven by his parents to the Atlanta suburb of East Lake. The purpose was to seek for him a more healthy lifestyle so as to improve his fragile health. Happily, the family settled alongside the East Lake Country Club and, early on, Bob started watching and imitating the Scottish pro at the club, Stewart Maiden. Quickly, Bob proved to be a natural athlete and became so competent that at age fourteen he qualified and played in his first United States Amateur Championship.

Bob was a determined competitor who in his earlier days often lost his temper. The nadir of this habit was when he tore up his card while competing in the British Open at St. Andrews. What a great story it is that he conquered those early outbursts and became the epitome of all that a sportsman should be.

Bob's Boswell was the Atlanta sportswriter O. B. Keeler who divided Bob's competitive career into two parts. First, were his seven lean years where he never won a major championship. Then came seven fat years. In this brief span of time he won thirteen majors – the British Open and Amateur and the United States Open and Amateur. Then in 1930, after always competing as an amateur, Bob retired from tournament golf at the tender age of 28. In that final competitive year we saw him winning the immortal "Grand Slam".

It was my great good fortune that our family moved alongside the fourth hole at East Lake in 1917 when I was four. Bob was ten years old at the time and I really can't remember when I first slipped across the fence onto the club grounds so as to watch and follow him. He was always so kind to me. I remember the time as if it were yesterday when he took me into the locker room and gave me my first taste of that great elixir of Atlanta – Coca-Cola.

There was no practice area around the course at East Lake and Bob's game was honed solely by his playing of the actual course. How different this is from today when the top players spend hour after hour pounding away at the little pellet. Obviously, Bob was blessed with a God-given talent.

Certainly, I was also blessed to have known Bob as long as I did. In the early

1930's until his health caused him to quit playing in 1948, I had many friendly games with him. He was still an unmatched competitor with desire nevertheless kept under strict control. I cherish my memories of things he said to me. At the top of the list is that time in 1925 when he returned to East Lake after losing the United States Open by one stroke. I walked up to him and said, "I am sorry you lost." His reply, "Don't worry about it, son, you never really know who your friends are until you lose."

In 1958, in St. Andrews, Bob was given the Freedom of the City and at that time he stated that if everything was taken out of his life except his experiences at this home of golf, he would have had a full and rewarding life. He hit his last golf shot at age 46 because of a neurological problem that finally caused a complete degeneration of his spinal cord. He brushed aside statements made to him by his friends who expressed their regrets at his condition. His reply, "Just remember you always play the ball as it lies."

In closing these comments let me relate that in Bob's office there were only two displays involving golf. The first was a line drawing of the layout of the Old Course at St. Andrews. The second was a picture of an attic scene where we see a beat-up golf bag leaning against a chair. Alongside was this poem written by Grantland Rice.

> For when the one great scorer comes to write against your name,
> He writes not that you won or lost but how you played the game.

Results and Statistics

by

John Littlewood

INTRODUCTION – THE ENTRANTS

The analysis of the entrants, largely done from Peter Ryde's "Royal and Ancient Championship Records", has needed some guesswork. A single initial J. might be J. E. a year or two later, or J. H. becomes J. N. and back to J. H. followed by a change of club. Allowing for these problems, the tally of individual entrants is an exact 7,600, led by 81 Smiths, 50 Browns and 48 Jones's, the last remarkably in third place, because it only first appeared in 1921 with the famous Bobby. The list of surnames continues with 40 Taylors, 38 Walkers and 35 Wilsons, all names with good golfing connections, and 35 Andersons of whom eight appeared together in 1950. These 7,600 golfers have played 15,839 matches and 6,758 qualifying rounds. 4,244 golfers, or rather more than half, entered only once, perhaps achieving an ambition to say that they played in the Amateur. More than one-third of all entrants played without ever winning a match or qualifying, some trying as many as eight and ten times.

There were only 40 competitors in the first year, and as few as 29 in 1887, but the entry grew steadily to reach 100 in 1899 and a record 220 played in 1914. Thereafter it was largely a battle to restrict numbers to a manageable size. Following an all time record of 304 in 1950, lower limits have been set and regulated by balloting out higher handicaps. Since the 36 hole qualifying competition was introduced in 1983, the limit has been 288.

Since 1900 there have been two significant changes in the character of the entry. The home entry has widened and the overseas entry has grown to some 40% of the total.

The home entry has mirrored the story of amateur golf, evolving from the early days when a few names dominated an exclusive game for long periods to the present spread of mostly younger golfers for whom the championship has become so brief a stepping stone to a professional career that the last 16 finals have been contested by 32 different golfers.

The expansion of the game has been reflected in the clubs providing the entrants. Before the Great War the entry was dominated by members from the famous golf clubs of the day, with 117 individual entrants from the Royal and Ancient, 71 from Royal Liverpool and 64 from Royal St. Georges. Members from the home club would sometimes swamp the field. 15 out of 40 entrants in 1890 were from Royal Liverpool; 40 members of the R & A played at St. Andrews in 1907; and 22 members entered from Royal North Devon when first played at Westward Ho! in 1912. A difference from today was that entries were received from clubs that would now be regarded as Societies. F. G. Tait twice won the Championship entering from his regiment, the Black Watch, and two other winners entered from their University. The Oxford & Cambridge Golfing Society and the Insurance and Banking Club of Edinburgh also provided many entrants.

In the twenties and thirties the emphasis in both the list of winners and the entrants shifted away from Scotland and the north of England to the south. The R & A still dominated with 86 entrants, more than twice any other, but Sunningdale was now in second place. Entries from the traditional clubs, Royal Liverpool, Royal St. Georges and Royal North Devon were at half the pre-war levels and closely matched by the likes of Addington, Walton Heath and St. Georges Hill from the south. In those pre- war years the draw would often reveal a sprinkling of Viscounts and Lords, Admirals and Generals, Reverends and M.P.s, and Counts from Europe.

Since the Second World War the competitive time span of the top amateurs of the day has gradually shortened, and the entry has been drawn from many more clubs. The entry is now defined by exact handicaps which has returned some overall stability to the field, but reduces the number of eligible entrants from each club. Two recent rare examples of golfing excellence have been Ealing in 1989 and Sand Moor in 1993, both with three members reaching the match play stages.

The second major feature has been the growth of the overseas entrants. The first were from Hong Kong in 1894 and Calcutta in 1896, but these and another thirty or so from clubs in India, and from cities such as Singapore, Shanghai, Manila, Cairo and Buenos Aires were almost certainly British golfers home on leave whilst working overseas. Four golfers from France and one from Sweden were the first European entrants.

The first entrant from the United States came from Staten Island in 1898 and another six in 1904 might have been touring together. From the outset the United States has provided much the largest contingent of overseas golfers and before the Great War five U.S. Amateur champions came over to play but only Walter Travis met with success in 1904. After modest beginnings the overseas entrants grew to one-fifth of the total during the inter-war years, led by the Americans, who added great status to the event every fourth year when it was held immediately after the Walker Cup, attracting the entry of their entire team.

Other overseas entries continued to be dominated by British golfers home on leave from an ever widening list of countries and cities around the world. India and Ceylon, Malaya and Singapore, Sarawak and British North Borneo, Bangkok and Rangoon, Abadan and Baghdad, Argentina and Brazil, Chile and Cuba would colour the entry from faraway places during the inter-war years, but pride of place belongs to the Royal Calcutta Golf Club which alone provided 17 individual entrants.

Since the Second World War the overseas entry has continued to grow, quickly reaching one-quarter of the total and in the latter half rising to 40% of total entrants. Although still dominated by U.S. golfers, large numbers were now entering from Australia, Canada and South Africa. France led the European entry, closely followed by the entry from German clubs who were mostly British and American golfers serving in the forces. There were now far fewer entries from those exotic corners of the Empire seen before the war.

The feature of recent years has been the growth in numbers and the rise in quality of the entry from Europe. From 1946 to 1970 there were only 82 entrants from Europe, but since 1970 there have been 219 from a wide range of countries and France, Holland, Spain and Sweden have each supplied a champion since 1980.

United States golfers have won the championship 20 times in all, but none since Jay Sigel in 1979. Subsequently, although three have reached the final, there has been a decline in their fortunes and in 1993 only one out of 30 U.S. entrants qualified for the match play stages.

In recent years many of the top amateurs have turned professional, so longevity can no longer be a feature of the modern amateur game. Of recent winners, only Peter McEvoy with eighteen appearances and Gary Wolstenholme with eleven consecutive amateurs can compare with earlier years. John Ball and Harold Hilton played in championships forty two and forty years apart. Robert Sweeny first played in 1929 and last in 1974, forty-five years later. Five golfers, Rex Crummack, Chick Evans, Denys Scott, Michael Scott and Edward Tipping played before the First World War and after the Second, with the widest spread of all – 1898 to 1946 – by Denys Scott.

MEDAL WINNERS

Year	Venue	Winner	Club	Score	Runner-Up	Semi-Finalists	
1885	Hoylake	A.F. Macfie	Royal & Ancient	7/6	H.G. Hutchinson	J. Ball	–
1886	St. Andrews	H.G. Hutchinson	Royal & Ancient	7/6	H.A. Lamb	C. Chambers	J. Ball
1887	Hoylake	H.G. Hutchinson	Westward Ho	1 hole	J. Ball	J. Ball Sen.	J.G. Tait
1888	Prestwick	J. Ball	Royal Liverpool	5/4	J.E. Laidlay	A. Stuart	L.M. Balfour
1889	St. Andrews	J.E. Laidlay	Honourable Company	2/1	L.M. Balfour	J. Ball	W.S. Wilson
1890	Hoylake	J. Ball	Royal Liverpool	4/3	J.E. Laidlay	L.M. Balfour	D. Leitch
1891	St. Andrews	J.E. Laidlay	Honourable Company	19th	H.H. Hilton	T. Gilroy	W. Ballingall
1892	Sandwich	J. Ball	Royal Liverpool	3/1	H.H. Hilton	L.M. Balfour	J.E. Laidlay
1893	Prestwick	P.C. Anderson	St. Andrews Univ.	2 holes	J.E. Laidlay	S.M. Fergusson	F.G. Tait
1894	Hoylake	J. Ball	Royal Liverpool	1 hole	S.M. Fergusson	J.E. Laidlay	F.G. Tait
1895	St. Andrews	L.M. B-Melville	Royal & Ancient	19th	J. Ball	L. Auchterlonie	F.G. Tait
1896	Sandwich	F.G. Tait	Black Watch	8/7	H.H. Hilton	H.G. Hutchinson	J. Graham Jnr.
1897	Muirfield	A.J.T. Allan	Edinburgh Univ.	4/2	J. Robb	L.M. B-Melville	J.L. Low
1898	Hoylake	F.G. Tait	Black Watch	7/5	S.M. Fergusson	J.L. Low	J. Robb
1899	Prestwick	J. Ball	Royal Liverpool	37th	F.G. Tait	G.C. Whigham	J.M. Williamson
1900	Sandwich	H.H. Hilton	Royal Liverpool	8/7	J. Robb	J. Graham Jnr.	J.A.T. Bramston
1901	St. Andrews	H.H. Hilton	Royal Liverpool	1 hole	J.L. Low	H.G. Hutchinson	J. Graham Jnr.
1902	Hoylake	C. Hutchings	Royal Liverpool	1 hole	S.H. Fry	J. Robb	R. Maxwell
1903	Muirfield	R. Maxwell	Tantallon	7/5	H.G. Hutchinson	H.W. de Zoete	A. Macdonald
1904	Sandwich	W.J. Travis	U.S.A.	4/3	E. Blackwell	H.G. Hutchinson	J.E. Laidlay
1905	Prestwick	A.G. Barry	St. Andrews Univ.	3/2	Hon. O. Scott	J. Graham Jnr.	A.R. Aitken
1906	Hoylake	J. Robb	Prestwick St. Nicholas	4/3	C.C. Lingen	H.S. Colt	E.A. Smirke
1907	St. Andrews	J. Ball	Royal Liverpool	6/4	C.A. Palmer	G. Campbell	R. Harris
1908	Sandwich	E.A. Lassen	Lytham St. Annes	7/6	H.E. Taylor	C.E. Dick	J. Graham Jnr.
1909	Muirfield	R. Maxwell	Tantallon	1 hole	C.K. Hutchison	B. Darwin	R. Andrew
1910	Hoylake	J. Ball	Royal Liverpool	10/9	C.C. Aylmer	A. Mitchell	H.H. Hilton
1911	Prestwick	H.H. Hilton	Royal Liverpool	4/3	E.A. Lassen	G. Lockhart	L.B. Stevens
1912	Westward Ho	J. Ball	Royal Liverpool	38th	A. Mitchell	A.V. Hambro	C.B. Macfarlane
1913	St. Andrews	H.H. Hilton	Royal Liverpool	6/5	R. Harris	C.C. Aylmer	E.P. Kyle
1914	Sandwich	J.L.C. Jenkins	Troon	3/2	C.O. Hezlet	E. Martin Smith	R.P. Humphries
1920	Muirfield	C.J.H. Tolley	Rye	37th	R.A. Gardner	G.L. Mellin	Hon. M. Scott
1921	Hoylake	W.I. Hunter	Walmer & Kingsdown	12/11	A.J. Graham	B. Darwin	H.S.B. Tubbs
1922	Prestwick	E.W.E. Holderness	Walton Heath	1 hole	J. Caven	W.I. Hunter	R. Scott
1923	Deal	R.H. Wethered	Worplesdon	7/6	R.Harris	F. Ouimet	D. Grant
1924	St. Andrews	E.W.E. Holderness	Walton Heath	3/2	E.F. Storey	W.A. Murray	R.H. Wethered
1925	Westward Ho	R. Harris	Royal & Ancient	13/12	K.F. Fradgley	E.N. Layton	R.H. Hardman
1926	Muirfield	J. Sweetser	U.S.A.	6/5	A.F. Simpson	Hon. W. Brownlow	A. Jamieson
1927	Hoylake	W. Tweddell	Stourbridge	7/6	D.E. Landale	R.H. Wethered	R.H. Jobson
1928	Prestwick	T.P. Perkins	Castle Bromwich	6/4	R.H. Wethered	W. Tulloch	E.B. Tipping
1929	Sandwich	C.J.H. Tolley	Rye	4/3	J.N. Smith	R.W. Hartley	J. Dawson
1930	St. Andrews	R.T. Jones	U.S.A.	7/6	R.H. Wethered	G.J. Voigt	W.L. Hartley
1931	Westward Ho	E. Martin Smith	R. St. Georges	1 hole	J. de Forest	J.D. MacCormack	W. Tulloch
1932	Muirfield	J. de Forest	Addington	3/1	E.W. Fiddian	L.O. Munn	E.A. McRuvie
1933	Hoylake	Hon. M. Scott	R. St. George's	4/3	T.A. Bourn	G.T. Dunlap	C.J.H. Tolley
1934	Prestwick	W. Lawson Little	U.S.A.	14/13	J. Wallace	L.G. Garnett	G.T. Dunlap
1935	Lytham	W. Lawson Little	U.S.A.	1 hole	W. Tweddell	R. Sweeny	T.A. Torrance
1936	St. Andrews	H. Thomson	Williamwood	2 holes	J. Ferrier	C. Ewing	G.A. Hill
1937	Sandwich	R. Sweeny	Royal & Ancient	3/2	L.O. Munn	C. Stowe	A. de Bendern
1938	Troon	C.R. Yates	U.S.A.	3/2	C. Ewing	H. Thomson	C.R. Somerville
1939	Hoylake	A.T. Kyle	Sand Moor	2/1	A.A. Duncan	W.E. Holt	C. Stowe

Medal Winners Continued

Year Venue	Winner	Club	Score	Runner-Up	Semi-Finalists	
1946 Birkdale	J. Bruen	Cork	4/3	R. Sweeny	H.E. Walker	G.H. Micklem
1947 Carnoustie	W.P. Turnesa	U.S.A.	3/2	R.D. Chapman	J.G. Campbell	S.L. McKinlay
1948 Sandwich	F.R. Stranahan	U.S.A.	5/4	C. Stowe	D.H.R. Martin	W.P. Turnesa
1949 Portmarnock	S.M. McCready	Sunningdale	2/1	W.P. Turnesa	K.G. Thom	E.B. Millward
1950 St. Andrews	F.R. Stranahan	U.S.A.	8/6	R.D. Chapman	C.J.H. Tolley	J.B. McHale
1951 Porthcawl	R.D. Chapman	U.S.A.	5/4	C.R. Coe	J.B. Carr	A.D. Evans
1952 Prestwick	E. Harvie Ward	U.S.A.	6/5	F.R. Stranahan	J.B. Carr	J.R. Cater
1953 Hoylake	J.B. Carr	Sutton	2 holes	E. Harvie Ward	C.H. Beamish	A.H. Perowne
1954 Muirfield	D.W. Bachli	Australia	2/1	W.C. Campbell	W.A. Slark	J.B. Carr
1955 Lytham	J.W. Conrad	U.S.A.	3/2	A. Slater	P.F. Scrutton	A.H. Perowne
1956 Troon	J.C. Beharrell	Little Aston	5/4	L.G. Taylor	R. Reid Jack	G.G. Henderson
1957 Formby	R. Reid Jack	Dullatur	2/1	H.B. Ridgley	A.F. Bussell	A. Walker
1958 St. Andrews	J.B. Carr	Sutton	3/2	A. Thirlwell	M.F. Bonallack	T. Holland
1959 Sandwich	D.R. Beman	U.S.A.	3/2	W. Hyndman	G.B. Wolstenholme	B. Magee
1960 Portrush	J.B. Carr	Sutton	8/7	B. Cochran	J. Walker	G. Huddy
1961 Turnberry	M.F. Bonallack	Thorpe Hall	6/4	J. Walker	M.J. Christmas	R.L. Morrow
1962 Hoylake	R.D. Davies	U.S.A.	1 hole	J. Povall	R. Foster	B.H.G. Chapman
1963 St. Andrews	M.S.R. Lunt	Moseley	2/1	J.G. Blackwell	E.R. Updegraff	R. Luceti
1964 Ganton	G.J. Clark	Whitley Bay	39th	M.S.R. Lunt	M.J. Christmas	J. Hall
1965 Porthcawl	M.F. Bonallack	Thorpe Hall	2/1	C.A. Clark	R. Foster	M.J. Christmas
1966 Carnoustie	R.E. Cole	South Africa	3/2	R.D.B.M. Shade	H. de Lamaze	G.B. Cosh
Y1967 Formby	R.B. Dickson	U.S.A.	2/1	R.J. Cerrudo	G.J. Clark	M. Fleckman
1968 Troon	M.F. Bonallack	Thorpe Hall	7/6	J.B. Carr	G.C. Marks	R.L. Glading
1969 Hoylake	M.F. Bonallack	Thorpe Hall	3/2	W. Hyndman	W.C. Davidson	D. Hayes
1970 County Down	M.F. Bonallack	Thorpe Hall	8/7	W. Hyndman	B. Critchley	T.B.C. Hoey
1971 Carnoustie	S. Melnyk	U.S.A.	3/2	J. Simons	P.H. Moody	T. Kite
1972 Sandwich	T.W.B. Homer	Walsall	4/3	A. Thirlwell	R.P. Revell	M.F. Bonallack
1973 Porthcawl	R.L. Siderowf	U.S.A.	5/3	P.H. Moody	H. Ashby	H.K. Clark
1974 Muirfield	T.W.B. Homer	Walsall	2 holes	J.R. Gabrielsen	H.B. Stuart	M.A. Poxon
1975 Hoylake	M.M. Giles	U.S.A.	8/7	M. James	R.L. Siderowf	G.C. Marks
1976 St. Andrews	R.L. Siderowf	U.S.A.	37th	J.C. Davies	A. Brodie	I.A. Carslaw
1977 Ganton	P. McEvoy	Copt Heath	5/4	H.M. Campbell	P.J. McKellar	M.F. Bonallack
1978 Troon	P. McEvoy	Copt Heath	4/3	P.J. McKellar	D.R. Suddards	J.C. Davies
1979 Hillside	J. Sigel	U.S.A.	3/2	S. Hoch	D. Roxburgh	A.Y. Gresham
1980 Porthcawl	D. Evans	Leek	4/3	D.R. Suddards	A.D. Pierse	D. Lindsay-Smith
1981 St. Andrews	P. Ploujoux	France	4/2	J. Hirsch	J. Carr	A.Y. Gresham
1982 Deal	M.S. Thompson	Middlesbrough	4/3	A.K. Stubbs	P.J. Hedges	A.P. Parkin
1983 Turnberry	A.P. Parkin	Newtown	5/4	J. Holtgrieve	S.D. Keppler	P. Deeble
1984 Formby	J-M. Olazabal	Spain	5/4	C.S. Montgomerie	D. Gilford	D.H. Curry
1985 Dornoch	G.M. McGimpsey	Bangor	8/7	G. Homewood	P. Hall	D. James
1986 Lytham	D.H. Curry	Prudhoe	11/9	G.S. Birtwell	P. McEvoy	B. Shields
1987 Prestwick	P.M. Mayo	Newport	3/1	P. McEvoy	L. Mattiace	R. Claydon
1988 Porthcawl	C. Hardin	Sweden	1 hole	B. Fouchee	C. Suneson	N. Graves
1989 Birkdale	S. Dodd	Brynhill	5/3	C. Cassells	S.H. McCraw	G.M. McGimpsey
1990 Muirfield	R. Muntz	Netherlands	7/6	M.A. Macara	C. Cassells	R. Johnson
1991 Ganton	G. Wolstenholme	Bristol & Clifton	8/6	B. May	W.S. Bryson	D. Duval
1992 Carnoustie	S. Dundas	Haggs Castle	7/6	B. Dredge	S.J. Gallacher	M. Stanford
1993 Portrush	I.D. Pyman	Sand Moor	37th	P.J. Page	N.H. Anderson	R. Russell
1994 Nairn	L. James	Broadstone	2/1	G. Sherry	A. Turnbull	K. Brink

Note – First named semi-finalist was defeated by the winner.

CAREER RECORDS – MINIMUM 30 MATCHES

Name	Club	A	M	W	L	%	W	RU	SF	Years Played
F.R. Stranahan	U.S.A.	9	50	43	7	86.00	2	1	0	1946-1954
F.G. Tait	R. & A.	8	36	30	6	83.34	2	1	3	1892-1899
J. Ball	R. Liverpool	30	121	99	22	81.82	8	2	3	1885-1927
W. Hyndman	U.S.A.	6	33	27	6	81.82	0	3	0	1959-1971
J.B. Carr	Sutton	26	119	96	23	80.67	3	1	3	1948-1973
D.H. Curry	Prudhoe	7	31	25	6	80.65	1	0	1	1981-1988
M.F. Bonallack	Thorpe Hall	28	117	94	23	80.34	5	0	3	1956-1983
E.W.E. Holderness	Walton Heath	10	39	31	8	79.45	2	0	0	1914-1931
R.H. Wethered	Worplesdon	16	71	56	15	78.87	1	2	2	1920-1935
R.D. Chapman	U.S.A.	13	54	42	12	77.78	1	2	0	1935-1971
C. Stowe	Penn	8	36	28	8	77.78	0	1	2	1937-1957
R.L. Siderowf	U.S.A.	11	40	31	9	77.50	2	0	1	1972-1989
R. Maxwell	Tantallon	12	44	34	10	77.27	2	0	1	1897-1920
P. McEvoy	Copt Heath	18	70	54	16	77.14	2	1	1	1974-1993
H.H. Hilton	R. Liverpool	33	124	95	29	76.61	4	3	1	1887-1927
J. Graham Jnr.	R. Liverpool	16	68	52	16	76.47	0	0	5	1896-1914
R.D.B.M. Shade	Duddingston	8	34	26	8	76.47	0	1	0	1961-1968
A.T. Kyle	Sand Moor	14	54	41	13	75.93	1	0	0	1938-1964
J.B. McHale	U.S.A	8	33	25	8	75.76	0	0	1	1950-1961
C.J.H. Tolley	Rye	25	94	71	23	75.53	2	0	2	1920-1955
G.B. Wolstenholme	Kirby Muxloe	8	32	24	8	75.00	0	0	1	1953-1960
M.J. Christmas	W. Sussex	9	35	26	9	74.29	0	0	3	1961-1982
T.W.B. Homer	Walsall	10	31	23	8	74.19	2	0	0	1964-1974
G.B. Peters	Fereneze	9	34	25	9	73.53	0	0	0	1931-1952
G. Wolstenholme	Bristol & C.	11	37	27	10	72.97	1	0	0	1984-1994
A.H. Perowne	R. Norwich	9	33	24	9	72.73	0	0	2	1946-1958
A. Brodie	Balmore	13	47	34	13	72.34	0	0	1	1968-1981
C.O. Hezlet	R. Portrush	12	43	31	12	72.09	0	1	0	1914-1930
H.G. Hutchinson	R. N. Devon	23	74	53	21	71.63	2	2	3	1885-1912
R. Harris	R. & A.	28	95	68	27	71.58	1	2	1	1901-1936
J.E. Laidlay	Hon. Co.	28	91	65	26	71.43	2	3	3	1885-1920
C.H. Beamish	R. Portrush	11	38	27	11	71.05	0	0	1	1946-1960
S.L. McKinlay	Western Gailes	17	58	41	17	70.69	0	0	1	1928-1952
J. de Bendern	Addington	16	51	36	15	70.59	1	1	0	1929-1955
P. Deeble	Alnmouth	15	51	36	15	70.59	0	0	1	1973-1990
G.C. Marks	Trentham	15	51	36	15	70.59	0	0	2	1962-1978
D.A. Blair	Nairn	18	61	43	18	70.49	0	0	0	1938-1971
G.J. Clark	Whitley Bay	15	47	33	14	70.21	1	0	0	1961-1989

Note – Qualification since 1983 for the last 64 match play places is counted as equal to two wins and failure to qualify as one defeat.

Name	Club	A	M	W	L	%	W	RU	SF	Years Played
W. Tweddell	Stourbridge	24	77	54	23	70.13	1	1	0	1921-1955
C.R. Dalgleish	Helensburgh	9	30	21	9	70.00	0	0	0	1978-87
G. Lockhart	P'wick St. Nicholas	9	30	21	9	70.00	0	0	1	1907-20
A.D. Pierse	Tipperary	9	30	21	9	70.00	0	0	1	1980-93
P.F. Scrutton	Sunningdale	9	30	21	9	70.00	0	0	1	1946-58
J.L.C. Jenkins	Troon	18	56	39	17	69.64	1	0	0	1903-38
J. Robb	P'wick St. Nicholas	17	52	36	16	69.23	1	2	2	1897-22
L.M.B-Melville	R.& A.	25	77	53	24	68.83	1	1	4	1886-20
L.O. Munn	R. Cinque Ports	13	41	28	13	68.29	0	1	1	1908-37
J.C. Davies	R. Mid-Surrey	15	47	32	15	68.09	0	1	1	1968-84
C.C. Aylmer	Sidmouth	17	53	36	17	67.92	0	1	1	1906-29
W.L. Hope	St. George's Hill	10	31	21	10	67.74	0	0	0	1922-32
I. Caldwell	Sunningdale	13	40	27	13	67.50	0	0	0	1950-82
T.A. Bourn	Sunningdale	14	43	29	14	67.44	0	0	1	1925-38
M.S.R. Lunt	Moseley	15	43	29	14	67.44	1	1	0	1957-74
Hon. M. Scott	R. St. George's	21	61	41	20	67.21	1	0	1	1911-46
R. Sweeny	Princes	25	72	48	24	66.67	1	1	1	1929-74
H.D. Gillies	Woking	21	63	42	21	66.67	0	0	0	1906-31
C.W. Green	Dumbarton	20	60	40	20	66.67	0	0	0	1961-84
E.W. Fiddian	Stourbridge	16	48	32	16	66.67	0	1	0	1928-55
H.S. Colt	Sunningdale	16	48	32	16	66.67	0	0	1	1895-12
D.M. Moffat	City of Newcastle	12	36	24	12	66.67	0	0	0	1958-76
F.W.G. Deighton	Hilton Park	10	30	20	10	66.67	0	0	0	1950-63
C.E. Dick	R. Liverpool	22	65	43	22	66.15	0	0	1	1890-22
W.C. Campbell	U.S.A.	12	35	23	12	65.71	0	1	0	1949-88
S.B. Roberts	Prestatyn	12	35	23	12	65.71	0	0	0	1932-53
C.K. Hutchison	Honourable Co.	11	32	21	11	65.63	0	1	0	1903-22
A. Slater	Wakefield	11	32	21	11	65.63	0	1	0	1952-64
D. Grant	R. St. George's	19	55	36	19	65.45	0	0	1	1910-37
W.A. Murray	West Hill	15	43	28	15	65.12	0	0	1	1907-34
R. Foster	Bradford	20	57	37	20	64.91	0	0	2	1962-82
D.M. Marsh	Southport-Ainsdale	13	37	24	13	64.86	0	0	0	1957-73
E. Blackwell	R.& A.	23	65	42	23	64.62	0	1	0	1901-30
A. Thirlwell	Gosforth	26	73	47	26	64.38	0	2	0	1951-79
J.G. Simpson	Scotscraig	20	56	36	20	64.29	0	0	0	1901-36
R.W. Hartley	R. St. George's	15	42	27	15	64.29	0	0	1	1924-38
W. Tulloch	Cathkin Braes	15	42	27	15	64.29	0	0	2	1923-38
E.N. Layton	Walton Heath	14	39	25	14	64.10	0	0	1	1920-34
A. Jamieson	Pollok	13	36	23	13	63.89	0	0	1	1926-50
G.H. Micklem	Wildernesse	17	47	30	17	63.83	0	0	1	1933-59
P.J. Hedges	Langley Park	16	44	28	16	63.64	0	0	1	1969-90
M.J. Kelley	Scarborough N. Cliff	12	33	21	12	63.64	0	0	0	1964-92
C.A. Palmer	Handsworth	12	33	21	12	63.64	0	1	0	1904-20
B. Darwin	Woking	25	68	43	25	63.24	0	0	2	1898-33
W.L. Hartley	Chislehurst	13	35	22	13	62.86	0	0	1	1923-37
C.D. Lawrie	Honourable Co.	16	43	27	16	62.79	0	0	0	1946-61

Name	Club	A	M	W	L	%	W	RU	SF	Years Played
S.M. Fergusson	R. & A.	18	48	30	18	62.50	0	2	1	1885-11
J.W. Jones	Grange Park	14	37	23	14	62.16	0	0	0	1933-62
F.C. Black	Prestonfield	13	34	21	13	61.76	0	0	0	1961-78
T.A. Torrance	R. & A.	25	65	40	25	61.54	0	0	1	1920-59
A.R. Aitken	Prestwick	20	52	32	20	61.54	0	0	1	1899-37
E.A. Lassen	R. Lytham	23	57	35	22	61.40	1	1	0	1899-26
A.F. Macfie	R. & A.	13	31	19	12	61.29	1	0	0	1885-07
H.G. Bentley	Hesketh	21	54	33	21	61.11	0	0	0	1929-62
R. Rutherford	R. Wimbledon	14	36	22	14	61.11	0	0	0	1926-50
A.A. Duncan	Southerndown	16	41	25	16	60.98	0	1	0	1937-59
J.D. MacCormack	Hermitage	16	41	25	16	60.98	0	0	1	1923-49
J.B. Beddard	South Staffs	13	33	20	13	60.61	0	0	0	1920-35
J.L. Low	R. & A.	13	33	20	13	60.61	0	1	2	1896-10
J. Glover	Clitheroe	23	58	35	28	60.34	0	0	0	1957-83
D. Cameron	Kirkintilloch	14	35	21	14	60.00	0	0	0	1934-63
G.B. Cosh	Cowglen	14	35	21	14	60.00	0	0	1	1961-83

OTHER CAREER RECORDS – MINIMUM 10 MATCHES

Name	Club	A	M	W	L	%	W	RU	SF	Years Played
W. Lawson Little	U.S.A.	2	16	16	0	100.00	2	0	0	1934-1935
E. Harvie Ward	U.S.A.	2	17	16	1	94.12	1	1	0	1952-1953
C. Hardin	Sweden	2	13	12	1	92.31	1	0	0	1987-1988
M.S. Thompson	Middlesbrough	2	13	12	1	92.31	1	0	0	1982-1983
J.W. Conrad	U.S.A.	2	12	11	1	91.67	1	0	0	1955-1956
C.R. Yates	U.S.A.	2	11	10	1	90.91	1	0	0	1938-1939
R.T. Jones	U.S.A.	3	18	16	2	88.89	1	0	0	1921-1930
I.D. Pyman	Sand Moor	3	17	15	2	88.24	1	0	0	1991-1993
P.M. Mayo	Newport	4	24	21	3	87.50	1	0	0	1984-1987
J. Sigel	U.S.A.	4	24	21	3	87.50	1	0	0	1979-1991
M.M. Giles	U.S.A.	3	16	14	2	87.50	1	0	0	1971-1976
S.M. McCready	Sunningdale	3	15	13	2	86.67	1	0	0	1949-1956
W.P. Turnesa	U.S.A.	5	28	24	4	85.71	1	1	1	1947-1951
W.I. Hunter	Walmer & Kingsdown	4	21	18	3	85.71	1	0	1	1914-1922
G.T. Dunlap	U.S.A.	2	14	12	2	85.71	0	0	2	1933-1934
T.P. Perkins	Castle Bromwich	3	14	12	2	85.71	1	0	0	1927-1929
R.D. Davies	U.S.A.	5	25	21	4	84.00	1	0	0	1954-1969
A.P. Parkin	Newtown	5	25	21	4	84.00	1	0	1	1980-1984
S. Dodd	Brynhill	4	18	15	3	83.33	1	0	0	1986-1989
C.A. Clark	Ganton	2	12	10	2	83.33	0	1	0	1964-1965
J. Holtgrieve	U.S.A.	2	12	10	2	83.33	0	1	0	1979-1983
A.K. Stubbs	Leek	2	12	10	2	83.33	0	1	0	1981-1982
G.J. Voigt	U.S.A.	2	12	10	2	83.33	0	0	1	1930-1931
P.H. Moody	Notts	4	23	19	4	82.61	0	1	1	1969-1973
J. Walker	Irvine	4	22	18	4	81.82	0	1	1	1952-1961
A.Y. Gresham	Australia	3	16	13	3	81.25	0	0	2	1979-1981
C. Cassells	Murcar	4	21	17	4	80.95	0	1	1	1987-1992
J. Bruen	Cork	4	15	12	3	80.00	1	0	0	1937-1960

OTHER CAREER RECORDS – 20 APPEARANCES

Name	Club	A	M	W	L	%	Years Played
H.E. Taylor	R. Mid-Surrey	30	71	41	30	57.75	1899-1937
J.B. Pease	Alnmouth	34	79	45	34	56.96	1893-1935
R.W. Crummack	Lytham St. Annes	24	54	30	24	55.56	1908-1946
M.J. Burgess	West Sussex	20	45	25	20	55.56	1956-1978
S.H. Fry	R. Mid-Surrey	25	51	26	25	50.98	1898-1931
E.B. Tipping	R. Ashdown F.	22	43	21	22	48.84	1909-1949
F. Strafaci	U.S.A.	25	45	20	25	44.44	1950-1981
D. Scott	R. St. George's	32	50	18	32	36.00	1898-1946
W. Doleman	Glasgow	20	29	9	20	31.03	1885-1912
H.M. Cairnes	Portmarnock	21	28	7	21	25.00	1902-1932

OTHER NOTABLE RECORDS

Most Matches Played

124	H.H. Hilton
121	J. Ball
119	J.B. Carr
117	M.F. Bonallack
95	R. Harris
94	C.J.H. Tolley
91	J.E. Laidlay
79	J.B. Pease
77	L.M. Balfour-Melville
77	W. Tweddell

Most Matches Won

99	J. Ball
96	J.B. Carr
95	H.H. Hilton
94	M.F. Bonallack
71	C.J.H. Tolley
68	R. Harris
65	J.E. Laidlay
56	R. H. Wethered
54	P. McEvoy
54	W. Tweddell

Consecutive Matches Won

23	M.F. Bonallack	1968-70
17	P. McEvoy	1977-79
16	H.H. Hilton	1900-02
16	W. Lawson Little	1934-35
16	E. Harvie Ward	1952-53
15	J.B. Carr	1953-54
14	W.I. Hunter	1921-22
14	R.H. Wethered	1923-24
14	H. Thomson	1936-38
14	M.S.R. Lunt	1963-64

Most Appearances

34	J.B. Pease	28	M.F. Bonallack
33	H.H. Hilton	28	R. Harris
32	Hon. D. Scott	28	J.E. Laidlay
30	J. Ball	26	J.B. Carr
30	H.E. Taylor	26	A. Thirwell

Biggest Final Victories

1934	W. Lawson Little beat J. Wallace	14/13	Prestwick
1925	R. Harris beat K.F. Fradgley	13/12	Westward Ho!
1921	W.I. Hunter beat A.J. Graham	12/11	Hoylake

Closest Finals

1964	G.J. Clark beat M.S.R. Lunt	39th	Ganton
1912	J. Ball beat A. Mitchell	38th	Westward Ho!

Closest Semi Finals (36 holes)

1959	W. Hyndman beat B. Magee	38th	Sandwich
1960	B. Cochran beat G. Huddy	38th	Portrush

Closest Semi Finals (18 holes)

1977	H.M. Campbell beat M.F. Bonallack	24th	Ganton
1898	F.G. Tait beat J.L. Low	22th	Hoylake
1987	P.M. Mayo beat L. Mattiace	22th	Prestwick
1993	I. Pyman beat N. Anderson	22th	Portrush

Longest Matches – Any Round

1908	C.A. Palmer beat L.O. Munn	28th	Sandwich
1989	P. McEvoy beat A.J. Elliott	28th	Birkdale
1936	J.L. Mitchell beat L.O. Munn	26th	St. Andrews
1970	A. Brodie beat R. McClure	26th	County Down

ANALYSIS OF ENTRY BY COUNTRY

Individual Overseas Entrants (Year first played)

	1885/1914	1920/39	1946/70	1971/94	Total
U.S.A.	34	127	365	638	1,164
Australia	8	16	36	50	110
Canada	7	21	23	72	123
India	10	27	5	9	51
South Africa	1	21	49	78	149
Other Commonwealth	6	14	40	34	94
	32	99	153	243	527
France	4	20	27	58	109
Germany	0	4	25	20	49
Italy	1	0	2	20	23
Spain	0	3	2	23	28
Sweden	1	0	6	38	45
Other Europe	0	7	20	60	87
	6	34	82	219	341
Rest of World	5	26	18	13	62
Total Overseas	77	286	618	1,113	2,094
Total U.K.	1,049	1,073	1,725	1,659	5,506
TOTAL Entry	1,126	1,359	2,343	2,772	7,600
Overseas %	6.8	21.0	26.4	40.2	27.6

Medals Won by Overseas Entrants by Country

	Winner	Runner-Up	Semi-Final
USA	20	18	18
South Africa	1	2	4
Australia	1	1	3
France	1	–	1
Sweden	1	–	1
Holland	1	–	–
Spain	1	–	–
Canada	–	–	2

248

VENUES

16	Hoylake	1885-1975	3	Westward Ho	1912-1931	
				Lytham	1935-1986	
15	St. Andrews	1886-1981		Formby	1957-1984	
				Ganton	1964-1991	
11	Sandwich	1892-1972				
			2	Deal	1923-1982	
10	Prestwick	1888-1987		Birkdale	1946-1989	
				Portrush	1960-1993	
9	Muirfield	1897-1990		Turnberry	1961-1983	
			1	Portmarnock	1949	
5	Porthcawl	1951-1988		Co. Down	1970	
				Hillside	1979	
4	Carnoustie	1947-1992		Dornoch	1985	
	Troon	1938-1978		Nairn	1994	

Note – Figure on left represents number of times played at each venue.

QUALIFYING ROUNDS (1983-1994)

Year	Qualifying Courses	Leading Qualifier	Score	Qualifying Score	Winner	Qualifying Rank of Winner
1983	Turnberry Ailsa/Arran	A.P. Parkin	140	150	A.P. Parkin	1
1984	Formby/Southport & Ainsdale	A.P. Parkin	141	150	J-M. Olazabal	5=
1985	Dornoch/Golspie	D.V. Banke	137	147	G.M. McGimpsey	6=
1986	Lytham/St. Anne's Old	D.V. Banke	142	152	D.H. Curry	4=
1987	Prestwick/Prestwick St. Nicholas	A.D. Hare	136	145	P.M. Mayo	2=
1988	Porthcawl/Pyle & Kenfig	S. Dodd L. MacNamara	145	155	C. Hardin	31=
1989	Birkdale/Hillside	J.W. Milligan	141	152	S. Dodd	46=
1990	Muirfield/Luffness	A. Hart	138	148	R. Muntz	22=
1991	Ganton/Scarborough N. Cliff	F. Andersson D. Duval	141	148	G. Wolstenholme	3=
1992	Carnoustie/Panmure	M.L. Welch	148	163	S. Dundas	5=
1993	Portrush Dunluce/Valley	C.R. Watson	141	152	I. Pyman	11=
1994	Nairn/Nairn Dunbar	S. Gallacher	145	155	L. James	37=

Note – On only two occasions has the leading qualifier reached as far as the quarter-final stages of the match-play, Parkin, winner in 1983, and Duval, Semi-Finalist in 1991.

INDEX OF COMPETITORS BY YEARS

Aaron T. 1959
Abercrombie J. 1927.31
Aitken A. 1905
Alexander B. 1987
Alexander D. 1958
Alexander H. 1909
Alexander M. 1956
Allan J. 1897
Allen D. 1967
Anderson Dr.N. 1993
Anderson P. 1893
Andersson E. 1914
Andrade B. 1987
Andrew R. 1906.07.09
Andrews G. 1956.58
Arend E. 1953
Ashby H. 1973
Attenborough M. 1967.68
Auchterlonie L. 1895
Aylmer C. 1910.13.27

Bachli D. 1954.85
Baker D. 1993
Baker P. 1985.86
Balfour L.(Melville)
    1886.87.89.92
    1895-1909.11.14
Ball J.Snr. 1887
Ball J.Jnr. 1885-99.1902-14
    1920.21.27.33
Banke D. 1985.86
Barker H. 1907
Barrie G. 1985
Barry A.G. 1905-08.20
Baugh R. 1929
Beamish C. 1953
Beddard J. 1921
Beharrell J. 1956.57.78
Behrend J. 1975
Beman D. 1959.63
Bendern de J.
    (See Forest de J)
Bennett S. 1977
Bennett W. 1994
Bentley M. 1977
Bergman W. 1978
Berridge D. 1994

Berry P. 1972
Bethell Hon.R. 1911
Biggs R. 1975
Birtwell G. 1986
Bishop P. 1908
Bishop S. 1947
Black F. 1965.72
Black J. 1935
Blackey M. 1994
Blackwell E. 1902-07.13.14
Blackwell J. 1963.64
Blair D. 1952.53.55.58.61
Blocker G. 1964
Bonallack M. 1958-74.
    77.80.82
Bond F. 1912
Bone D. 1888
Bostwick P. 1969
Bourn Dale. 1933.34
Boxall R. 1982
Brabazon Lt.Col.L. 1937
Bradshaw I. 1979.80
Brady P. 1964
Braid H. 1924
Bramston J. 1900.02.04
Brand G. 1975
Brand G.Jnr. 1979
Brannan M. 1990
Bremner W. 1985
Brink K. 1994
Bristowe O. 1924
Broadhurst P. 1987
Broadwood C. 1896
Brodie A. 1973.76.78-80
Brooks C. 1984
Brown C. 1936
Brownlow Hon.W. 1926
Bruen J. 1937-39
    46.47.49.60
Bryson W. 1991
Bucher A.Melville. 1953
Burn Capt.W. 1901
Burns G. 1975
Burns R. 1992
Bussell A. 1957
Byers E. 1907

Cage S. 1993
Cairns H. 1910
Caldwell I. 1953.56
Campbell F. 1978
Campbell G. 1907
Campbell H. 1971.77
Campbell J. 1947
Campbell P. 1949
Campbell W. 1950-54.
    1965-67.75.88
Carlow C. 1952
Carr. Joe. 1947-70
Carr. John. 1981
Carr R. 1970-72
Carrick D. 1983.86
Carslaw I. 1976-78
Carter Capt.E. 1920.22.27
Carvill J. 1990
Cassells C. 1989.90
Cater R. 1952.55
Caven J. 1922.24
Cerrudo R. 1967
Chambers C. 1886
Chandler A. 1971
Chapman B. 1960-62
Chapman R.D. 1936.37.39.
    47-52.65
Chapman Roger. 1980
Charles R. 1958
Cherry D. 1955
Chesses N. 1975
Christmas M. 1961-65.82
Cisco S. 1980
Clark C. 1965.66
Clark G. 1964.65.67.68.73.88
Clark H. 1973
Claydon R. 1987.89
Cobley P. 1971
Cochran B. 1960
Coe C. 1951.59.63
Cole R. 1966
Colt H. 1896.1906.08
Conrad J. 1955.56
Cook J. 1989
Cosh G. 1966.68.69
Cox D. 1924
Craddock T. 1967

Cradock-Hartopp J. 1950
Crane J. 1928
Crawley L. 1932.38.39.46
Critchley Brig.A. 1937.49
Critchley B. 1962.70
Crosby B. 1950
Crosby N. 1982
Crow T. 1958
Cruikshank R. 1920
Cruikshank J. 1925
Cullen Capt.J. 1885
Culligan T. 1973
Curry D. 1984.86-88

Dalgleish C. 1981.82.85
Dalton E. 1954
Darwin B. 1902.04.05.08.11
    20.21
Davidson D.P. 1974.80
Davidson W. 1969
Davies J. 1973.75-79.81
Davies R. 1962.63
Dawson J. 1928
Deeble P. 1974.81-84
Deighton Dr.F. 1956
Dick C. 1893.98.1901.05.08.12
    1920.21
Dickson R. 1967
Dodd S. 1988.89
Doe D. 1954
Doleman W. 1912
Douglas J. 1921
Downes P. 1980
Dredge B. 1992-94
Drew B. 1923
Duke C. 1994
Duncan A. 1939.49.59
Duncan J. 1960
Dundas S. 1992.93
Dunlap G. 1933.34
Duval D. 1991
Dyke J.M. 1935.36

Edlund D. 1987
Edmond O. 1990
Egan C. 1934
Elliott D. 1989
Ellis H. 1902.04.14
Ellison T.F. 1927.28

Elm G.Von. 1926
Els E. 1988.89
Enderby K. 1952
Ericsson K. 1991
Erlandsson M. 1994
Evans A.D. 1951
Evans A.J. 1928.37
Evans C. 1911.14.21.46.55
Evans D. 1979-81
Evans G. 1990
Evans H. 1980
Everard H. 1887
Ewing C. 1936.38.49
Eyles R. 1973

Fairbanks D. 1931
Fairlie F. 1892
Fairlie W. 1895
Faldo N. 1975
Falkenberg R. 1966.69
Fehr R. 1983
Ferguson W. 1975
Fergusson Mure S.
    1886.87.92-94.
    96.98.1900.02.
    04.14
Ferrier J. 1936
Fiddian E. 1930.32-35
Fischer J. 1938
Fisher D. 1994
Flaherty P. 1964
Fleckman M. 1967
Foggo J. 1886
Forbes K. 1932
Foreman T. 1983
Forest A.de 1937
Forest J.de 1929.31-33.51.85
Foster L. 1961
Foster R. 1962.65.67.68.71-73
Fouchee B. 1988
Fowler W.H. 1901.09
Fownes W.C. 1921.26
Fox C. 1951
Fradgley K. 1925
Fry S. 1902.03.11
Fuhrer F. 1982

Gabrielson J. 1971.74.76
Gairdner J. 1899

Gallacher B. 1967
Gallacher S. 1992.94
Garbutt I. 1992
Gardner R. 1965
Gardner R.A. 1920.23.26
Garnett L. 1934
Genese B. 1992
Giddins A. 1982
Giles M. 1971.75.76
Gilford D. 1982.84
Gillies H. 1906.07.10.
    1913.14.24.27.28
Girand E. 1988
Givens D. 1968
Glading R. 1968
Glover J. 1970.78
Godwin G. 1980.81
Gonzales M. 1948
Goodloe W. 1950
Goodman J. 1934
Gordon K. 1946.53
Goulding N. 1993
Grace J. 1975
Graham A. 1921
Graham J.Jnr. 1896-1901
    1904-08.10.14.20
Graham J.A. 1939
Grant D. 1923.29.33
Grant P. 1909
Graves N. 1988
Gray A.Downing 1967
Green C. 1966.68.70.72.73.75
Greig W. 1895.97.1913
Gresham A. 1979-81
Groenwald E. 1980
Guilford J. 1921
Gunn W. 1926

Haas J. 1975
Haglund A. 1988
Hales P. 1965
Haley E. 1927
Hall P. 1985
Hambro A. 1912
Hamilton A. 1900
Hamlet E. 1921
Hannay G. 1933
Hardin C. 1988
Harding D. 1989

251

Hardman R. 1925.33
Hare A. 1987
Harrington P. 1991-93
Harris R. 1907.10.12-14
    1921.23-27.34
Harrison C. 1980
Hart A. 1990
Hartley R. 1929
Hartley W. 1930
Hattersley H. 1938
Hay G. 1991
Hayes D. 1969
Hayes Jimmy. 1966
Hayes John. 1962
Heard P. 1954
Hedges P. 1982.85
Henderson G. 1956
Henderson W. 1909
Hezlett C. 1914.28
Hill G.A. 1936.38
Hill W. 1959
Hilton H. 1887-94.1896-1907.
    1911-14.20.27.28
Hirsch J. 1981.82
Hoch S. 1979
Hodgson C. 1922
Hoey T. 1970
Hoffer B. 1983
Holden H. 1933
Holderness E. 1921-26.28
Holland T. 1958.60
Holt P. 1975
Holt W. 1939
Holtgrieve J. 1983
Homer T. 1971-74
Homewood G. 1985.94
Hope. Bob. 1951
Hopkinson H. 1971
Hornby W.P. 1922
Howard B. 1994
Huddy G. 1960.61
Hughesdon M. 1975.76.81
Huggan J. 1981.85
Humphreys R. 1914
Humphreys W. 1972
Hunter N. 1904.09.12
Hunter W. 1920-22
Hutcheon I. 1971.74.78.85

Hutchings C. 1890.96.98
    1900-2.08
Hutchinson H.
    1885-90.92.94.96.
    1900-05.07.08.
    1910-12.14
Hutchison Capt.C. 1909
Hyndman W.
    1956.65.66.68-70.72

Ingram J. 1922

Jack R. 1954.56.57
Jackson B. 1989
James D. 1985
James L. 1994
James M. 1975
Jamieson A. 1926.27.36
Jenkins L. 1914.20.21.38
Jobson Capt.R. 1927
Johnson R. 1990
Johnston H. 1930
Jonas P. 1978
Jones R.T. 1921.26.28.30.38

Kelley M. 1970.75
Kelley P.D. 1964
Kennedy G. 1990
Keppler S. 1982.83
Kinell K. 1982
King M. 1972.73
Kinloch F. 1910
Kirk J. 1886.88.91
Kite T. 1971
Koch G. 1975
Kocsis C. 1938
Kyle A. 1939.46.61.64
Kyle D. 1924
Kyle E. 1913

Laidlay J. 1886-93.96.99.
    1900-09.11.14
Lamaze de H. 1947.64
Lamb H. 1886
Lambie J. 1953
Landale E. 1927
Langley J. 1936.53
Langridge R. 1965
Lassen E. 1903.08-11.13.24

Lawrence M. 1959
Lawrie C. 1948.59
Lawrie G. 1988
Layton N. 1925
Leitch D. 1890
Lemaire P. 1977
Levenson G. 1975.78
Levet T. 1988
Lewis. Bob. 1987
Lewis J.W. 1967
Liddle A. 1974
Lincoln A. 1908
Lindsay-Smith D. 1980
Lingen C. 1906
Little E. 1994
Little Lawson. 1934.35
Locke A.D. 1936.39
Lockhart G. 1911
Loeffler W. 1987
Long J. 1975
Lopez J. 1981
Low A. 1965
Low J. 1897.98.1901.02.04
Lowery E. 1947.49
Lucas P.B. 1936.38.49
Luceti Dr.R. 1963
Lundberg M. 1993
Lunt M. 1963-65.67
Lygate M. 1970.73
Lyle A. 1975-77
Lyon G. 1905.08

Macara M. 1990
MacCallum Dr.A. 19287
McCallum H. 1932.35
McClue L. 1957.68
McCormack M. 1966.70
MacCormack J.D. 1927.31.48
McCraig Dr.D. 1886
McCraw S. 1989
McCrea W. 1970
McCready M. 1949.50
MacDonald A. 1903
McDonald R.H. 1965
Macdonald S. 1971.74
McEvoy P. 1977-82.84-89.
    1992.93
MacFarlane C. 1912.14
Macfie A. 1885.86.88

McGimpsey G. 1985-87.89.93
McGregor G. 1971
McHale J. 1950.52.55.58
McHugh J. 1928
McInally H. 1947.49
McIntosh K. 1980
McIntyre G. 1976
McKellar P. 1977.78
McKenzie F. 1901
Mackenzie R. 1926
Mackenzie W. 1923
McKibbin H. 1992
McKinlay S. 1932.47
McLachlan C. 1981
McLean J. 1933-35.38
McNair A. 1927.29
McNamara L. 1988
McNulty M. 1977
McRuvie E. 1932
Maddern J. 1955
Magee I.t.B. 1959
Mahon J. 1955
Maidstone Viscount 1922
Mann L. 1983
Mansfield J. 1888
Marchbank B. 1976.77.79
Marks G. 1968.69.1975-77
Marr D. 1966
Marsh D. 1964.73
Marston M. 1934
Martin D. 1932
Martin Ham. 1934
Martin L. 1932
Martin-Smith Eric. 1931.32
Martin-Smith Everard. 1914
Mathews W. 1904
Mattiace L. 1987
Maxwell R. 1897.99-1908.
   1914.20
Maxwell W. 1952
May B. 1991
Mayfair B. 1987
Mayo P. 1984-87
Meehan M. 1992
Meldrum B. 1977
Mellin G. 1908.20
Melnyk S. 1971
Micklem G. 1946.48.53-55.
   1957.66.69.76

Miller A. 1971
Miller M. 1974
Milligan J. 1987.89-91
Millward E. 1949.54
Mitchell A. 1910.12.13
Mitchell I. 1936
Mitchell J. 1936
Moe K. 1982.84
Mohta R. 1981
Moir A. 1984
Montgomery B. 1987
Montgomery C. 1984.85.87
Moody P. 1971.73
Moreland G. 1934
Morey D. 1955.57.64.68.69.73
Morgan G. 1947
Morman R. 1977
Morrison A. 1891
Morrison R. 1899
Morrow R. 1961
Mulcare P. 1975
Munn L. 1908.32.36.37
Muntz R. 1990.92.93
Murphy R. 1967
Murray G. 1977.78
Murray J. 1922
Murray S. 1963
Murray W.A. 1926
Murray W.B. 1967.69
Muscroft D. 1986

Nelford J. 1977
Nettlefold L. 1927
Newton S. 1928
Nicklaus G. 1991
Nicklaus J. 1959
Nicklaus J.Jnr. 1986
Norval L. 1979

O'Brien M. 1969
O'Carroll C. 1992
Olazabal J-M. 1984.85.93
Oldcorn A. 1983
Oosterhuis P. 1967.68
Oppenheimer R. 1929.56
Orr G. 1987
Orr J. 1950
Orr R. 1906
O'Sullivan W. 1949.50

Ouimet F. 1914.21.23.26
   1934.47.49
Owens J. 1974

Pakenham Walsh G. 1934
Page P. 1993
Palmer C. 1907-09.11.14
Parker T. 1935
Parkin P. 1982-84
Pate J. 1976
Patey I. 1946
Patton W.J. 1955.59
Payne J. 1989
Pearce B. 1911
Pearson M. 1953.69
Pease J.B.(Lord Wardington)
   1910.20.28.38.46
Peattie R. 1926
Peel M. 1964
Peers D. 1950
Pegler F. 1913.21
Pennink F. 1937
Perkins P. 1928.29
Perowne A. 1953.55
Peters G. 1936.37.46
Pierse A. 1980
Pirie A. 1966.67
Planchin T. 1978
Player W. 1978.81
Ploujoux P. 1981.82.93
Pollock V. 1908
Potter T. 1885
Povall J. 1962.65
Poxon M. 1974
Prat A. 1993
Pressley J. 1946
Price N. 1975
Pullan M. 1991
Pyman I. 1993

Quick S. 1947

Rae M. 1970
Rafferty R. 1980.81
Randall C. 1955
Randall L. 1959
Reid D. 1951
Reinach U. 1949
Revell R. 1972

Richardson K. 1972
Richardson S. 1985
Ridgley H. 1957.59
Ridley F. 1977
Robb J. 1897-1900.
  1902-04.06.08
Robertson D. 1972
Robinson P. 1989
Robinson S. 1922
Robson S. 1979
Roderick R. 1984
Rogers A. 1987
Rolland D. 1885
Roper S. 1930.31
Ross A. 1889
Roxburgh D. 1978.79.81
Runcie S. 1922
Russell R. 1993
Ryan M. 1938

Saddler S. 1961.67
Samek H. 1925
Sander B. 1977
Sanders D. 1956
Sanger M. 1972
Schmidt H. 1913
Schofield S. 1953
Schunk M. 1933
Scott Hon.D. 1911.12
Scott Hon.M. 1911.12.20.
  1925.33.34
Scott Hon.O. 1905.11
Scott R. 1922.26
Scroggie Dr.F. 1910
Scrutton P. 1948.55.58
Sewell D. 1955
Shade R. 1962-64.66-68
Shankland C. 1929
Sharp R. 1891
Sharp W. 1955
Shepperson A. 1962
Sherry G. 1994
Shields B. 1986.90
Siderowf R. 1972-77.79.81
Sigel J. 1979.83.87.91
Simons J. 1971
Simpson A. 1926
Simpson G. 1920
Sinclair A. 1957

Singh L. 1979
Slark W.A. 1954.57
Slater A. 1955.56
Smirke E. 1906
Smith C. 1908
Smith D. 1972
Smith G. 1902
Smith Nelson J. 1929
Smith P. 1974
Somerville R. 1932.35.38
Sorenson J. 1987
Speight F. 1979
Spencer E. 1987.88
Stadler C. 1975
Stanford M. 1992.93
Steel W. 1960
Stephenson I. 1985
Stephenson J. 1938
Stevens H. 1914
Stevens L. 1911.12
Stewart J. 1888
Storey E. 1924
Stowe C. 1937.46.48
Strafaci F. 1978
Stranahan F. 1946-50.52-54
Stranahan R. 1949
Strange C. 1975.76
Stroyan Capt.J. 1929
Stuart A. 1888.92.95
Stuart H. 1971.73.74
Stubbs A. 1982
Suddards D. 1978-80.82
Sullivan K. 1970
Sundelson N. 1974
Suneson C. 1988
Sutton H. 1979
Sutton N. 1927
Sutton W. 1929
Sweeny R. 1935-37.46.64
Sweetser J. 1923.26
Sym A. 1978
Szewczul D. 1991

Taggart J. 1962
Tait F. 1893-99.1914
Tait J. 1887
Tait P. 1950
Tataurangi P. 1993
Tate J.K. 1954

Taylor H. 1908
Taylor J. 1957
Taylor L. 1956.78
Taylor R. 1954
Tentis D. 1983
Thirlwell A. 1958.64.72.73
Thom K. 1949
Thomas I. 1933
Thompson M. 1982.83.93
Thomson H. 1935-38.46
Thomson J. 1983
Thorburn K. 1929
Thornhill J. 1958
Tipping E. 1928
Tolley C. 1920-30.33.36-38.50
Toogood P. 1954
Torrance T.A. 1935
Toussaint P. 1969
Townsend P. 1965-67
Travers J. 1909.14
Travis W. 1904.05
Tubbs H. 1921.25
Tulloch W. 1928.31.32
Turnbull R. 1994
Turner A. 1956
Turnesa W. 1947-51
Turpie W. 1895
Tuten B. 1983
Tutwiler E. 1972
Tweddell Dr.W. 1927.28.33.
  1935.38.46

Updegraff Dr.E. 1963
Urzetta S. 1951

Vandersluis R. 1988
Vanier G. 1993
Van Ingen P. 1972
Van Niekerk R. 1979
Vannet L. 1993
Venturi K. 1955
Vincent (St) Viscount. 1911
Voges M. 1991
Voigt G. 1930.31

Wadkins L. 1971
Waldorf D. 1985
Walker A. 1955.57
Walker H. 1946

Walker J. 1952.60-62
Walker L. 1977
Wallace J. 1934
Ward B. 1947
Ward E.Harvie. 1952.53
Watson C. 1993.94
Way P. 1981
Weaver F. 1906.10
Wehrle W. 1937
Welch M. 1992
West R. 1969
Westland J. 1934
Westwood L. 1992
Wethered R. 1920-25.27-31.33
Wheeler F. 1920
Whigham G. 1899.1900
Whigham W. 1905

White L. 1990
White R.J. 1946.47.49.51.52
Whitelaw (Viscount) W.
    1969.94
Whitton I. 1914
Williams Major A. 1909
Williamson J. 1899.1900
Wilson J.A. 1987
Wilson J.C. 1947
Wilson J.K. 1950
Wilson John. 1923
Wilson W. 1889.93
Winninger B. 1951
Winsnes W. 1982
Winter G. 1990
Wolstenholme Gary.
    1990-93

Wolstenholme Guy.
    1955.57-59.
    1961
Wood D. 1987
Woosnam I. 1976
Wragg B. 1920
Wright F. 1921
Wyatt S. 1907

Yates C. 1938.85
Yates D. 1992
Yost R. 1955

Zahringer G. 1991
Zoete H. de 1903
Zoete W. de 1885